Commentary on the

Minor Prophets

Volume I
Joel, Amos, and Jonah

James Burton Coffman

Author of the Firm Foundation Series of
Commentaries on the New Testament

Houston, Texas

1981

Published By
THE FIRM FOUNDATION PUBLISHING HOUSE
P. O. Box 610, Austin, Texas 78767

DEDICATION

This first volume on the Minor Prophets is lovingly dedicated to the Elders of the Garden Oaks Church of Christ, Houston, Texas:

PAUL BARNETT
DAVID BENNETT
RALPH W. ENGLEHARDT
T.C. (Bill) MILLER

These are men whose dedication and ability have won the admiration of all who know them.

CONTENTS

PREFACE

Why these particular three prophecies in this first volume? A certain element of chance entered into it. When these studies were begun, there was no intention of doing more than one of the Minor Prophets; but the widespread need for a believing, conservative exegesis of the Book of Jonah led to the production of the commentary on that much maligned prophecy. The work proved to be so exciting and rewarding that we were led to project a larger work, comprehending all of the Minor prophets. Joel and Amos were also long-standing old friends; and so it came about that these three are in volume 1.

The biblical text followed is that of the American Standard Version, the choice resulting from the fact that this was the version followed in the series of commentaries on the NT, and from the conviction that persists to the effect, as F. F. Bruce stated it, that this version "is the most accurate for purposes of detailed studies" of the Bible.

Every effort has been made to address the questions which any serious Christian student of the holy scriptures would encounter when reading or studying these prophecies.

We praise God for his blessing of my wife Thelma and me in the privilege of launching this new venture. We are profoundly grateful for the widespread acceptance of the NT series, and for the continued encouragement of our publisher, George Showalter. It is our humble prayer, that the Lord may, through these studies, enable good to be done and souls to be won for the Lord Jesus Christ.

Burton Coffman
2108 Branard Street
Houston, Texas 77098
Autumn, 1980.

ABBREVIATIONS

ca.	=	Circa (about).
cf.	=	compare.
ch.	=	chapter.
f.	=	verse following.
ff.	=	verses following.
Ibid.	=	the author just quoted.
op. cit.	=	book cited above.
vol.	=	volume.
v.	=	verse.
vv.	=	verses.
ABC	=	Abingdon Bible Commentary.
ABS	=	American Bible Society.
A.D.	=	The year of Our Lord.
AV.	=	Authorized Version.
ASV.	=	American Standard Version.
B.C.	=	Before Christ.
BBC.	=	Broadman Bible Commentary.
CBC.	=	Cambridge Bible Commentary.
IB.	=	Interpreter's Bible.
ISBE.	=	International Standard Bible Encyclopaedia.
JFB.	=	Commentary on the Bible by Jamieson, Faussett & Brown.
LXX.	=	The Septuagint Translation of the Bible.
MHC.	=	Matthew Henry's Commentary.
MT.	=	Masoretic Text.
NBCR.	=	New Bible Commentary Revised.
NLBC.	=	New Layman's Bible Commentary.
NEB.	=	New English Bible.
NT.	=	New Testament.
OT.	=	Old Testament.
RV.	=	Revised Version.
RSV.	=	Revised Standard Version.
WBC.	=	Wycliffe Bible Commentary.
WBE.	=	Wycliffe Bible Encyclopaedia.

Book titles by James Burton Coffman:

CM	=	Commentary on Matthew.
CMK	=	Commentary on Mark.
CL	=	Commentary on Luke.
CJ	=	Commentary on John.
CA	=	Commentary on Acts.
CR	=	Commentary on Romans.
CC	=	Commentary on the Corinthians.
CG	=	Commentary on Galatians-Colossians.
CT	=	Commentary on Thessalonians-Philemon.

CH = Commentary on Hebrews.
CJA = Commentary on James-Jude.
CRE = Commentary on Revelation.
GG = Gospel in Gothan.
CD = The Decalogue.
CMY = The Mystery of Redemption.

Joel

INTRODUCTION

Efforts exerted against the authorship and unity of the prophecy of Joel have failed, and the most dependable scholars everywhere are in agreement that it is the work of one author and that that author is the prophet whose name identifies the book. Some critical conclusions, however, have only been modified to the extent of making the prophecy, in such views, a "collection" of the sayings of Joel, put together by some later collector; but even such an incorrect notion as that still leaves intact the conviction that here, indeed, we have the true words of one of the great prophets of God.

As to the identity of Joel, nothing is definitely known except the very meager information which appears in the prophecy itself. The name Joel, which means "Jehovah is God," was popular among the Hebrew people, no less than twelve persons of this name being mentioned in the OT during a period of history reaching from 1,000 B.C. to 536 B.C., some fifty years after the Babylonian captivity.[1] The author of this prophecy is further identified as the "son of Pethuel"; but this is the only mention of a person with that name in the entire Bible.

Date. The date of Joel is vigorously disputed, the dates assigned by commentators ranging all the way from the tenth century B.C. to the second century B.C.[2] All of these "guesses" tend to polarize around two primary dates which have been proposed, i.e., (1) during the reign of King Joash of Judah (ca. 837 B.C.), and (2) the second around postexilic times (ca. 400 B.C.).[3] The early date is preferred and will be followed in this study, the late date being rejected because the principal support of it rests upon what must be considered as inaccurate interpretations of certain key passages. For example, some have cited the mention of "the captivity" in 3:1 as an infallible indicator that the Babylonian captivity was history at the time Joel was written; and yet

---

[1]*Unger's Bible Dictionary* (Chicago: Moody Press, 1957), p. 594.
[2]*Ibid.*, p. 595.
[3]J. Hardee Kennedy, *BBC, Vol. 7* (Nashville: Broadman Press, 1972). p. 64.

the passage itself clearly identifies what is spoken of in that verse as occurring at a time *after* the day of Pentecost! Many other such things will be cited in the notes. Perhaps a little fuller discussion of the alleged reasons for the support of a late date would be appropriate:

1. There is no mention of a king, and this is alleged to mean that a postexilic period is indicated; but the times of Joash, when that king was in his infancy and the affairs of the nation were in the hands of his regent, the priest Jehoida (2 Kings 11:1-17), fit just as well.

2. The fact of the Northern Kingdom not being mentioned is interpreted to mean that the Ten Tribes had long ago disappeared, as in the postexilic period; but the early date would explain this as easily as the later date.

3. The alleged quotation from some 27 other OT books is said to favor a late date; but the question of who quoted whom is difficult, if not impossible, to determine; and it is just as likely that many of the later books which Joel is said to have quoted were instead quoting him! No dependence whatever should be put in such arguments. Even in those biblical passages in which a writer says, "Thus saith the Lord," there is no evidence from such an expression that he is quoting *another* sacred author, it being just as likely that he is accurately delivering the message which God gave *him*. This is observed quite frequently in the writings of Paul. "Who borrowed from whom is a question subject to forceful argument on either side."[4]

4. The mention of "elders" is said to point to postexilic times when the nation was governed by official "elders"; but no such officialdom is referred to in Joel. They were merely the "old men"; and, "They stand as the experienced citizens of the community, not as state officials, and in 2:16 are set over against children and sucklings."[5]

5. There is no mention of Assyria, and this is said to point to a period when Assyria had already been overthrown; but there is no mention of Assyria in Amos!

6. Sounding the "trumpet" or the ram's horn to summon the people points to a very small community in Jerusalem

---

[4]*Ibid.*

[5]George I. Robinson, *The Twelve Minor Prophets* (Grand Rapids: Baker Book House, 1926), p. 41.

after the exile and after the temple had been rebuilt, allegedly;[6] but this is a symbolical thing, and is applied in scripture to the summoning of all nations to the Final Judgment
(1 Corinthians 15:1-10). The imagery was derived from the
period of the wilderness wanderings, long prior to the days
of Joel.

There is really no need to multiply this type of investigation. There are no valid objections to the early date of this
prophecy, ca. 836 B.C., as many able present-day scholars
have pointed out. It actually comes down to what men
prefer to accept. In this connection, it should also be
pointed out that no world-shaking importance attaches to
the question in the first place. *Whenever* it was written, it is
universally received by both Jews and Christians as a valid
portion of God's word; and practically none of the prophecy's marvelous teachings are dependent in any way upon
the determination of exactly when the book was written;
although it is true that acceptance of the latest dates assigned to it almost automatically results in some erroneous
interpretations of certain passages.

The style and beauty of the prophecy are such that, "It
may be reckoned among the classics of Hebrew literature."[7]
The dramatic and powerful presentation of its content is so
concise, clear, and understandable that, "The need of a
commentary for details, as in the case of Amos and Hosea,
is here hardly felt."[8]

Our preference for the early date is definitely influenced
by the opinion of Hebrew scholars who placed it so early in
the Canon, a fact not easily reconciled with the later dates.
In principle, we have long been convinced that men of the
20th century are simply too late, by many centuries, to
claim any trustworthiness in the matter of dating biblical
books.

The theme of Joel is quite clearly "The Day of the Lord,"
an expression applied in scripture, not merely to great visi-
tations of God in the punishment of wicked men, or nations,
but also, by extension, to the great and final day of the

---

[6]John H. Thompson, *IB, Vol. VI* (New York, Abingdon Press, 1957), p. 732.
[7]James Robertson, *ISBE* (Chicago: Howard-Severance Company, 1915), p.
1688.
[8]*Ibid.*

Eternal Judgment. Joel is, in a sense, a source, from which the holy apostles and the Lord Jesus himself derived their holy teachings regarding "That Day," of course, expanding and developing the thoughts through means of their own unqualified inspiration. This makes Joel one of the most important books in the Bible, despite its smallness.

The purpose of Joel is direct and simple. He discerned that the terrible locust plague that devasted the land and reduced the people to poverty and despair was a judgment of God upon them, brought about by their sinful lives. It is the conviction of this writer that what Joel saw in that national disaster was exactly that which is inherent in all natural calamities of every kind which again and again inflict suffering and despair upon mankind. All such natural disasters, which are symbolically presented under the trumpet series of visions in the book of Revelation, are actually continuations and extensions of the primeval curse upon Adam (and his posterity) imposed by God himself, and never withdrawn (Genesis 3:17-19). God's continual and unremitting interference with human comfort and complacency through a long and unbroken chain of historical natural disasters has the same benign purpose of the original sentence upon Adam, which was "for Adam's sake," i.e., that of inducing repentance and return to God on the part of rebellious and wicked mankind. Joel clearly discerned this, and therefore, in keeping with that perception, he so interpreted the locust plague; but he went beyond that. He remembered that God had also warned Adam and Eve that "in the day" that they ate of the forbidden tree, they would "surely die," another divine sentence that God never withdrew, commuted, or repealed. It is still in force and will ultimately be executed upon Adam and Eve in the person of their total posterity at the time of the Final Judgment, the unique exceptions to that terminal sentence being those who shall have been redeemed in Christ Jesus. "The day" that God spoke of still continues. Much misunderstanding exists with regard to "day" as used in the Bible; but, regardless of what interpretation one wishes to place upon the six days of creation, "God rested on the seventh day; and God is still resting; and, therefore we are still living in the *seventh day*, as indicated in Hebrews 4:1-5.

This is "the day" in which God promised to destroy Adam and Eve; and the sentence will yet be executed. By tying all these things together, Joel gives the clue to understanding the recurring nature of "The Day of the Lord" as used in the Bible, and of his unhesitating use of the locust plague as a prototype of the final judgment day.itself. The truth of this is further emphasized by the apostle John's use of "locusts" as the symbol of the final and terminal rebellion of the race of men against God, culminating in the judgment day (Revelation 9). In fact, chapter 9 of Revelation is an excellent supplementary commentary upon the prophecy of Joel.

In keeping with what is conceived of as Joel's purpose, we shall not hesitate to interpret the second chapter, not as a mere re-hash of the locust plague, but as its extension and application to further calamities which were prophesied to come upon the Hebrew people because of their rebellion against God. In a sense, this is true of all the calamities that come upon men, the greatest ones serving particularly as prototypes of the Final Judgment, the destruction of Jerusalem by the Romans in A.D. 70 being an outstanding example of this. Numerous judgments of God upon wicked men have already fallen, as evident in Tyre and Sidon, Sodom and Gomorrah, Babylon and Nineveh, Jerusalem and Rome. Historically, such things as the Black Death of the fourteenth century and the devastating wars of the 20th century must also surely be included.

Jesus our Lord used the imagery of this prophecy in speaking of his Second Advent and the final judgment; the apostle John used it specifically in his series of trumpet visions; and the apostle Peter ushered in the gospel age with an appeal to the words of this very prophet. In view of its small size, it is almost incredible how this small prophecy has been quoted and referred to by so many. Surely, there is an indescribably rich mine of significant spiritual truth in the prophecy of Joel.

CHAPTER 1

This whole chapter (1-20) relates to a terrible and destructive locust plague that came upon Israel, particularly Judah, a disaster so overwhelming that no escape was possible. The fact of it is dramatically stated (1-4); the prophet's admonition to the people is given in three terse commandments: (1) "Awake ..." (5-7), (2) "Lament" (8-12), and (3) "Gird yourselves with sackcloth ..." (13-14). Despite the fact of these appeals being directed to three different classes, namely, the drunkards, the agricultural community, and the priests, they should be understood as applicable generally to all the people, and not merely to specific groups.

As in many another human disaster resulting from natural causes, the prophets of God, and all persons with spiritual discernment, have invariable associated such things with the wrath of God, due to divine disapproval of human sin and wickedness. Joel at once concluded that the locust disaster was a harbinger of "the day of the Lord," a truth that is not nullified by the fact that the Final Judgment was not to occur for at least 2,700 years! That disaster which so long ago brought fear and despair to a portion of the earth's population *was* a type of the final and eternal judgment that shall overwhelm all men; and significantly, many other such natural disasters since that time (as well as before that time) should be understood in exactly the same way! We must therefore reject the superficial interpretation of the final paragraph of this chapter (15-20) which views it merely as Joel's foolish fear that the end of time was at hand.

Verse 1, The word of Jehovah that came to Joel the son of Pethuel.

"The word of Jehovah ..." This phrase identifies the content of this prophecy as the inviolate and eternal word of Almighty God, and so we receive and interpret it. It had an immediate and compelling relevance to the first generation that received it and is no less pertinent and relevant to

9

our own times. Great natural disasters are still taking place
on earth, in the face of which men are just as powerless and
helpless as were the ancient Jews who struggled against an
overwhelming invasion of devastating locusts. God wanted
his people to see in that natural catastrophe something far
more than merely an awesome natural phenomenon; and
therefore God moved to reveal through his holy prophet
what the genuine significance of such an event really is.
This significance still should be recognized in all physical
disasters that torment and destroy men upon earth, as was
beautifully discerned by Boren:

> It is my conviction that the eruption of Mt. St.
> Helens is an awesome display of the omnipotent power
> of God, and one of the countless warnings of God to
> humankind of impending judgment! Certainly, God
> warns through his word; but he also warns through the
> observable cataclysmic happenings of the natural
> world.[1]

One of the reasons, therefore, why God gave his word to
Joel upon the occasion of a great natural disaster is that
men of all subsequent centuries should know how to interpret such things.

It is wrong to refer the judgments and conclusions that
are set forth in Joel as merely the judgments and conclusions of the prophet himself. On the day of Pentecost, an
inspired apostle of Christ said:

> This is that which hath been spoken through the
> prophet Joel: And it shall be in the last days, saith
> God, I will pour forth of my Spirit. . . . etc. (Acts 2:16-
> 17).

Note particularly the words "spoken through the prophet
Joel . . . saith God . . ." We may be certain therefore that no
merely naturalistic origin of the great conclusions in Joel is
possible. The words spoken and the conclusions given are of
God himself, and not merely based upon the prophet's
fears, interpretations and discernments. For this reason,

---

[1]Maxie B. Boren, *The Messenger* (Corsicana, Texas, Church Publication,
1980), June 8, p. 1.

such interpretations as the following should be rejected:

> So terrible was the devastation that the prophet
> feared that Yahweh's Day, the judgment of Yahweh's
> people, was near at hand.² Joel regards the locust
> plague as comparable to any other mightly act of Is-
> rael's history.³

It was not merely Joel's *fears* that connected the locust
plague with the Day of the Lord; it was not merely Joel's
private conclusion that the locust plague was comparable
to any other mighty act of God in the history of Israel.
These conclusions were part of the "word of Jehovah"
which came to Joel.

"Joel the son of Pethuel . . ." Despite the fact of there
being a dozen persons named "Joel" in the OT, the name
"Pethuel" is found nowhere else. It has the utility, thus, of
dissociating Joel from others of the same name in Hebrew
history. The use of expressions like, "son of . . . etc." "was
analogous to our use of second names."⁴

**Verse 2, Hear this, ye old men, and give ear, all ye inhabit-
ants of the land. Hath this been in your days, or in the days
of your fathers?**

"Old men . . ." This is not a reference to some special
class of leaders among the people, but merely an appeal to
those of the most advanced age who could more readily
confirm the uniqueness of the disaster that was upon them.

"All ye inhabitants of the land . . ." The whole prophecy
is addressed to all the people, and not merely, to special
classes.

"Hear this . . ." The prophet, having himself heard God's
word is constrained to share it with others.

> God's word is never for our selfish enjoyment; it
> brings with it a responsibility for others. Perhaps that

²J. Lindblom, *Prophecy in Ancient Israel* (Philadelphia: Fortress Press,
1965), p. 276.
³R.A. Cole, *NBCR* (Grand Rapids: Wm. B. Eerdmans Publishing Company,
1970), p. 718.
⁴Derward Deere, *WBC* (Chicago: Moody Press, 1962), p. 820.

is why, in the NT, so much stress is laid on oral confession of Jesus Christ (Romans 10:9)[5]

The NEB is obviously correct in rendering "aged men" in this verse instead of "elders," since it is not of "the rulers" of the people that the prophet speaks here, but merely of those of great age, who neither in their own lives or that of their ancestors as communicated to them had there ever occured anything of the magnitude of that overwhelming infestation of locusts.

Verse 3, Tell ye your children of it, and let your children tell their children, and their children another generation.

Locust plagues were ordinary experiences in that part of the world during the times of Joel, and for centuries prior to and subsequently to his times, as indeed they still are; but this was not an ordinary locust plague.

> The special significance of this one related not only to its severity, but also to the fact that it is seen as a prelude to the devine devastation the prophet envisions for the disobedient people of God, and those nations which have oppressed her.[6]

"Tell ye your children . . . etc." "There is unmistakable allusion to Exodus 10:2, where the Lord charges Moses to tell Pharaoh that he will do signs,"[7] with similar instructions for Pharaoh to tell his sons, etc. This indicates that this mighty plague was comparable in gravity and origin to the plagues of Egypt and the deliverance of God's people through the Red Sea. It must not be understood as merely an extraordinary natural phenomenon, but as a direct judgment of God upon wickedness. The reason why the details of this disaster were to be remembered and passed on to succeeding generations was rightly stated by Myers, "as a deterrent to sin."[8]

[5]R.A. Cole, *op. cit.*, p. 718.

[6]Paul E. Leonard, *NLBC* (Grand Rapids: Zondervan Publishing House, 1979), p. 942.

[7]C.F. Keil, *Commentary on the OT, Vol. 10* (Grand Rapids: Wm. B. Eerdmans Publishing Company), p. 175.

[8]Jacob M. Myers, *The Layman's Bible Commentary* (Richmond, Va.: John Knox Press, 1959), p. 77.

The proper understanding and interpretation of such natural disasters as that recounted in Joel must always include the discernment of God's hand in them.

> God would ever have his children recognize his hand in all such visitations. For the believer, there are no second causes. The Lord has said, "I Jehovah create peace, and create evil." And he asks the question, "Shall there be evil in a city, and the Lord hath not done it?" (Isaiah 45:7; Amos 3:6).[9]

Verse 4, That which the palmer-worm hath left hath the locust eaten; and that which the locust hath left hath the canker-worm eaten; and that which the canker-worm hath left hath the caterpillar eaten.

The two great problems of interpretation encountered in this verse regard (1) the four different names applied to the destroying insects, and (2) the question of whether or not this was a literal infestation.

As to the four different names, they have been supposed to refer to the locust at various stages of its development; but the most thorough studies of that insect do not reveal four different phases in its life cycle. As Keil said, "These words never appear in simple plain prose,"[10] and all of them may therefore be poetic references to the same insect. "The four names are not names applied in natural history to four distinct species."[11]

The question about whether this was a literal disaster, or perhaps a symbolical depiction of some future event prophesied by Joel, is decided by verse 3, where there is an undeniable reference to Exodus 10:2, with the mandatory deduction that this disaster was comparable to the Egyptian plagues, which, of course, were literal events.

The allegorical interpretation of these locusts, however, has been very attractive to whole generations of interpretators.

---

[9]H.A. Ironside, *Notes on the Minor Prophets* (Neptune, N.J.: Loizeaux Brothers, Inc., 1909), p. 114.

[10]C.F. Keil, *op. cit.*, p. 181.

[11]*Ibid*, p. 180.

On the margin of the Greek Codex Marchalianus (Q) of the sixth century, the words for locusts in 2:25 are identified with the Egyptians, Babylonians, Assyrians and Greeks ... According to Merx, Joel's locusts are supernatural apocalyptic creatures in chapter 1, and symbols of the invading armies of the end times in chapter 2.[12]

The denial that the locusts were a literal disaster is totally frustrated by "before our eyes" (1:16). That the recapitulation of the disaster in chapter 2 indeed has overtones of the end times can hardly be discounted, due principally to the manner of the apostle John's treatment of the locusts in Revelation 9th chapter.

The palmer-worm, locust, canker-worm, and caterpillar may therefore be understood in this chapter as saying that, "One swarm of locusts after another has invaded the land, and completely devoured its fruit."[13]

The notion that plagues in successive years are meant is from the mention of "the years that the locust hath eaten" (2:25); but, again, from Keil:

We cannot possibly think of the field and garden fruits of two successive years, because the fruits of the second year are not the leavings of the previous year, but have grown afresh in the year itself.[14]

Before leaving this verse, it is of interest that Deere translated the four names as, "shearer, swarmer, lapper, and devourer, describing four of the eighty or ninety species of locusts in the East."[15] This understanding of the terms as different kinds of locusts is widely accepted; but the view preferred here is that the words are poetic descriptions of wave after wave of the devouring insects.

Verse 5, Awake, ye drunkards, and weep; and wail, all ye drinkers of wine, because of the sweet wine; for it is cut off from your mouth.

[12]John H. Thompson, *IB, Vol. VI* (New York: Abingdon Press, 1957), p. 733.
[13]C.F. Keil, *op. cit.*, p. 182.
[14]*Ibid.*, p. 181.
[15]Derward Deere, *op. cit.*, p. 821.

Joel viewed the locust plague as a manifestation of God's displeasure due to the sins of his people; and, quite appropriately, he directed his first great admonition, "Awake," to a prominent class of sinners always present in any wicked society, i.e., the drunkards. Naturally, the destruction of all vegetation, including the vineyards, would have interrupted and cut off the supply of intoxicants. Notably, Joel did not address this class as unfortunates overcome by some innocent disease. Ah no. The biblical view of drinking intoxicants and wallowing in drunkenness relates such conditions to wickedness, and not to disease. Our own current society has repudiated this view; but it is nevertheless correct. As Shakespeare put it:

> O thou invisible spirit of wine,
> If thou hast no name to be known by, let
> Us call thee devil.[16]

Thomas' comment on this whole verse is pertinent:

> *Awake*, you are sleeping on the bosom of a volcanic hill about to burst and engulf you. *And weep*, because of the blessings you have abused, the injuries you have inflicted upon your own natures, and upon others; weep because of the sins you have committed against yourself, society, and God. *Howl, all ye drinkers of wine* . . . If you were aware of your true situation, you would howl indeed, howl out your soul in confession and prayer![17]

Verse 6, For a nation is come up upon my land, strong, and without number; his teeth are the teeth of a lion, and he hath the jaw-teeth of a lioness.

"For a nation . . ." This expression, of course, has been made a basis of advocating a symbolical interpretation of the locusts. Such a personification of locusts is in keeping with the biblical description of ants and conies as "folk" and "people" (Proverbs 30:25-27), and it is interpreted here as metaphorical description of

[16]William Shakespeare, *Othello, Act II, Sc. 3, Line 285.*
[17]D. Thomas, *Pulpit Commentary, Vol. 13, Joel* (Grand Rapids: Wm. B. Eerdmans Publishing Company, 1950), p. 17.

the locusts. However, there very well may be here an overtone of the wider application of the locust invasion that appears in chapter 2.

As Kennedy said, "Viewed collectively, they were like an invading army. Such indeed is the suggestion of the phrase *has come up against my land* (cf. 2 Kings 18:13)."[18] Barnes was probably correct in his understanding that:

Here it is used, in order to include at once, the irrational invader, guided by a Reason above his own, and the heathen conqueror. For this enemy is come up upon my land, i.e., the Lord's land.[19]

Verse 7, He hath laid my vine waste, and hath barked my fig-tree: he hath made it clean bare, and cast it away; the branches thereof are made white.

"Barked" may also be translated "splintered"; and some commentators have viewed this as hyperbole. "The locusts could not splinter the fig-tree";[20] but such a view is due to a failure to take into consideration what would happen to a soft and brittle branch of a fig-tree when overloaded with an incredibly large swarm of locusts which would literally break it off. Certainly the devastation of locusts is too widely known in the East to make possible any claim of exaggeration on Joel's part, even for the sake of emphasis.

Verse 8, Lament like a virgin girded with sackcloth for the husband of her youth.

"Like a virgin girded with sackcloth for the husband of her youth . . ." This refers to the mourning of a virgin espoused to her husband whose life ended before the consummation of the marriage, a grief that was considered to be particularly anguished by the Hebrews. It is, of course, the Jewish ancient customs regarding marriage that appear in such a reference as this. It will be remembered that Joseph, the husband of Mary, was troubled by what he at

---

[18]J. Hardee Kennedy, *BBC, Vol. 7* (Nashville: Broadman Press, 1972), p. 69.
[19]Albert Barnes, *Notes on the OT, Minor Prophets, Vol. 1* (Grand Rapids: Baker Book House, 1953), p. 161.
[20]Derward Deere, *op. cit.*, p. 821.

first thought to be a reflection upon the chastity of his wife during their espousal, and before the marriage had really begun (Matthew 1:18-24).

Also, there is a reminder here that the chosen people themselves, the nation of Israel, were frequently compared to a beautiful virgin. "The real subject here is the congregation or people of Judah, as suggested in the Chaldee."[21]

Verse 9, The meal-offering and the drink-offering are cut off from the house of Jehovah; the priests, Jehovah's ministers, mourn.

Naturally, with the total destruction of all crops and vegetation, the usual sacrifices in the temple were curtailed and eliminated. Joel's speaking of the priests here in the third person is taken to indicate that he was not of their number. It is incorrect to make Joel's concern for this interruption of the sacrifices as the basis of postulating a late post-exilic date when the congregation in Judah was very small; because the total devastation inflicted by the locusts would have produced a similar effect whenever it might have occurred. The seriousness of this cessation of the daily offerings was inherent in the people's conviction that by the means of those sacrifices their fellowship with God was perpetuated and maintained. "Without those offerings, the people felt loss of contact with the Lord; and the priests, who understood their significance, mourned."[22] In spite of the reluctance of the people to cut off the supplies necessary to the faithful observances of the sacrifices, however, "there was no food left for man or beast."[23] No wonder that the priests mourned, for their very livelihood depended upon the offerings out of which they lived.

Verses 10-12, The field is laid waste, the land mourneth; for the grain is destroyed, the new wine is dried up, the oil languisheth. Be confounded, O ye husbandmen. Wail, O ye vinedressers, for the wheat and for the barley; for the harvest of the field is perished. The vine is withered, and the

[21]W.J. Deane, *Pulpit Commentary, Vol. 13, Joel* (Grand Rapids: Wm. B. Eerdmans Publishing Company, 1950), p. 3.
[22]Jacob M. Myers, *op. cit.*, p. 78.
[23]Robert Jamieson, *JFB* (Grand Rapids: Zondervan Publishing House, 1961), p. 784.

fig-tree languisheth; the pomegranate-tree, the palm-tree also, and the apple-tree, even all the trees of the field are withered: for joy is withered away from the sons of men.

This paragraph depicting the devastation of the locust scourge is as moving and dramatic a presentation as can be imagined. There is no need of help of any kind in understanding the full meaning of such a description; it is a classic. Something in it reminds us of that sorrowful and heart-moving speech delivered by Sir Winston Churchill at a low water mark of Great Britain's struggle against Hitler in World War II: "Singapore has fallen. The Prince of Wales is lost. The Repulse is at the bottom of the sea!" There is something of that same epic tragedy in Joel's wonderful words here. As Deane commented:

> "The field is wasted; the ground mourns; the corn is wasted; the new wine is spoiled; the oil decays!" — What a scene of desolation! yet how briefly and forcibly depicted! We see it all; we want nothing more to present it to our eyes.[24]

Not merely the fruit-bearing trees, but "even all the trees" of the field had been denuded and left bare and white in the sun, with even the bark stripped off.

> Pictures taken after a locust plague in 1915 show branches of trees completely devoid of bark and glistening white in the heat of the sun.[25]

A marvelous description of the locust plague is given in the National Geographic Magazine for August, 1969, under the title, "The Teeth of the Wind." A heavy locust flight actually darkens the sun and brings utter devastation in its wake.

Verses 13-14, Gird yourselves with sackcloth, and lament, ye priests; wail, ye ministers of the altar; come, lie all night in sackcloth, ye ministers of my God: for the meal-offering and the drink-offering are withholden from the house of your God. Sanctify a fast, call a solemn assembly, gather

---

[24]W.J. Deane, *op. cit.*, p. xi.
[25]Jacob M. Myers, *op. cit.*, p. 78.

the old men and all the inhabitants of the land unto the house of Jehovah your God, and cry unto Jehovah.

This appeal for the priests of God's religion to bestir themselves upon behalf of arousing the nation to repentance, prayer, and fasting indicates that it had been the wickedness of the people which had precipitated the onset of the plague. This interpretation of great natural calamities and disasters is not superstitious, at all, but biblical. God is still concerned with the behavior of his human creation; and, beginning with the primeval curse upon the ground for Adam's sake (Genesis 3:17-19), the Lord has continually ordered the affairs of his world in such a manner as to prevent man's becoming too complacent and comfortable in his earthly environment. It is this basic fact which underlies this appeal to the priests to stir up the people in the direction of righteousness and more wholehearted observance of their religious duties.

The calling of a solemn public assembly, the proclamation of a fast, and the public and private prayers offered to God for the alleviation of their distress were an entirely appropriate response to the threat of starvation and death which had come upon them in the locust plague. What other response should sinful, fallible and helpless men make to a situation which is totally beyond their control? It was a very similar thing which the Ninevites did under the threat of the preaching of Jonah. This is the way that Jehoshaphat responded to the impending attack by the allied armies of Moab, Ammon, and Edom; and this is exactly what Jehoiakim and Ezra did in the face of dangers which, without the help of God, they knew would destroy them. Modern men sometimes imagine that they are able to deal with everything that may happen, feeling no need for prayers and supplications to God; but this is an erroneous and short-sighted blindness, which, historically, God has repeatedly moved to correct; and one may feel sure that he will do so again.

The priests and leaders of the people were called upon to lead the way in this national response to the threat of death and destruction; and this was probably done for two reasons. First, the priests and national leaders were sinners in exactly the same way as the rest of the nation; and secondly, their example was sorely needed in order to arouse as nearly unanimous response as possible.

The reference to meal-offering and drink-offering in this verse has been alleged to indicate a post-exilian date; but one should be very wary of such allegations. Scholars, in their enthusiasm to maintain their postulations, sometimes go overboard in making deductions from totally insufficient premises. Regarding this, Robertson wrote:

> The only ritual references (in Joel) are to the meal-offering and the drink-offering, and these were characteristically not post-exilian. Indeed, they may be regarded as primitive forms of offerings![26]

Verse 15, Alas for the day! for the day of Jehovah is at hand, and as destruction from the Almighty shall it come.

In this verse, Joel went a step beyond the terrible visitation of the locusts threatening starvation and death to the whole nation; and he prophesied that "the day of Jehovah is at hand!" The biblical use of this expression is enlightening; and we shall devote some space to a discussion of it.

"The day of the Lord" has two meanings in the prophetic use of the expression. (1) It means any time of severe visitation inflicted upon either nations or upon all mankind by the judgment of God upon human sin and unrighteousness. In his famed Olivet discourse, the Lord Jesus clearly referred to the fall of Jerusalem and the destruction of the Jewish temple as his "coming" in judgment upon Israel, a summary judgment which followed as the direct result of their terminal rebellion against God in the rejection and crucifixion of the Messiah. From this, it is clearly seen that other great historical judgments upon such wicked cities as Tyre, Sidon, Ninevah, Babylon, Sodom, and Gomorrah were exactly the same type of visitation that fell upon Jerusalem.

(2) The ultimate meaning of "day of the Lord" identifies it with the final and terminal destruction of the entire posterity of Adam and Eve upon the great occasion of the

---

[26]James Robertson, *ISBE* (Chicago: Howard-Severance Company, 1915), p. 1692.

eternal Judgment Day, when the dead shall be raised, the righteous redeemed, and the wicked turned aside for ever. These distinctively different meanings were not always clear to the prophets who used the phrase (which actually came from God); indeed, it is safe to assume that they might never have known the full meaning of what they prophesied, as detailed by the apostle Peter in 1 Peter 1:10-12. The holy prophets were not concerned with fully understanding what the message from God might have been, but with delivering it accurately to their fellow men.

The nature of the "day of the Lord," whatever the specific situation foretold, is clearly given in this verse. "As destruction from the Almighty shall it come."

From this it is plain that the "day of the Lord" never referred to a benign and peaceful event, but to "destruction." This is what it meant for the ante-deluvian world which was destroyed from the face of the earth because of their wickedness; and that is what it invariably meant in all the other instances of it which have been cited. Furthermore, this is what it will ultimately mean at the Final Judgment at the Second Coming of Christ. That will be the occasion when the primeval sentence imposed upon the progenitors of the human race for their rebellion in the Garden of Eden will be finally and irrevocably executed upon them in the person of their total posterity, the unique exceptions to the universal destruction of that Day being only those who have been redeemed through the blood of Christ.

Thus, when one of the ancient prophets referred to "the day of Jehovah," it always referred, not merely to the Final Arraignment and Punishment of mankind, but to any lesser judgment that might be imposed upon specific sectors of humanity (or even upon all of it) in the period intervening before that Final Day. "For Joel, as for the other prophets, 'the day of the Lord' is always at hand."[27] "Joel did not mean that the day of the Lord, in its full prophetic sense, of the revelation of Christ ... was really to occur in their times."[28] However, Joel did see in that terrible locust plague

---

[27]Paul E. Leonard, *NLBC* (Grand Rapids: Zondervan Publishing House, 1979), p. 943.
[28]H.A. Ironside, *op. cit.*, p. 119.

"a warning of 'the day of Jehovah' which was to come."[29]
Furthermore, it was a warning that other occasions of 'the
day of Jehovah' were in store for Israel. Historically, it was
only a little while before the Assyrians and the Babylonians
would come and execute "the day of Jehovah," not merely
upon the northern kingdom, but upon the southern kingdom of Israel as well. Thus Joel very accurately foretold
future judgments upon Israel, taking the locust disaster as
an omen, or an earnest, of an even greater judgment (or
judgments) yet to come. Deane correctly discerned this:

> "The day of the Lord," first mentioned, it is said, by
> Joel, is the day when God inflicts punishment upon
> sinners, as in the present instances; it may be a pres-
> age of that judgment that brought ruin to their city,
> temple, and nation. It may be an emblem of that judg-
> ment that wound up their nation by the destruction of
> their capital, or even of the final judgment when God
> shall destroy the impenitent sinners and deliver his
> saints.[30]

It is totally wrong to allege that Joel himself understood
all that was indicated by his prophecy here of "the day of
the Lord"; nor is it possible to suppose that even today
students of the holy scriptures have any complete knowledge of all that is meant.

In view of the unmistakable overtones associated with
"the day of Jehovah," full agreement is felt with Jamieson
who noted that, "Here the transition begins from the
plague of locusts to the worse calamities (ch. 2) from invading armies about to come on Judea, of which the locusts
were the prelude."[31] As Barnes put it, "All judgment in
time is an image of the judgment for eternity."[32]

**Verses 16-18, Is not the food cut off before our eyes, yea,
joy and gladness from the house of God? The seeds rot
under their clods; the garners are laid desolate, the barns
are broken down; for the grain is withered. How do the**

[29]Homer Hailey, *A Commentary on the Minor Prophets* (Grand Rapids:
Baker Book House, 1972), p. 46.
[30]W.J. Deane, *op. cit.*, p. 6.
[31]Robert Jamieson, *op. cit.*, p. 784.
[32]Albert Barnes, *op. cit.*, p. 167.

beasts groan! the herds of cattle are perplexed, because they have no pasture; yea, the flocks of sheep are made desolate.

This is a further emphasis upon the severity of the plague; and it is evident that the scourge of the locusts has been compounded and multiplied by drouth. The situation appeared to be utterly hopeless. Without food or pasture, the herds of sheep and cattle would soon die; a disaster of the greatest magnitude was upon them.

> What with the locusts devouring all that appeared above ground, and the drouth destroying the seeds sown under the surface, the havoc was complete; famine and distress afflicted both man and beast.[33]

Verses 19-20, O Jehovah, to thee do I cry; for the fire hath devoured the pastures of the wilderness, and the flame hath burned all the trees of the field. Yea, the beasts of the field pant unto thee; for the water brooks are dried up, and the fire hath devoured the pastures of the wilderness.

We do not see any need whatever to understand "fire" and "flame" in these verses as a metaphorical reference to the locusts and the drouth; the danger of fire increases in direct proportion to the dryness of the vegetation and the atmosphere, as any forest ranger knows; and with the extended devastation and drouth already described, the breakout of terribly destructive fires would have been certain. If nothing else was available to set them off, a stroke of lightning would have been sufficient. For that reason, we feel it necessary to disagree with Keil, who wrote:

> Fire and flame are the terms used by the prophet to denote the burning heat of the drouth, which consumes the meadows and even scorches the trees. This is very obvious from the drying up of the water brooks.[34]

[33]W.J. Deane, *op. cit.*, p. 7.
[34]C.F. Keil, *op. cit.*, p. 188.

Summarizing what the chapter reveals about the cataclysmic disaster: it resulted from wave after wave of devouring locusts who ate up every green thing, and was made more complete by the ravages of a drouth so severe that the very watercourses became dry, and then was climaxed by forest and dry-grass fires which raged out of control in the super-dry "trees of the field" and the "pastures of the wilderness." No greater calamity could be imagined in a society predominantly agricultural and pastoral.

"O Jehovah, to thee do I cry . . ." In the last analysis, there is none other, except God, to whom the helpless and the hopeless may appeal. Even the rabbit cries out in the clutches of the hawk! Man instinctively cries to his Creator in the face of death and destruction.

CHAPTER 2

This chapter begins with the announcement that "the day of Jehovah cometh," and the summons of all of the people to a solemn convocation in the presence of God (1-3). There is a strong eschatalogical overtone in verse 1, a note which is echoed again and again in the chapter. "The eschatalogical warning already sounded in 1:15 is several times repeated (2:1,2,10 and 11)."[1] "A more terrific judgment than that of the locusts is foretold, under imagery drawn from that of the calamity then engrossing the afflicted nation."[2] Next comes a description of the threatened judgment, "in metaphors more distinctly military in nature,"[3] (4-11). A solemn appeal for genuine heart-felt repentance is then made, based upon the premise that, "Who knoweth whether he (God) will repent, and leave a blessing behind him?" (12-14). The call for a solemn assembly is repeated (15-17); a reaffirmation of God's care for his people and a promise of his blessing are given (15-20); a continued affirmation of the favored status of Israel as God's chosen people appears (21-27); and, finally, the chapter has, "a promise of the Holy Spirit in the last days under the Messiah, and the deliverance of all believers in Him,"[4] (28-32). This last paragraph is written as a separate chapter in the Hebrew Bible, giving four chapters instead of three in that version of Joel.

Verse 1, Blow ye the trumpet in Zion, and sound an alarm in my holy mountain; let all the inhabitants of the land tremble: for the day of Jehovah cometh, for it is nigh at hand.

"Blow ye the trumpet of Zion . . ." This verse interprets the awful calamity that had come upon the people, "as a

---

[1]John H. Thompson, *IB, Vol. VI* (New York: Abingdon Press, 1957), p. 743.

[2]Robert Jamieson, *JFB* (Grand Rapids: Zondervan Publishing House, 1961), p. 784.

[3]Paul E. Leonard, *NLBC* (Grand Rapids: Zondervan Publishing House, 1979), p. 943.

[4]Robert Jamieson, *op. cit.*, p. 784.

warning of 'the day of Jehovah' which was to come, the dawn of which was already breaking."[5] The blowing of the trumpet was used in the early history of Israel to call the people to the door of the tent of meeting (the tabernacle) during the wilderness wanderings, as a signal to start their journey from one station to another, or as means of calling the people together for a great assembly. This "horn blowing" therefore became a symbol connected with such occasions in all the subsequent history of Israel, and at times long after there was any possibility that "all the inhabitants of the land" would actually be able literally to hear the sound of a trumpet blown in Jerusalem. The NT writers extended the imagery of this "blowing of the trumpet" in a number of references to the final judgment, a usage that goes back to Christ himself who said, "And he shall send forth his angels with a great sound of a trumpet, and they shall gather together his elect from the four winds, from one end of heaven to the other" (Matthew 24:31). (See 1 Corinthians 15:52, 1 Thessalonians 4:16, and Hebrews 12:19). In the light of this, how unreasonable are the interpretations which insist that because of Joel's using this figure, the entire nation of the Jews was only a small community when he wrote, and actually living within earshot of Jerusalem! This is one of those "interpretations" relied upon heavily as evidence of a late post-exilian date.

"Sound an alarm in my holy mountain ..." The holy mountain here is the same as Zion, both being poetic references to the high hill (2,539' above sea level)[6] in Jerusalem upon which the temple was built. It was also called Mt. Moriah and is the same as the mountain where Abraham offered up Isaac, and where David returned the ark of the covenant from Obed-Edom, and where the cross of the Son of God was lifted up. As Deane said, "This mountain was the visible symbol of the divine presence";[7] and therefore the spiritual impact of this blowing of the trumpet (or ram's

---

[5]Homer Hailey, *A Commentary on the Minor Prophets* (Grand Rapids: Baker Book House, 1972), p. 46.

[6]W.J. Deane, *Pulpit Commentary, Vol. 13, Joel* (Grand Rapids: Wm. B. Eerdmans Publishing Company, 1950), p. 12.

[7]*Ibid.*

horn) had the effect of a summons for the people to stand in the presence of the Lord.

"Let all the inhabitants of the land tremble . . ." Perhaps those whose place of residence made it possible for them would also have actually assembled in the city of Jerusalem.

"For the day of Jehovah cometh, for it is nigh at hand . . ." For discussion of "the day of Jehovah," see under 1:15, above. To the prophets of the OT, and even the NT for that matter, "the day of the Lord" is always "at hand," the same being profoundly true, if the expression be understood as signaling the impending judgment of God upon the grossly wicked, or if it is taken as a reference to that great and final day, when Almighty God shall rise in righteous wrath and throw evil out of his universe. The first is always an earnest of the second. No greater misunderstanding of the sacred scriptures is current in the world today than the notion that Christ himself, and all of his apostles, thought that "the end of the world" was just around the corner. Christ indeed mentioned "the end of the world" in Matthew 28:10, but he certainly did not indicate that *that* event was impending or immediate. The "day of the Lord" and the "day of judgment," in its last and final manifestation will indeed evidently occur at the end of the world; but the widespread assumption that every NT reference to such things as "the day of the Lord," "the day of judgment," or the coming of Christ (in judgment) is a certain reference to the end of time is absolutely incorrect. Many cities, nations and peoples have already experienced "the day of the Lord," as did Tyre, Sidon, Sodom, Gomorrah, Nineveh, Babylon, Jerusalem and Rome; and doubtless many others will also yet pass through similar "judgments" before the actual "end of time" is reached.

Verse 2, A day of darkness and gloominess, a day of clouds and thick darkness, as a dawn spread upon the mountains; a great people and a strong; there hath not been ever the like, neither shall be any after them, even to the years of many generations.

It would appear that far more than any locust plague is in view here. "The locusts are now pictured on a scale larger than life, and many commentators have understood them here as prefiguring some invading army from the north."⁸ We do not hesitate to interpret this as a prophecy of the invasion of Israel by the Assyrians, who usually entered Palestine from the north. Some commentators, of course, hesitate to accept this, due to their erroneous decision that Joel was written at a time when the Assyrian scourge had already disappeared from the earth.

"There hath not been ever the like . . ." The unique terror of the Assyrians is a historical phenomenon; even the friezes that decorated the palaces of Ashurbanipal, and Ashurnasipal depicted the slaves and captives without skin, exposing the muscles and tendons as articulating with the bones in such a manner as to indicate that the Assyrians were more familiar with the human anatomy without skin, than they were with the normal body.⁹ They customarily flayed their victims, and often did this while the unfortunates were still alive!

As has been repeatedly stressed in this series, the prophetic description of "the day of the Lord" invariably appears in the very darkest colors. Another example is Amos 5:18ff, where the impact of that day upon men will be like that of one who flees from a lion, but who meets a bear, and then, finally reaching what might have been supposed as the safety of his house, he went in and leaned against the wall; and a serpent bit him! The seven parallel presentations of the Judgment Day in the book of Revelation all follow this tragic and exceedingly distressing pattern.

Verse 3, A fire devoureth before them; and behind them a flame burneth: the land is as the garden of Eden before them, and behind them a desolate wilderness; yea, and none hath escaped them.

"None hath escaped them . . ." This is the key that unlocks the extended meaning of the locusts in this passage. The locusts never hurt *people*; and clearly the disaster

---

⁸R.A. Cole, *NBCR* (Grand Rapids: Wm. B. Eerdmans Publishing Company, 1970), p. 720.

⁹Merrill F. Unger, *Archeology and the OT* (Grand Rapids: Zondervan Publishing House, 1954), p. 251.

threatened here is against the population itself. The probability of this view being correct is greatly enhanced by the
dual presentation of the locusts in Revelation 9th chapter.
In phase I, there was no loss of human life; but in phase II,
the "locusts" became a murdering army of 200,000,000
with a commission to destroy a third of the human race!
The genius of the inspired writers in discerning these *two
phases* in the life-cycle of the actual locust is certainly
reflected in both Joel and the book of Revelation. This two-
phase phenomenon in the life of the locust was not known
to the scientific community for generations; because it was
not until 1921 that, "The centuries-old question posed by a
locust swarm was answered (in 1921) by Sir Boris
Uvarov."[10] The revelation of this "Secret of the Locust"
was elaborately discussed by Robert A. M. Conley in 1969
thus:

> He discovered that one of the familiar green grass-
> hoppers of the African and Asian bush is really the
> ravenous locust in another guise. When repeated rains
> dampen desert sands, thousands of eggs hatch. The
> hoppers constantly touch one another, triggering a
> change of behavior and color; they seek each other's
> company and turn yellow, black and red.[11]

Quite evidently the peculiar use of the locust as a "type" by
both Joel and the apostle John resulted from their inspiration in knowing what would remain unknown about the
locusts until long millenniums afterwards! The connection
that this portion of the Bible has with the book of Revelation is further pointed up by the mention here of the garden
of Eden, that being the place where human rebellion
against God began, where the sentence of death was imposed (and never repealed), and where God uttered his curse
upon the ground "for Adam's sake." That ancient paradise
(Eden) is also repeatedly mentioned in Revelation, and for
exactly the same reasons as here. This reference by the
prophet to the garden of Eden is laden with great significance.

[10]*National Geographic Magazine, Vol. 136, No. 2, August, 1969* (Washington
D.C.: National Geographic Society), p. 209.
[11]*Ibid.*

30   *Commentary on the Minor Prophets*

"Fire devoureth before them, and behind them a desolate wilderness . . ." There is no need whatever to see this as any kind of metaphor. An invading army always burns everything in its path, leaving nothing behind except desolation.

Verse 4, The appearance of them is as the appearance of horses; and as horsemen, so do they run.

Revelation 9:7-12 has a remarkable elaboration of this same comparison of the locusts to "many horses rushing to war," even the sound of the locust's wings being compared to the noise of a cavalry charge. The impossibility of understanding John's words in Revelation as a reference to any literal locusts greatly enhances the probability that the true interpretation of them in this chapter is that they represent an impending military disaster coming soon to Israel in the invasion of the Assyrians.

These verses (4-11) describe disaster which Joel prophesied in much of the imagery of the locust plague, but there are the strongest military overtones throughout. "He must be speaking of real warriors under the figure of real locusts."[12]

To be sure, there were characteristics and appearances of the locusts which suggest horses rushing to war; but it is our conviction that it was God's word regarding this which was delivered by the prophet; he was not merely describing the way the locusts seemed to him. This does not deny the appropriateness of the comparison. As Jamieson said, "The locust's head is so like that of a horse that the Italians call it (the locust) *cavalette*."[13] It is also said that, "The amazing noise of the locusts can be heard six miles off!"[14]

Verse 5, Like the noise of chariots on the tops of the mountains do they leap, like the noise of a flame of fire that devoureth the stubble, as a strong people set in battle array.

This is a continuation of the prophecy of a military invasion, presented in the strongest military imagery. Horses

---

[12]George I. Robinson, *The Twelve Minor Prophets* (Grand Rapids: Zondervan Publishing House, 1926), p. 37.
[13]Robert Jamieson, *op. cit.*, p. 785.
[14]Derward Deere, *WBC* (Chicago: Moody Press, 1962), p. 823.

were, above all other animals, the instruments of war, as were also the chariots. The passage in Revelation 9:7-12 should be consulted in connection with what is said here.

Verse 6, At their presence the people are in anguish; all faces are waxed pale.

It is clearly not the destruction of vegetation that is indicated here; it is a prophecy of the appearance of "the breakers," the ruthless and savage army of Assyria that was capable of striking the fear of death into every heart and blanching the faces of all the people with paleness. As Keil said, "Joel is no doubt depicting something more here than the devastation caused by the locusts in his own day."[15]

Verse 7, They run like mighty men; they climb the wall like men of war; and they march every one on his own ways, and they break not their ranks.

The mention of "ranks" again suggests the military, not a swarm of insects; and, although it is true enough that the locusts move in a straight trajectory, turning aside neither to the right or the left, and even scaling walls and houses in their procedure, it has never been alleged by anyone that the locusts were definitely arrayed in "ranks" and "echelons." The prophecy throughout this section (4-11) moves beyond the locust plague to something more terrible. However, the locust plague was also terrible in its own right:

> When a wall or a house lies in their way, they climb straight up, going over the roof. When they come to water, whether a puddle, river, lake, or the open sea, they never attempt to go around it, but unhesitatingly leap in and are drowned; and their dead bodies floating on the surface make a bridge (over lesser bodies of water) for their companions to pass over. Thus the scourge often ends, causing a stench which sometimes produces a fearful plague.[16]

---

[15]C.F. Keil, *Commentary on the OT, Vol. 10* (Grand Rapids: Wm. B. Eerdmans Publishing Company), p. 192.
[16]W.J. Deane, *op. cit.*, p. iv.

This also has its counterpart in the stench of battlefields with the rotting of the dead bodies of men and horses.

Verses 8,9, Neither doth one thrust another, they march every one in his path; and they burst through the weapons, and break not off their course. They leap upon the city; they run upon the wall; they climb up into the houses; they enter in at the windows like a thief.

"Burst through the weapons . . ." is another stern military term, the weapons in view being the defensive weapons employed in warfare, not any kind of clubs used against locusts. The people visited by a locust plague already know the hopelessness of attacking the swarms with any type of "weapons," such things as fire, smoke, poisons, insecticides, and trenches filled with water being the usual defenses. The imagery here is that of a city's defenses being overwhelmed with military force.

Verse 10, The earth quaketh before them; the heavens tremble; the sun and the moon are darkened, and the stars withdraw their shining.

This terminology is invariably associated with the coming of Christ, or God, in judgment upon mankind. Jesus said, "The sun shall be darkened, and the moon shall not give her light, and the stars shall fall from heaven, and the powers of the heavens shall be shaken; and then shall appear the sign of the Son of Man in heaven" (Matthew 24:20,30). Fanciful illustrations of how a great swarm of locusts may cut off the light of sun, moon and stars, together with the denomination of this passage as hyperbole, fail to fill the bill here. The whole passage must be applied to "the day of Jehovah." Furthermore, as Hailey said, such a description as this verse, "became the prophetic description of Jehovah's judgments by the prophets that followed Joel,"[17] and was also adopted by the sacred writers of the NT as a description of the final judgment day, as seen repeatedly in Revelation (cf. Revelation 6:12-14).

This verse is a picture of the dreadful consequences of the present and temporary locust plague; but it is also a picture of the future judgment of God upon Israel, being also, even

[17]Homer Hailey, *op. cit.*, p. 49.

a type of the final judgment of all humanity on the Last Day.

Verse 11, And Jehovah uttereth his voice before his army; for his camp is very great; for he is strong that executeth his word; for the day of Jehovah is great and very terrible; and who can abide it?

Revelation 6:17 has this: "For the day of their wrath (that of God and the Lamb) is come, and who shall be able to stand?" The passage there is a reference to the eternal judgment. As Keil observed:

> That these words affirm something infinitely greater than the darkening of the lights of heaven by storm-clouds is evident from the predictions of the wrath of the Lord . . . at which the whole fabric of the universe trembles and nature clothes itself in mourning.[18] "These words give a theological and eschatalogical interpretation of the locust invasion."[19]

Verse 12, Yet even now, saith Jehovah, turn ye unto me with all your heart, and with fasting, and with weeping, and with mourning.

The contingency of all God's warnings of impending judgments is seen in this. No matter how closely a rebellious people might have moved toward that hidden boundary between God's mercy and God's wrath, the Father will even then be deterred from the execution of his wrath, if only the people will truly repent and turn to him with all their hearts.

Contrary to the widely advocated notion that it is *merely* the inward response alone that is important, this passage shows that a genuine turning to God with all the heart was an absolute essential; but so also was an acceptable outward manifestation of it, "fasting, weeping and mourning." "Genuine sorrow and shame for sin were to be accompanied by fasting, tears of penitence, and other *indications* of mourning."[20]

---

[18]C.F. Keil, *op. cit.*, p. 195.
[19]John A. Thompson, *IB, Vol. VI* (New York: Abingdon Press, 1957), p. 746.
[20]W.J. Deane, *op. cit.*, p. 22.

We should not leave this verse without noting that, "When the Bible says *heart* it means man's thinking powers, not his emotions."[21] Jesus once asked the Pharisees, "Why think ye evil in your hearts?" indicating clearly enough, that in the Bible, the heart is actually *the mind*. Emotions are always exposed in the sacred text as very unreliable.

Verse 13, And rend your heart, and not your garments, and turn unto Jehovah your God; for he is gracious and merciful, slow to anger, and abundant in lovingkindness, and repenteth him of the evil.

"And not your garments . . ." The prohibition in this is not directed against the demonstration of adequate external signs of repentance, for such *indications* of the inward condition of penitence had just been commanded in the preceding verse; what is forbidden, therefore, is the reliance upon such outward things *in the absence of* the truly penitent condition they were designed to demonstrate.

Joel here spoke of the same qualities of God's infinite graciousness, mercy, and lovingkindness that were known to Jonah (4:2), but it is very unlikely that either writer had received much information from the other, the same being a part of the heritage of Israel, and fully known to long generations prior to either Joel or Jonah.

"And repenteth him of evil . . ." Such an expression as this is a source of question to some; but the meaning is quite simple, beautifully stated thus by Hailey:

> God's repentance is a change of his will toward the people and is the result of a change of will and conduct on their part. Their repentance would cause God to pour out a blessing instead of judgment.[22]

Coupled with such terrible judgments as Joel had been proclaiming, was the possibility that the people might become overly discouraged and think that all was lost, no matter what they did; but in this great verse, Joel showed

[21]R.A. Cole, *op. cit.*, p. 721.
[22]Homer Hailey, *op. cit.*, p. 50.

himself ready to, "claim the covenant promise and hold it out as a lifeline to the people of his day."[23]

The tremendously beautiful message of this wonderful verse is given a musical treatment in *Elijah*, by Felix Mendelssohn.

Thompson also observed that the expression "and not your garments" "does not absolutely forbid this common sign of grief."[24] However, it is not forbidden at all, being one of the things commanded in the immediately preceding verse. What is meant by this passage is that no reliance should be placed in either the heart-felt repentance, or the outward observance of the actions indicating it, in the absence of the other. The genuine repentance without any outward tokens of it would fail as an example to others, for they would not be aware of it; and the outward tokens of it without the true repentance itself, would likewise fall utterly short of God's approval.

Verse 14, Who knoweth whether he will not turn and repent, and leave a blessing behind him, even a meal-offering and a drink-offering unto Jehovah your God?

"Who knoweth . . ." This was exactly the response of the people of Nineveh to the preaching of Jonah. They said: "Who knoweth whether God will not turn and repent, and turn away from his fierce anger, that we perish not?" (Jonah 3:9). This very likely indicates knowledge on the part of the Ninevites of this very passage in Joel; because all of the ancient Gentile nations were fully aware of God's special dealings with Israel, of his bringing them up out of Egypt; and they had, perhaps, also a knowledge of what their prophets had said. It is very difficult to believe that the Ninevites would have made exactly this response without a prior knowledge of Joel; a fact that advocates of a post-exilian date of Joel cannot explain at all.

Verses 15-17, Blow the trumpet in Zion, sanctify a fast, call a solemn assembly; gather the people, sanctify the assembly, assemble the old men, gather the children, and those that suck the breasts; let the bridegroom go forth

---

[23]John A. Thompson, *op. cit.*, p. 747.
[24]*Ibid.*

from his chamber, and the bride out of her closet. Let the priests, the ministers of Jehovah, weep between the porch and the altar, and let them say, Spare thy people, O Jehovah, and give not thy heritage to reproach, that the nations should rule over them: wherefore should they say among the peoples, Where is their God?

This passage is an elaboration of 2:1 and indicates that the utmost participation in the solemn assembly must be achieved, even bridegrooms who by Jewish custom were exempted from all public duties during the first year of marriage (even war), as well as brides and infant children were required to attend. See Deuteronomy 24:5.

The duties of priests, even including the exact prayer they were to pray, were included. Significantly, that prayer was not for the alleviation of the locust plague, but that God should avert the delivery of Israel into the hands of "the nations that they should rule over them." If proof were needed that this 2nd chapter deals with a great judgment symbolized by the locust plague, and not merely with such a plague itself, it surely appears here.

"Between the porch and the altar . . ." This and other related expressions in these verses have been made the basis of postulating a late post-exilian date; but as Robertson said:

> Too much is made of the references to ritual, as if they necessarily implied a post-exilian date. It is not legitimate here. . . . The meaning of "old men" or "elders" is no such indication. The expression everywhere in Joel means nothing more than "old men"; and, even if it had an official connotation, the official elders are an old tribal institution in Israel.[25]

"Give not thy heritage to reproach . . . Wherefore should they say, Where is their God? . . ." Such expressions as this "are all anterior to the earliest possible date of Joel, and prove that at an early time there was a consciousness in Israel that the fortunes of the people were bound up with

[25]James Robertson, *ISBE* (Chicago: Howard-Severance Company, 1915), p. 1691.

the honor of God."[26] Such an idea was certainly very much older than the times of the exile. As a matter of fact, this particular idea goes back to Moses himself who used exactly this same appeal in his plea to God to avert the threatened destruction of the nation upon the occasion of their worshipping the golden calf. He said:

> Wherefore should the Egyptians speak, saying, For evil did he bring them forth, to slay them in the mountains, and to consume them from the face of the earth? Turn from thy fierce anger, and repent of this evil against thy people. Remember Abraham, Isaac, and Israel, thy servants (Exodus 32:12,13).

Also, the book of Deuteronomy casts a great deal of light on this prophecy. Moses specifically warned the people of their becoming a "byword" among all nations, and that locusts would destroy their harvests (Deuteronomy 28:36-46); and, in the light of Moses' warning, it was actually no difficult thing to connect the present locust plague with the ultimate dispersion of Israel as a reproach among all nations as foretold by Moses.

Verse 18, Then was Jehovah jealous for his land, and had pity on his people.

Whether viewed as a prophecy of Joel of relief for the penitent people or as an exclamation of praise after the event of his mercy, this section (15-17) is rich with a portrayal of God's abundant blessings upon the covenant nation (not the secular state, as such, but the spiritual remnant who, in scripture, were always equated with the "true Israel"). "Apparently Joel had been successful in inspiring the people of Judah to repent sincerely, for here we are told that, 'The Lord became jealous for his land.' "[27] Two motives may be assigned to God as reasons for his "repentance" of the threatened disaster:

> The first is jealousy, the dishonor done to his name must be forever removed; the second, his pity, which

---

[26]*Ibid.*, p. 1693.
[27]Jacob M. Myers, *Layman's Bible Commentary, Vol. 14* (Atlanta: John Knox Press, 1959), p. 86.

has been stirred by the penitence of his afflicted people.[28]

It should be observed that none of this could be applied to the locust plague, a disaster which was already present; but it indicates that the ultimate destruction of Israel and their removal to other nations as captives, the more terrible judgment of which the locust plague was a symbol,—that disaster was indeed averted *for the time*.

The failure to see this second chapter as the prophecy of a far greater judgment than that of the locusts results in the interpretation of these verses (18-27) as a statement of God's promise to remove the terrible scourge of the locusts, or to bring about the cessation of it. Deere commented thus:

> Evidently the people responded to the prophet's invitation. The solemn convocation was convened; the people repented; and the Lord forgave them. Consequently, he now promises to remove the locusts and restore the prosperity of the land. Now all will know that God himself dwells with his people.[29]

This is, of course, correct as far as it goes; but the great damage of the locust plague still remained; and it is better to view the removal of the locusts as a symbol of a lifting of that greater doom impending, which eventually came, in the invasion of Assyrians and Babylonians.

Verses 19,20, And Jehovah answered and said unto his people, Behold, I will send you grain, and new wine, and oil, and ye shall be satisfied therewith; and I will no more make you a reproach among the nations; but I will remove far off from you the northern army, and will drive it into a land barren and desolate, its forepart into the eastern sea, and its hinder part into the western sea; and its stench shall come up, and its ill savor shall come up, because it hath done great things.

"I will remove far off from you the northern army . . ."

[28]W. Gladstone Watson, *ABC* (New York: Abingdon Press, 1929), p. 772.
[29]Derward Deere, *WBC* (Chicago: Moody Press, 1962), p. 824.

This is a prophetic *double entendre*, rather than a prob-lem."[30] Not only did the worst locust plagues usually de-scend on Jerusalem from the north,[31] but, "It was also true that Israel's main invaders: Aram, Assyria, Bablyon, Per-sia, Greece and Rome all attacked from the north."[32] What is evidently in view in this passage is that the summary end of the locust plague which resulted from their being carried by strong winds into the seas, is cited as a pledge that the greater judgment of invasion has also been averted. The use of the military words "the northern army" precludes the limitation of this to the locust scourge. Even the expres-sions "forepart" and "hinder part" are "more applicable to a human army's van and rear, than to locusts."[33]

"Stench shall come up . . . ill savor . . ." "One of the most refreshing things about the Bible is its frankness; a bad smell is still a bad smell, even in scripture."[34] As in other things in these verses, the words here have a double mean-ing, applying first to the bad odor resulting from the drown-ing death of millions of locusts, and secondly to the terrible odor of a battlefield with its unburied corpses of men and horses.

It should be pointed out that many eminent biblical com-mentators insist on seeing nothing in these verses of chap-ter 2, except a recapitulation of the prophet's very thorough description of the locusts in chapter 1. Deane, for example, said, "The army of this verse we still hold to be the tribes of locusts";[35] but even he admitted that, "The Assyrian ene-mies of Judah who advanced from the north are in a subsid-iary sense represented."[36] Despite the disagreement of many, however, it seems to us that the quality of the lan-guage in this chapter, coupled with the fact that there was no necessity whatever for any re-hash of the very adequate depiction of the locusts in chapter 1, compels the view which has been adopted here.

---

[30]R.A. Cole, *op. cit.*, p. 722.
[31]John D. Whiting, *National Geographic Magazine, Vol. 84, No. 12* (Washing-ton D.C.: National Geographic Society, 1915).
[32]R.A. Cole, *op. cit.*, p. 722.
[33]Robert Jamieson, *op. cit.*, p. 785.
[34]R.A. Cole, *op. cit.*, p. 722.
[35]W.J. Deane, *op. cit.*, p. 24.
[36]*Ibid.*

Verses 21,22, Fear not, O land, be glad and rejoice; for Jehovah hath done great things. Be not afraid, ye beasts of the field; for the pastures of the wilderness do spring, for the tree beareth its fruit, the fig-tree and the vine do yield their strength.

These verses are a beautiful description of the physical blessings which followed the removal of the locusts; and the mention that "Jehovah hath done great things" shows that the continuing act of God's provision for mankind through the abundance of his creation is no less a "great thing," than any of his more spectacular judgments against Israel's enemies. Just as the swarms of locusts were said to have "done great things" in v.20, the actions of God's benefits are no less so.

Verses 23,24, Be glad then, ye children of Zion, and rejoice in Jehovah your God; for he giveth you the former rain in just measure, and he causeth to come down for you the rain, the former rain, and the latter rain, in the first month.

These verses, continuing the theme of the whole section (18-27), are the praise of God for the temporal and physical blessings which were given to mankind, and to Israel in particular, because they were the covenant people.

Modern man supposes that he is above attributing any such physical benefits as rain and sunshine to God; and, as the mayor of a north New Jersey township objected to a public prayer meeting "for rain," brought about by a six-year drouth which had threatened the water supply of the whole section, "The water supply is too important to be left up to God!" there are many in the current culture who do not believe that God has anything to do with such things; but this is a frightfully short-sighted and inaccurate notion. In the last analysis, everthing depends upon the Father's will. The great climatic changes which can change a rain-forest into a petrified forest, or through drouth destroy the civilization of Frijoles Canyon are finally and absolutely of God himself. His will is back of everything.

Verses 25,26, And I will restore to you the years that the locust hath eaten, the canker-worm, and the caterpillar, and the palmer-worm, my great army which I sent among you.

And ye shall eat in plenty and be satisfied, and shall praise the name of Jehovah your God, that hath dwelt wondrously with you; and my people shall never be put to shame.

It is of interest that the four names of locusts appearing here are the reverse order of their use in 1:4. God promised the complete recovery of all the losses incurred from the terrible visitation.

"My great army which I sent among you ..." This is a reference to the locusts, since that is the subject being discussed; but this isolated use of the expression here is not sufficient to deny its symbolical and figurative use earlier. It is rather a reminder of the greater disaster symbolized by the locusts. In fact, even this description of the temporal benefits of God's blessings upon Israel is freighted with intimations of the spiritual benefits accruing to God's people in all ages to come. Paul so interpreted this very verse in Romans 10:11,13, where he spoke of the blessings of believing in Christ, saying, "For the scripture saith, whosoever believeth on him shall not be put to shame; for there is no distinction between Jew and Greek."

One great fact regarding such precious promises was that in the ultimate and final sense, they were contingent upon Israel's continued penitence and obedience. One may be very sure that the first generation to receive these words failed to get that condition. "My people shall never be put to shame" was a promise which secular Israel mistakenly assumed to be their unique heritage, overlooking the truth that in every age, God's people are those who do his will. These promises then, both here and in the succeeding verse, did not promise unlimited security and blessing for secular Israel, but to God's true people, the *spiritual seed* of Abraham.

Verse 27, And ye shall know that I am in the midst of Israel, and that I am Jehovah your God, and there is none else; and my people shall never be put to shame.

As Cole said, the expression "and there is none else" "is as strong a statement of monotheism as anything in the second half of Isaiah, or anywhere else in the OT."[27]

---

[37]*Ibid.*

The ends-of-the-earth implication of these last verses in this section is further emphasized by the switch immediately afterwards to the glorious promises of the outpouring of God's Holy Spirit during the times of the Messiah and his kingdom.

Verse 28, And it shall come to pass afterward, that I will pour out of my Spirit upon all flesh; and your sons and your daughters shall prophesy, your old men shall dream dreams, your young men shall see visions.

"And it shall come to pass afterward . . ." The specific fulfilment of this passage occurred on the day of Pentecost, upon which occasion the apostle Peter referred to the outpouring of the Holy Spirit upon the twelve apostles as "this is that which was spoken by the prophet Joel" (Acts 2:17f). To be sure, as Hailey said, "Only the apostles received the outpouring of the Holy Spirit on that occasion";[38] but the infusion of the Holy Spirit that became available to mankind on that day was a much more extensive thing than his miraculous demonstration upon the Twelve. Peter on that same occasion promised that all who would repent and be baptized in the name of Jesus Christ for the remission of sins, "shall receive the gift of the Holy Spirit"; and this also is included in the prophecy. It is in this extended sense that it is "upon all flesh." Furthermore, there were many isolated examples as seen in the virgin daughters of Philip (Acts 21:9) in which "sons and daughters" alike received great measures of the Holy Spirit. It was Moses who first expressed the hope that God's Spirit would be upon all the people, saying, "Would that all the Lord's people were prophets, that the Lord would put his Spirit upon them" (Numbers 11:29). The fulfilment of this desire is seen in the truth that every Christian is endowed with an "earnest" of the Holy Spirit.

Verse 29, And also upon the servants and upon the handmaidens in those days will I pour out of my Spirit.

It should be noted that beginning with the previous verse 28, this portion of Joel (to the end of the chapter) forms a

---

[38]Homer Hailey, *op. cit.*, p. 53.

separate chapter in the Hebrew version of the Bible, giving four chapters instead of three in that version.

This refers to the universality of membership in the Lord's church and the consequent reception of a measure of God's Spirit in the hearts of all believers during the times of the Messiah. Many of the Christians to whom Colossians and Ephesians were originally addressed were slaves; and in that is a most accurate and extensive fulfilment of these very words. Of course, it is not necessary to suppose that even Joel fully understood the import of this prophetic word, as noted above. As Robinson said: "Joel probably had but a vague appreciation of what these words really meant in the great program of God."[39] Of course, there has never been any need to understand Joel's prophecy here as a promise that "all of God's people" will be supernaturally endowed with the Holy Spirit. It was not so in the days of the apostles, nor is it true now.

"Old men shall dream dreams . . . young men shall see visions . . ." The place of dreams in the new covenant is greatly downgraded by a number of considerations;

> No other dream is mentioned in the NT save those given to Joseph in the very beginning of the NT, before the full Gospel had come, and to the wife of Pilate, a *Gentile*.[40]

There is absolutely nothing in the NT to indicate that any Christian or any other person (exceptions noted above) ever relied upon a dream for anything whatsoever. Christians of all ages have refused to trust dreams.

Verse 30, And I will show wonders in the heavens and in the earth, blood and fire and pillars of smoke.

Myers' observation that the portents in the heavens "are frequently associated with the coming of great events"[41] is correct. There was also a moral implication. Such omens as are mentioned in these verses "are omens of the Day of

---

[39]George I. Robinson, *op. cit.*, p. 39.
[40]Robert Jamieson, *op. cit.*, p. 786.
[41]Jacob M. Myers, *op. cit.*, p. 786.

Judgment, the day of the destruction of evil in order that good may survive and flourish."[42]

On the day of Pentecost, the apostle Peter quoted this very passage as having already been fulfilled *as a prelude* to "the great and notable Day of the Lord," the day upon which salvation would be given to all who should "call on the name of the Lord." Since the day on which Peter said that was only fifty three days after the crucifixion of Christ, it is appropriate to look to that event as the time of the portents mentioned here.

"Wonders in the heavens . . ." The sun's light failed for a period of three hours, the most remarkable "portent" ever seen in the heavens by any generation.

"And in the earth . . ." These would surely have included a number of wonders such as the rending of the veil of the temple, the earthquake that opened the graves of the righteous, the saints who came out of their graves after Jesus' resurrection, and the undisturbed grave clothes of Jesus. All of these things were surely among the wonders on earth beneath.

"Blood and fire and vapor of smoke . . ." These expressions almost certainly indicate one of the great Jewish national festivals as the occasion when God's wonders would be done. The sacrifice of many thousands of animals, the roaring fires of the sacrifices, and the "vapor of smoke" inevitably associated with those great occasions would appear to be adequate identification. Christ was crucified at the Passover festival, and the Holy Spirit came upon Pentecost, some seven complete weeks later; and thus the "blood, fire, vapor of smoke" reference was fully applicable to both occasions. See CA, pp. 44-48.

The crucifixion of Christ was a day when evil was destroyed (Satan was destroyed through the death of Christ, Hebrews 2:14), and was therefore an occasion fully important enough to be heralded by the portents mentioned here.

The echoes of the final judgment are also in these verses, but this should not be surprising. The Final Day actually began with the crucifixion of Christ and will be consumated at his Second Coming.

---

[42]*Ibid.*

"The last days" began with Christ's first advent and will end with the second advent. They are the days during which the age to come overlaps the present age; hence the assurance with which Peter quoted Joel's words and declared, "This is that."[43]

Peter's use of this passage is most significant. "He equated the gift of the Spirit with the dawning of the Messianic age, which was to usher in the final judgment."[44] It is very likely that Peter and all of the apostles regarded the final judgment as an event to occur in their own times, or shortly thereafter; although, in all fairness, it must be pointed out that no sacred writer ever said so! What the apostolical group "thought" is therefore a very poor basis for interpreting their words, which were not of themselves, but of God. The fact that the Final Judgment is still future, after nearly two thousand years, is no grounds whatever for supposing that the prophets were mistaken. Indeed no! The great and terrible judgment of all mankind will yet occur, as Jesus Christ and all of the apostles and prophets have warned. What appears to be "the delay" is merely the mercy and forbearance of God, "who is not willing that any should perish, but that all should come to repentance."

The Judgment Day will finally occur, and it will, in all probability, be ushered in by these same portents, on a cosmic scale, of which the occurrences known to Peter and the people who heard him were only the dim and feeble types.

Verse 31, The sun shall be turned into darkness, and the moon into blood, before the great and terrible day of Jehovah cometh.

The NT does not mention the light of the moon having failed during the wonders that attended the crucifixion; but Luke's assertion that "the sun's light failed" would necessarily also have involved the moon. Pagan testimony to the fact of both having occurred was cited in NT Apocrapha. Pontius Pilate wrote to the Emperor Tiberius that:

---

[43]F.F. Bruce, *The Book of Acts* (Grand Rapids: Wm. B. Eerdmans Publishing Company, 1954), p. 68.

[44]R.A. Cole, *op. cit.*, p. 723.

And when he had been crucified, there was darkness
over the whole earth . . . so that the stars appeared . . .
as I suppose your reverence is not ignorant of, because
in all the world they lighted lamps from the sixth hour
until evening. And the moon, being like blood, did not
shine the whole night, and yet she happened to be in
the full.[45]

Similar words are likewise used to describe the final judgment day in Revelation 6:12-17; and therefore, the events
connected with the Passion of Christ are most likely symbols of even more terrifying wonders that shall mark the
arrival of the Final Assize itself. That those events, foretold
by Joel, and mentioned as having already occurred by the
apostle Peter, were generally known throughout the Roman
empire would seem to be indisputable. Tertullian, in his
Apology directed to the "Rulers of the Roman Empire," in
paragraph 21, has this:

In the same hour, too, the light of the day was
withdrawn, when the sun at the very time was in his
meridian blaze. Those who were not aware that this
had been predicted of Christ, no doubt thought it was
an eclipse. You yourselves have the account of the
world-portent still in your archives.[46]

That Tertullian appealed to the rulers of the empire as
having a record of the very things prophesied by Joel and
fulfilled at the Passion of Jesus Christ would appear to be
of the very greatest significance. Tertullian would not have
dared to make such an appeal unless it had been generally
known and recognized as the truth.

A very excellent statement of the full meaning of this
passage was given thus by R. J. Knowling:

St. Peter saw in the outpouring of the Spirit the
fulfilment of Joel's prophecy (2:28-32) and the dawn of
the period preceding the return of Christ in glory.[47]

---

[45]Ante-Nicene Fathers, *Vol. VIII, Report of Pontius Pilate to Tiberius Caesar*
(Grand Rapids: Wm. B. Eerdmans Publishing Company, 1951), p. 463.

[46]Tertullian, *Apology, No. xxi* (Grand Rapids: Wm. B. Eerdmans Publishing
Company, 1951), *p. 35 in Vol. III of Ante-Nicene fathers.*

[47]R.J. Knowling, *Expositor's Greek NT, Vol. II* (Grand Rapids: Wm. B.
Eerdmans Publishing Company, 1967), p. 78.

"The last days . . ." A misunderstanding of this phrase clouds many of the interpretations. Ironside thought that, "all this can never be fulfilled till the people of Israel are restored to their land."[48] Others are querulous about how it could have been "the last days" so long ago; but, of course, Peter meant the dispensation of the last days; and besides that, in a very dramatic and genuine sense it was the "last days" for Israel. Their long occupancy of a favored role as God's chosen people ended with what was prophesied here. It was the end of their whole religious system, which, within forty years would be wiped off the face of the earth, never more to appear again. It was the "last days" of their secular state which soon would perish and never rise again until millenniums afterwards; it was "the last days" of the highpriesthood of Aaron and the Levites; it was "the last days" of the daily sacrifices, of the temple, and of the state and nation of Israel.

The ultimate fulfilment in the great and final Day of the Lord cannot, therefore, be in any way contingent upon secular Israel getting possession of "their land." Their status as "God's chosen people" ended forever when they crucified Christ; and there are no promises whatever regarding Israel in the NT, except as they may be realized by some of their number accepting Christ and thus establishing themselves as "seed of Abraham."

The proximity of the "great and terrible day of the Lord" was real enough for the generation to whom Peter applied these words. Christ had foretold the doom of Jerusalem, and from his understanding of Joel, Peter knew that the judgment against Jerusalem could not be long delayed, nor was it. It was executed by the armies of Vespasian and Titus who besieged and ravished the city of Jerusalem in August, A.D. 70. "That destruction, which fulfilled the prophecy, in turn became a prophetic type of the ultimate end of the world and of the judgment of God on the world of the ungodly."[49]

Thus, in the instance of "that great and notable day of the Lord," as in many of God's prophecies, there were two

[48]H.A. Ironside, *Notes on the Minor Prophets* (Neptune, N.J.: Loizeaux Brothers, 1909), p. 129.
[49]Homer Hailey, *op. cit.*, p. 54.

fulfilments, an immediate, and a remote fulfilment. The immediate fulfilment was the destruction of Jerusalem, and the remote fulfilment (yet to be) will appear at the end of the world, the Second Coming of Christ, and the final judgment.

Verse 32, And it shall come to pass, that whosoever shall call upon the name of Jehovah shall be delivered; for in mount Zion and in Jerusalem there shall be those that escape, as Jehovah hath said, and among the remnants those whom Jehovah doth call.

In the light of Peter's use of this passage, the primary meaning of it is applicable to salvation from sin, with the attendant indication that just a few, a "remnant" will actually participate in this salvation. In the extended meaning of the prophecy, "mount Zion and Jerusalem" stand for the church or kingdom of Jesus Christ which began there. In the spiritual sense, it is still true that "the word of the Lord goeth forth from mount Zion and Jerusalem."

This verse has been cited as "the clearest example in the whole book of one author quoting another";[50] but it should be particularly noted that Joel did not say, "Obadiah saith," but that "Jehovah saith." Joel says that he was giving God's word; and it is not necessary at all to make a portion of this passage a "quote" from Obadiah 17. As Cole freely admitted, "It is, however, possible that both Joel and Obadiah are quoting some earlier anonymous prophetic saying."[51] Of course, such a thing is easily possible; but there is yet another possibility that should never be ruled out by one who actually believes that the prophets were writing what they said they were writing, i.e., the "word of Jehovah"; and that is the possibility that Jehovah himself gave identical words to different authors. Why should such a possibility as this be ruled out? Certainly, any adequate theory of "inspiration" must always include it!

One familiar with the Bible knows that the standard formula for one sacred author's quoting another is that of giving the quoted prophet's name, as Peter did when he

---

[50]R.A. Cole, *op. cit.*, p. 723.
[51]*Ibid.*

quoted this passage. In the light of this, many so-called "quotes" cited by commentators are no such thing at all.

This prophecy looks beyond the time of restoration and rehabilitation of Joel's day, even beyond Pentecost which marked the inception of the new age, to a time of the final consummation of things visualized by the author of Revelation in his announcement of a new heaven and a new earth.[52]

The events of any prophetic fulfilment should be carefully studied for clues to possibilities in the ultimate fulfilment. Just as the Christians were warned prophetically of the destruction of Jerusalem, and all of them escaped it by retiring to Pella,[53] all who truly believe in Christ and obey him will escape the ultimate general destruction at the last day.

In view of the NT usage of this prophecy, it must be considered one of the most important sections of the OT.

---

[52]Jacob M. Myers, *op. cit.*, p. 91.
[53]Robert Jamieson, *op. cit.*, p. 787.

CHAPTER 3

The prophecy of this chapter is one of the most remarkable in the whole Bible; and, for centuries, interpreters have found no agreement in what to make of it. More than 150 years ago, Adam Clarke wrote that, "This is a part of the prophecy which is difficult to understand; all interpreters are at variance upon it,"[1] himself leaning toward the view that it referred to certain victories or changes in the fortunes of the secular state of Israel. It is our conviction that most of the failure to understand Joel 3 derives from a misunderstanding of the secular state and fleshly nation of the Jews as the principal, or even the sole, subject of God's concern and of his prophetic word, i.e., a confusion of the two Israel's of God, the one of the flesh alone, the other of the spirit and mind of Abraham. It is of this latter Israel, the true Israel alone, that the great prophecies of the OT are speaking, some notable exceptions occurring at a time when the two were commingled with a secular state which the fleshly Israel had injected into God's plans by their rebellion against him and their insistence upon having a king. As during the subsequent centuries the true Israel was necessarily mingled with the secular, and indeed confused with it, there were indeed many prophecies and references to "Israel" which applied to them *both*.

But in this chapter, one should forget all about the secular Israel, the Jewish state, the Hebrew nation, the fleshly Israel, the old Israel, etc. All of the references to Judah, Jerusalem, Zion, "my heritage Israel," etc. are used in a spiritual sense of the church and kingdom of Jesus Christ our Lord. The very first verse of this chapter dates everything in it subsequently to the Day of Pentecost; and that leaves the secular Israel completely out of it.

The first section of the chapter, in highly metaphorical language, speaks of the "true Israel" receiving the forgiveness of sins, and of the judgments of God upon the nations

---

[1]Adam Clarke, *Commentary on the Whole Bible, Vol. V* (New York: T. Mason & G. Lane, 1837), p. 667.

which opposed his purpose (1-7). Section two (9-13) has the same meaning as the gathering of the nations for the battle of Armageddon (Revelation 16); and it also has the summoning of all nations to the Final Judgment, presented under the figure of the sickle and the harvest as is also the case in Revelation 14. The reign of Christ is depicted in section three (14-17), during which time, the Lord "roars from Jerusalem" (in the NT which originated there), and also during which time the "people of Israel" (the church of Jesus Christ) will find their refuge in Jehovah (not in literal Jerusalem). All men during this phase of divine history will be caught up in "the valley of decision," where will be determined their destiny as servants either of Christ, or of the devil.

The final section of this chapter (18-21) is a figurative presentation of the wonderful spiritual blessings available in the kingdom of heaven.

Verse 1, For behold in those days, and at that time, when I shall bring back the captivity of Judah and Jerusalem.

"In those days, and at that time . . ." Cole said that this "points to the distant and vague future";[2] and, although that might be true as it seemed to the people of Joel's day, it is not so for us. What is clearly meant is that "in the times of the pouring out of God's Spirit upon all flesh," as prophesied immediately before these words, the captivity of Judah and Jerusalem will be "brought back." And of course, we know exactly when that time began, namely, on the first Pentecost after the resurrection of Christ. As Keil noted, "All of the views which refer these words to events before the Christian era are irreconcilable with the context."[3] Everything in this chapter is to occur after the outpouring of God's Spirit upon all flesh. Hailey correctly identified the time-frame of this chapter with "the dispensation following Pentecost."[4] All applications of these words to some future

[2]R.A. Cole,*NBCR* (Grand Rapids: Wm. B. Eerdmans Publishing Company, 1970), p. 724.
[3]C.F. Keil, *Commentary on the Whole Bible, Vol. 10* (Grand Rapids: Wm. B. Eerdmans Publishing Company), p. 219.
[4]Homer Hailey, *A Commentary on the Minor Prophets* (Grand Rapids: Baker Book House, 1972), p. 56.

millennium, or to pre-Christian episodes, are incorrect.

"I shall bring back the captivity of Judah and Jerusalem . . . ." One is at once aware of variations from this rendition, "The RSV (and a number of translations) rendering it in the more general sense of *restore the fortunes*."[5] This change was evidently made in order to accommodate the interpretation of this place as pertaining to secular Israel, an interpretation denied by the literal meaning of the words, because "even after the returns of the sixth and fifth centuries, many Jews still remained in exile."[6] However, the ASV and all of the ancient versions harmonize with the AV in this place, "bring again the captivity of Judah"; and "this is the literal translation."[7] It is therefore a very general and widespread captivity which is the subject of the prophecy. What is it? Jesus mentioned it in the first public sermon he ever preached:

He hath sent me to proclaim release to the captives,
And recovering of sight to the blind,
To set at liberty them that are bruised,
To proclaim the acceptable year of the Lord (Luke 4:18).

This is the only release of captives that can properly be identified with the dispensation of the Spirit of God; and it is clearly a release from bondage and servitude of sin that is meant. "It is the deliverance from the bondage of corruption into the glorious liberty of the Son of God."[8] The terrible captivity of the Jews (in the general sense) is to Satan, whose servants they chose to become when they cried, "We have no king but Caesar," and "his blood be upon us and upon our children." Likewise, the vast majority of the whole Gentile world as well are engaged in the very same servitude of the evil one. It is *that captivity*, preeminently, and above all others, with which God has always been concerned. In speaking of Jews and Gentiles, let it ever be remembered that all alike, both Jews and

---

[5]John A. Thompson, *IB* (New York: Abingdon Press, 1957), Vol. VI, p. 754.
[6]*Ibid.*
[7]R.A. Cole, *op. cit.*, p. 724.
[8]Albert Barnes, *Notes on the Minor Prophets, Vol. 1* (Grand Rapids: Baker Book House, 1953), p. 201.

Gentiles, are invited by the gospel of Christ to receive the turn of their captivity. Whosoever will may come! This sublime truth makes it impossible to suppose that God has in any manner wronged Israel by his refusal to accommodate to their carnal view of God's kingdom which identified it with *their state*! The fact that Amos "spoke of 'an entire captivity' (1:6,9),"[9] at a period long before either the Assyrian or Babylonian captivities occurred, shows the ancient prophets did not restrict this to a physical captivity. Then, as now, the problem was sin and rebellion against God.

"Turning again the captivity of Judah and Jerusalem" thus refers to the times of regeneration in the kingdom of Christ, that is, to this present dispensation of the gospel when all men, of every race and nation, if they so desire, may receive the forgiveness of their sins and the restoration of their broken fellowship with the Father.

Verse 2, I will gather all nations, and will bring them down into the valley of Jehoshaphat; and I will execute judgment upon them there for my people Israel, whom they have scattered among the nations; and they have parted my land.

"The valley of Jehoshaphat ..." "This is not to be thought of as a literal place in Palestine, but as an ideal place where judgment is to be executed."[10] This is the same as the place called Armageddon (Revelation 16); and in both cases, it is the place where God will execute his wrath upon evil men; and absolutely no "battle" of any kind is prophesied as occurring at either site. This judgment of God upon "all nations" who have persecuted God's people has already taken place repeatedly in history, as witnessed by Tyre, Sidon, Sodom, Gomorrah, Assyria, Nineveh, Babylon, Persia, Greece, Rome, and Jerusalem; and *it is still going on*! See in CRE, pp. 374-378.

"My people Israel whom they have scattered among the nations ..." Many expositors think only of the dispersion of the Jews; but more than that is meant.

[9]James Robertson, *ISBE* (Chicago: Howard-Severance Company, 1915), p. 1693.
[10]Homer Hailey, *op. cit.*, p. 56.

The people and inheritance of God are not merely the OT Israel as such, but the church of the Lord, (the true Israel) of both covenants, upon which the Spirit of God is poured out.[11]

The "scattering" here must then be applied to all of the many "scatterings" that were inflicted upon the old Israel, as well as to the "scatterings" of Christians all over the world, a very considerable number of which have resulted directly from vicious persecution by evil nations, as that which arose around the martyrdom of Stephen, the dispersion of the faithful that came about from the persecutions of the apostolical missionaries, as Paul, who fled from place to place, with a result of congregations being planted all over the Roman empire; and this pattern continues indefinitely and even into modern times; it was persecutions which drove the early colonies to the New World in the 17th century. Thus the scattering of God's people among the nations is not a one-shot episode that happened to ancient Israel. No wonder the commentators cannot decide what "scattering" is meant here!

"And have parted my land . . ." Here again, "my land" is wrongly read as "Palestine"; but the notion that any such place is any more "God's land" than North America or any other place on earth should have been laid to rest twenty centuries ago. "The earth is the Lord's, and the fulness thereof" (Psalm 24:1). The parting, or dividing of God's land therefore refers to the horrible divisions that have come upon the earth through the devices of wicked men. The whole world today is divided, because the only basis of unity through "one new man in Christ Jesus" has been denied and rejected by evil men. This passage teaches that the ultimate judgment of God will fall upon humanity for their sins. Deane was near the common consensus of opinions in this comment:

> This must be referred to the long subsequent time (from Joel) when Palestine became a Roman province, its capital levelled with the ground; then the great

---

[11]C.F. Keil, *op. cit.*, p. 222.

dispersion of the covenant people among the nations commenced, and continues to the present day.[12]

Apparently, however, Deane failed to include here the similar "scattering" of the true Israel and the "divisions" of mankind resulting from wickedness. They also, of course, are included.

Verse 3, And have cast lots for my people, and have given a boy for a harlot, and sold a girl for wine, that they may drink.

There have been many examples of the unconscionable wickedness represented by these examples of it. Significantly, fornication, drunkenness, and human slavery, especially child-abuse, are prominent here; and these are universally the hallmark of evil societies.

Verse 4, Yea, and what are ye to me, O Tyre, and Sidon, and all the regions of Philistia? will ye render me a recompense? and if ye recompense me, swiftly and speedily will I return your recompense upon your own head.

The omission of the names of many nations that were just as wicked as these cited has been widely misinterpreted, all kinds of allegations regarding the date of the prophecy being made to turn on the singular mention of just these; but these do not make up any kind of list, being merely well-known examples of horrible wickedness leading at last to God's judgment. Robinson spoke of this and other such data, as "obviously too indefinite to be of any great value in deciding the prophet's date."[13] It is significant that Amos also used these very examples of rampant wickedness. "Amos singles out the very nations mentioned by Joel, and reproaches them with such offences as Joel specifies (Amos 1:6-12)."[14]

"If ye recompense me . . ." Jamieson explained the meaning here thus: "If ye injure me (my people) in revenge for

[12]W.J. Deane, *Pulpit Commentary, Vol. 14, Joel* (Grand Rapids: Wm. B. Eerdmans Publishing Company, 1950), p. 47.
[13]George I. Robinson, *The Twelve Minor Prophets* (Grand Rapids: Baker Book House, 1926), p. 42.
[14]James Robertson, *op. cit.*, p. 1692.

fancied wrongs, I will requite you in your own coin, swiftly and speedily."[15] In all history, those nations which have undertaken to destroy Christianity have themselves been speedily destroyed. Secular Israel, pagan Rome, Assyria and Babylon are ancient examples, especially Jerusalem and Rome; but there are modern examples also. Hitler burned the Bibles at Nuremburg, but the fire did not go out till Berlin was totally ruined. God is still in control of his world.

Verses 5-8, Forasmuch as ye have taken my silver and my gold, and have carried into your temples my goodly precious things, and have sold the children of Judah and the children of Jerusalem unto the sons of the Grecians, that ye may remove them far from their border; behold, I will stir them up out of the place whither ye have sold them, and will return your recompense upon your own head; and I will send your sons and your daughters into the hand of the children of Judah, and they shall sell them to the men of Sheba, to a nation far off: for Jehovah hath spoken it.

This is merely an elaboration of the ancient divine principle that "whatsoever a man soweth, that shall he also reap"; and it applies to states and nations as well as to individuals. There is no hint in a passage like this of any divine approval of such things as slavery; Joel was merely citing some well-known examples of "retribution in kind" as prophecy of the way it would always be under the government of God. When a nation was victorious, they sold their captives as slaves; but, in turn, when they were defeated, their citizens were likewise sold into slavery. David took the sword of Goliath and hung it up in the temple (or tabernacle); and when Babylon took the Israelites captive, they looted the treasures of the temple and placed them in the temples of pagan deities. The prophecy is presented in the imagery of such things which were well known and understood by the ancients. Adoni-Bezek is a classical example of the retribution in kind that marked pre-Christian societies. He had his thumbs cut off and was compelled to

grovel for food under the king's table, because he had inflicted similar atrocities upon others. There is no need to
multiply examples of such things nor to attempt any specific detail of exactly what events Joel used here as the
source of his imagery, as they were very many indeed. The
selling into slavery here, "would not be literal or physical
selling, but an avenging by divine judgment of the shameful treatment inflicted upon the people of the Lord."[16]

**Verse 9, Proclaim ye this among the nations; prepare war;
stir up the mighty men; let the men of war draw near, let
them come up.**

"Here God is proclaiming that the nations themselves
will be the instruments of his judgment. The seeds of destruction are sown in the forces of destruction."[17] Furthermore, the destructive nations themselves will be destroyed,
and their gathering together for violence is a prophecy of
their own doom also. There is thus a forenotice here of that
episode in Revelation, chapter 16, where the evil spirits
went forth to gather the kings of the earth "unto the war of
the great day of God" (16:14). See CRE in the Firm Foundation series of NT Commentaries on the passage in Revelation, pp. 374-378.

**Verse 10, Beat your plowshares into swords, and your
pruning-hooks into spears: let the weak say, I am strong.**

This passage was once cited by President Truman when a
group of five preachers called upon him during the Korean
war and were received in the White House office. Some of
the area preachers in Washington, D. C. had been preaching
from the contrasting passage in Isaiah 2:4 about beating
swords into plowshares, etc.; and the President, asked,
"Why don't you preachers preach all the Bible?" He then
turned to this passage and read from the Bible which had
just been presented to him this very verse, adding, "I don't
think these are Minor Prophets at all; some of the most
important things in the Bible are found in these short
books." It was this writer's privilege to share in that visit,

---

[16]Homer Hailey, *op. cit.*, p. 58.
[17]*Ibid.*

and the President's words regarding the Minor Prophets have always been remembered as solemn truth.

Here again, one encounters the notion that the origin of this verse was in Isaiah, and that Joel was merely giving a "parody of what that prophet wrote";[18] and such an idea fits in nicely with opinions of a late post-exilian date; but the student should see again the comments under 2:32, above, for a discussion of the true origin of prophetic statements. There is absolutely no evidence whatever that either Isaiah or Joel quoted the other in these passages; as a matter of fact, if either of them had done so, he would have said so. "For Jehovah hath spoken it" (3:8) is a frequently recurring note in this prophecy.

Rather than being a command upon the part of the Lord that the nations of earth should arm for war, it would appear to be a prophecy of what they will, through their wickedness, actually do, converting the total economy of their societies to the making of instruments of destruction, even the humblest implements of agriculture being also involved in the perversion. Is not this a perfect picture of what is going on in the world at this very time? Conditions symbolized by this are a prelude to the great and final judgment itself. The language would appear to be similar to that which is said in Revelation 22:11:

> He that is unrighteousness, let him do unrighteousness still:
> And he that is filthy, let him be made filthy still:
> And he that is righteous, let him do righteousness still:
> And he that is holy, let him be made holy still . . .
> BEHOLD I COME QUICKLY!

What is indicated by such words as our verse (10), and also by this NT quotation, is that the time of the Final Judgment has almost arrived; and there is no need whatever for nations of the earth, which have hardly ever done anything else except prepare for war, to make any significant change; it is too late for that. The immediate reference in this very short paragraph in verses 12 and 13 to the

[18]R.A. Cole, *op. cit.*, p. 724.

"sickle" of judgment, and the "winepress" of God's wrath strongly supports this impression. The time indicated by Joel's words here is near the close of the era when, denying the benign teachings of the Saviour's kingdom, men shall beat plowshares into swords, etc.: it comes at a time when the final and irrevocable rebellion of all mankind shall be approaching its climax.

Myers gave a spiritual interpretation of this verse, reading it as equal to, "What Amos said to Israel, 'Prepare to meet your God (Amos 4:12).' The military terms employed to accentuate the seriousness of the conflict must not be allowed to obscure the real meaning."[19] Without doubt, this is an acceptable understanding of this place; but our own preference favors the view given above.

Verse 11, Haste ye, and come, all ye nations round about, and gather yourselves together: cause thy mighty ones to come down, O Jehovah.

The gathering of the nations in their opposition to God, which is prophesied to come at the general hardening of mankind that is prophesied as preceding the Final Judgment is here represented as an act of God himself, indicating judicial hardening. Thus, in the case of Judas, Jesus commanded him, "What thou doest, do quickly" (John 13:27).

"Thy mighty ones to come down . . ." Some expositors are inclined to view the assembled nations as an assembly convened to execute the will of God, but we believe the assembly here is a spiritual thing, referring to the unanimity with which human nations shall oppose God, and that this is a prophecy of their assembly not to execute God's wrath upon others, but as the occasion when God will execute his judgment *upon them*! The next two verses would appear to make that certain. Keil was of course correct in seeing something here far greater than a few neighboring nations of ancient Israel. He wrote:

These are not merely the neighboring nations to

---

[19]Jacob M. Myers, *The Layman's Bible Commentary* (Richmond, Va.: The John Knox Press, 1959), p. 93.

Judah, but all heathen nations who have come in contact with the kingdom of God, i.e., all the nations of the earth without exception, inasmuch as before the last judgment the gospel of the kingdom is to be preached in all the world for a testimony to all nations (Matthew 24:14, Mark 13:10).[20]

Verse 12, Let the nations bestir themselves, and come up to the valley of Jehoshaphat; for there will I set to judge all the nations round about.

"Jehoshaphat . . ." has the meaning of, "The Lord judges, or has judged."[21] The scene, therefore is the eternal judgment, not that of any earthly event at all. The language is metaphorical. "The figure of a great battle between the nations and the warriors of God is joined to that of the nations gathered around before the judge of all the earth."[22]

"Cause thy mighty ones to come down . . ." is a reference to the angels of God, always mentioned in connection with judgment scenes, especially in the NT. The "mighty ones" are not therefore, in any sense, 'righteous nations' but the angels of heaven; and there is not going to be any kind of a literal conflict on earth to decide the fate of anything; God's fiat will determine that.

Verse 13, Put ye in the sickle; for the harvest is ripe: come tread ye; for the winepress is full, the vats overflow; for their wickedness is great.

Revelation 14:14-20 appears to be founded entirely upon this conception introduced in these few verses of Joel. See CRE for extensive comment on this, for practically all of it is applicable here.

This verse surely supports the view that the "mighty ones" from above, spoken of as "coming down" in the preceding verse, must be the angels of God, for, "Down to NT times the eschatalogical harvesters are usually the angels (Matthew 13:39, Revelation 14:14-20)."[23] This double

---

[20]C.F. Keil, *op. cit.*, p. 226.
[21]Jacob M. Myers, *op. cit.*, p. 91.
[22]*Ibid.*, p. 93.
[23]R.A. Cole, *op. cit.*, p. 725.

figure of the judgment under the imagery of the grain harvest and of the grape harvest suggests much important truth regarding God's final judgment of humanity. It will come at a time when human wickedness has run its course, borne its fruit, and arrived at a state where there is nothing else left to do except to reap it! There has been some refinement of the double figure by subsequent sacred authors who used the treading of the winepress as particularly indicative of God's wrath, and the gathering of the wheat into the garner as indicating the salvation of the righteous.

Verse 14, Multitudes, multitudes in the valley of decision! for the day of Jehovah is near in the valley of decision.

The tumult of the nations in the valley of decision is not accidental, nor of their own volition; it is because they have been summoned there by the Lord, "for the day of the Lord is near."[24]

"The valley of decision is the same as the valley of Jehoshaphat, the repetition heightens the effect."[25]

On the fact of God's causing the nations to move into the valley of decision, two facts are pertinent: (1) in the very nature of man's probation, he is always in the valley of decision as long as he is on earth, and (2) when either individuals or whole nations exhibit a final and stubborn attitude of rebellion against God, judicial hardening always occurs eventually, as in the classical instance of Pharaoh, or of Judas, or of secular Israel.

Every man is in the valley of decision *now*; and his "battle of Armageddon" is a thing of the heart and mind and soul, and not a matter of nations and battlefields.

Verse 15, The sun and the moon are darkened, and the stars withdraw their shining.

Such terminology as this is used in Revelation 6:12:17, following the pattern throughout the Bible in references to the judgment of the Final Day. We do not pretend to know

---

[24]Jacob M. Myers, *op. cit.*, p. 94.
[25]Robert Jamieson, *op. cit.*, p. 788.

what this means; but it would appear to be certain that
cosmic disturbances of the very greatest magnitude will
attend God's final arraignment and judgment of the prince
of his creation, namely, man.

That the final day is always considered "near" (v. 14) by
the inspired authors appears to derive from two things: (1)
in the sense of recurring judgments upon the incorrigibly
wicked, as seen in so many historical examples, notably the
destruction of Jerusalem, that day in its immediate application and impending sense is indeed always near, always
impending and threatening to occur at any time; (2) all such
lesser judgments are likewise omens or tokens of the great
and final event that shall consummate all things and usher
in the new heaven and the new earth. Furthermore, this
ultimate and final event is uncertain as to the time. Not
even Christ in the limitation of his flesh knew when it would
be; and, therefore, the thoughtful of every generation have
received it in the words of the prophets as "near at hand."
There is a sense, too, in which it is indeed "near" to every
generation; because, for all practical purposes, the day of
death for every man may be equated with the day of judgment as far as it pertains to him.

**Verse 16, And Jehovah will roar from Zion, and utter his
voice from Jerusalem; and the heavens and the earth shall
shake; but Jehovah will be a refuge unto his people, and a
stronghold to the children of Israel.**

The figure of the Lord roaring out of Zion and Jerusalem
is a reminder of "how " the Lord does his roaring, namely,
through his word, which traditionally, and even in the instance of the gospel, comes not from Rome, Salt Lake City,
Boston, or Moscow, but from Jerusalem! The shaking of
the heavens and the earth show that the figure of the final
judgment is still being used. The author of Hebrews specifically equated the shaking of the earth with its "removal"
(12:26-28) at the time of the great judgment. See CH,
pp.334-336.

"Jehovah will be a refuge to his people . . . a stronghold to
the children of Israel . . ." There is no reference here to the
fleshly members of Abraham's descendants; it is the spiritual remnant, the genuine children of Abraham, the spiritual

Israel which is meant. Note also, that their refuge and stronghold will not be a fortress in Jerusalem, but God himself, namely, as recipients of his blessings under the new covenant "in Christ." Those commentaries which explain this in fanciful terms of how the "Jews were victorious over their cruel foes under Antiochus,"[26] and envision this as a prophecy that God will come to Jerusalem and protect and promote Israel in the physical and secular sense have failed to see the eternal and world-wide proportions of this great passage in its truly spiritual sense.

Verse 17, So shall ye know that I am Jehovah your God, dwelling in Zion my holy mountain: then shall Jerusalem be holy, and there shall no strangers pass through her any more.

This is a description of the spiritual Zion, mentioned in the preceding verse. It was beautifully understood and commented upon by Hailey in these words:

> Spiritual Zion is impregnable; strangers will not pass through her as they did physical Jerusalem. The kingdom over which Jehovah reigns from Zion is one that cannot be shaken (Hebrews 12:28); it will stand forever(Daniel 2:44, 7:13,14).[27]

"Jerusalem shall be holy . . ." This, more than anything else, demands a spiritual application of these words. In no absolute sense was the literal Jerusalem ever "holy"; nor can there be any reasonable postulation of its holiness in the earthly sense, as long as the world stands. The only "holy Jerusalem" known to the word of God is that of "the new Jerusalem which cometh down from God out of heaven," which to be sure is a symbol of the glorified church of Jesus Christ.

Verse 18, And it shall come to pass in that day, that the mountains shall drop down sweet wine, and the hills shall flow with milk, and all the brooks of Judah shall flow with waters; and a fountain shall come forth from the house of Jehovah, and shall water the valley of Shittim.

[26]*Ibid.*
[27]Homer Hailey, *op. cit.*, p. 60.

This verse begins a paragraph concluding the whole prophecy in which there is a metaphorical description of the wonderful blessings available to the children of God in their service of Christ and his kingdom. It may well be admitted that it is very unlikely that Joel himself fully understood these words, that probably being the very reason that God gave him the description in metaphorical terms that he *could* understand. Joel was not writing for himself alone and his own generation merely, but he most certainly did know that the words he gave had implications for other generations to come; because, as an apostle expressed it:

> To whom it was revealed (that is, to the prophets), that not unto themselves, but unto you did they minister these things, which have now been announced to you through them that preached the gospel unto you by the Holy Spirit sent forth from heaven (I Peter 1:12).

What is seen in this verse is a picture of universal peace, security, plenty, and tranquility. It is appropriate to remember that even for Christians the blessings here are not literal, but spiritual. A literal view of this passage is impossible. It is a picture of the spiritual joys in the days of the outpouring of God's Spirit, namely, in the days of the present dispensation of the NT.

"The valley of Shittim . . ." was a very dry and unproductive area; and the imagery is that through the great spiritual blessings available in Christ, some of the most unpromising situations shall yield precious fruit for the kingdom.

Verse 19, Egypt shall be a desolation, and Edom shall be a desolate wilderness, for the violence done to the people of Judah, because they have shed innocent blood in their land.

This continues to be metaphor. Egypt and Edom were traditional enemies of God's people; and the ruin of such nations (all such) was here prophesied. It has continued to be fulfilled throughout all history. Those very nations on earth today where the gospel is not known are the very places where debauchery, poverty, wretchedness, violence and starvation are among their principal characteristics.

The Hebrew interpretation of this passage was cited by

Deane: "In the day of the Lord, God will make an end of all the nations in the valley of Jehoshaphat, and then great goodness shall accrue to Israel."[28] Of course, that is the same old carnal misunderstanding of God's word that resulted in the Jewish rejection of the Messiah to begin with; and it is exactly the view of all kinds of millenarians who have fallen into the same old error. As Deane pointed out, "This passage does not teach the earthly glorification of Palestine and desolation of Egypt and Idumaea."[29]

Verse 20, But Judah shall abide for ever, and Jerusalem from generation to generation.

Judah and Jerusalem here, as frequently, are symbols of God's true Israel upon earth (both the old and the new), that is, God's true covenant people of both the OT and the NT. It is the perpetual continuation of God's covenant people upon earth which is indicated by this, and the words may not be applied carnally to any heavenly guarantee of the inviolability of the secular state, whether that of Israel, or any other. The NT renewal of this promise is in Matthew 28: 18-20, where is recorded Christ's promise to "be with you always, even to the end of the world. Amen." The simple meaning of this whole passage is, "That in the days of the Spirit, God would establish his spiritual people and dwell among them."[30]

Verse 21, And I will cleanse their blood which I have not cleansed: for Jehovah dwelleth in Zion.

As Myers pointed out, "The Lord dwells in Zion" is almost a signature of validity with which Joel closes his book."[31] This word is one of assurance and encouragement and a guarantee of the eternal continuity and abiding presence of the Lord among his people. They will never be deserted or forsaken. No matter what may happen around them, nothing can really happen *to them*; for they are God's! Myers also observed the similarity of this and the

---

[28] W.J. Deane, *op. cit.*, p. 53.
[29] *Ibid.*
[30] Homer Hailey, *op. cit.*, p. 61.
[31] Jacob M. Myers, *op. cit.*, p. 96.

preceding verse to the concluding passage of Matthew cited under verse 20:

> This reminds the reader of the last verse in Ezekiel, "The Lord is there!" It is the most reassuring promise and truth of the Bible, comparable to the last promise of our Lord (Matthew 28:20).[32]

Thus is concluded this marvelous prophecy of times far beyond his own generation, and involving information regarding the fate of every man ever born upon the planet earth, or who may yet be born. There is indeed a sense of awesome appreciation for words so weighty and so charged with eternal significance to men. The climax of the prophecy came in this third chapter where are depicted in terms of the most amazing metaphor the blessings of the eternal kingdom of Jesus Christ our Lord.

---

[32]*Ibid.*

BIBLIOGRAPHY

The following books and periodicals have been referred to and quoted in this work. We express our appreciation for permission to quote from the following:

Aboot, Lyman A., ____ (New York: ____ Publishing Company)

Beacons, A Publication illuminating the ____ (Boston: ____)

Battle, Ralph, ____ (Grand Rapids: Thing Book Company)

Berne, Eric, ____ Games People Play (New York: ____, 1980)

Bruce, F. F., ____ (Grand Rapids: Wm. B. Eerdmans Publishing Company)

Clarke, Adam, ____ Commentary on the Bible, 1960 (New York: T. Mason & Co.)

Cole, R. A., ____ (Grand Rapids: Wm. B. Eerdmans Publishing Company, 1970)

Conley, Elizabeth, ____ The Book of the World in Revelation (Beaconsville ____, 1974) (Washington, D.C.: The National Geographic Society)

Deane, W. J., ____ (Grand Rapids: Wm. B. Eerdmans Publishing Company, 1950)

Deere, Derward, ____ (Chicago: Moody Press, 1974)

Heller, Homer, A Commentary on the Minor Prophets (Grand Rapids: Baker Book House, 1972)

Ironside, H. A., Notes on the Minor Prophets (Neptune, N.J.: Loiseaux Brothers, 1909)

Jamieson, Robert, JFB (Grand Rapids: Zondervan Publishing House, 1961)

Keil, C. F., Commentary on the O.T. (Vol. 10 (Grand Rapids: Wm. B. Eerdmans Publishing Company)

Kennedy, G., Harper, BBC, 1961 (Nashville: Broadman Press, 1973)

Knowling, R. J., Expositor's Greek N.T. Vol. IV (Grand Rapids: Wm. B. Eerdmans Publishing Company, 1967)

80

BIBLIOGRAPHY

The following authors and sources were quoted in the text of the commentary on Joel:

Apocrapha of the NT, Pilate's Report to Tiberius Caesar, in Ante-Nicene Fathers, Vol. VIII (Grand Rapids: Wm. B. Eerdmans Publishing Company, 1951).

Barnes, Albert, *Notes on the Minor Prophets, Vol. 1* (Grand Rapids: Baker Book House, 1953).

Boren, Maxie B., *Church Bulletin* (Corsicana, Texas, June 8, 1980).

Bruce, F. F., *The Book of Acts* (Grand Rapids: Wm. B. Eerdmans Publishing Company, 1954).

Clarke, Adam, *Commentary on the Whole Bible, Vol. V* (New York: T. Mason & G. Lane, 1837).

Cole, R. A., *NBCR* (Grand Rapids: Wm. B. Eerdmans Publishing Company, 1970).

Conley, Robert A. M., *The Teeth of the Wind, in National Geographic Magazine, Vol. 136, No. 2* (Washington, D.C.: The National Geographic Society, 1969).

Deane, W. J., *The Pulpit Commentary, Vol. 14, Joel* (Grand Rapids: Wm. B. Eerdmans Publishing Company, 1950).

Deere, Derward, *WBC* (Chicago: Moody Press, 1962).

Hailey, Homer, *A Commentary on the Minor Prophets* (Grand Rapids: Baker Book House, 1972).

Ironside, H. A., *Notes on the Minor Prophets* (Neptune, N.J.: Loizeaux Brothers, 1909).

Jamieson, Robert, *JFB* (Grand Rapids: Zondervan Publishing House, 1961).

Keil, C.F., *Commentary on the OT, Vol. 10* (Grand Rapids: Wm. B. Eerdmans Publishing Company).

Kennedy, J. Hardee, *BBC, Vol. 7* (Nashville: Broadman Press, 1972).

Knowling, R. J., *Expositor's Greek NT, Vol. II* (Grand Rapids: Wm. B. Eerdmans Publishing Company, 1967).

Leonard, Paul E., *NLBC* (Grand Rapids: Zondervan Publishing House, 1979).

Lindblom, J., *Prophecy in Ancient Israel* (Philadelphia: Fortress Press, 1965).

Myers, Jacob M., *The Layman's Bible Commentary, Vol. 14* (Richmond, Va.: The John Knox Press, 1959).

Robertson, James, *ISBE* (Chicago: Howard-Severance Company, 1915).

Robinson, George I., *The Twelve Minor Prophets* (Grand Rapids: Baker Book House, 1926).

Shakespeare, William, *Othello*.

Thomas, D., *Pulpit Commentary, Vol. 14, Joel* (Grand Rapids: Wm. B. Eerdmans Publishing Company, 1950).

Thompson, J. A., *IB, Vol. VI* (New York: Abingdon Press, 1957).

Tertullian, *Apology xxi, Ante-Nicene Fathers* (Grand Rapids: Wm. B. Eerdmans Publishing Company, 1951).

Unger, Merrill F., *Archeology and the OT* (Grand Rapids: Zondervan Publishing House, 1954).

Unger, Merrill F., *Unger's Bible Dictionary* (Chicago: Moody Press, 1957).

Watson, W. Gladstone, *ABC* (New York: Abingdon Press, 1929).

Whiting, John D., *Locusts, National Geographic Magazine, Vol. 52, No. 12* (Washington, D.C.: National Geographic Society, 1915).

Amos

INTRODUCTION

Amos was one of the great prophets of the eighth century B.C., "Whose book in the Bible is one of the most eloquent denunciations of injustice and cruelty in history."[1] Most of the prophets directed their message to only one or two nations, but Amos, "Took in a whole range of various nationalities, indicted them for their sins, and proclaimed the judgments of God alike upon nations and individuals."[2] Amazingly, he did not make a sharp distinction between Israel and Judah, because in his view, there was but one Israel and it included them both. Morgan summarized the denunciations of Amos as being directed against the following nations and their characteristic sins, as follows:

> The sin of Syria . . . cruelty.
> The sin of Philistia . . . the slave trade.
> The sin of Phoenicia . . . slave trade in spite of covenant.
> The sin of Edom . . . determined unforgiveness.
> The sin of Ammon . . . cruelty based upon cupidity.
> The sin of Moab . . . violent and vindictive hatred.
> The sin of Judah . . . Jehovah's laws despised.
> The sin of Israel . . . the corruption of a delivered people.[3]

The author. Amos, not to be confused with Amoz, the father of Isaiah, did not belong to any of the priestly or prophetical families of the chosen people, nor had he ever attended any of the schools of the prophets, being a herdsman and dresser of sycamore trees from Tekoa, a frontier town of Judah, situated about six miles south of Bethlehem on the range of hills stretching toward the Dead Sea.[4] The

---

[1]William P. Barker, *Everyone in the Bible* (Old Tappan, N.J.: Fleming H. Revell Company, 1966), p. 32.

[2]Herbert Lockyer, *All the Men of the Bible* (Grand Rapids: Zondervan Publishing House, 1958), p. 47.

[3]G. Campbell Morgan, *The Minor Prophets* (Old Tappan, N.J.: Fleming H. Revell Company, 1960), p. 56.

[4]Merrill F. Unger, *Unger's Bible Dictionary* (Chicago: Moody Press, 1957), p. 1074.

name of this village probably means "trumpet,"[5] suggesting the status of Tekoa as a fortified outpost. The occupation of Amos has been identified as that of shepherd of a particular breed of sheep noted both for their ungainly appearance and for the superior quality of their wonderful wool. He was also a dresser of the sycamore orchard which produced a fruit similar to the fig, and which had to be pierced before it would properly ripen. Keil affirmed that the language in 7:14 indicates that Amos was a person "who fed upon" this fruit,[6] supporting the following deduction:

> Consequently we have to regard Amos as a shepherd living in indigent circumstances, not as a prosperous man possessing both a flock of sheep and a sycamore plantation, which many commentators following the Chaldee and the Rabbins have made him out to be.[7]

Barnes also mentioned the Jewish opinion which followed the notion that, "Prophecy was bestowed by God only upon the rich and the noble."[8] Amos is a refutation of that opinion.

Amos did not deny the validity of his prophetic office by the declaration in 7:14, as is seemingly the case in the versions which read, "I am no prophet, neither the son of a prophet." The past tense is clearly correct in that passage and has reference to the status of Amos *before* he was called to his prophetic mission.

The name *Amos* occurs only in this prophecy and in Luke 3:25 where it is given as the name of one of our Lord's remote ancestors. The name means "burden, heavy, or bearer."[9]

Absolutely nothing is known of this prophet's life except the hints of it which may be gleaned from the prophecy that bears his name; and these shall be noted occasionally in the

---

[5]*Ibid.*

[6]C.F. Keil, *Commentary on the OT, Vol. X* (Grand Rapids: Wm. B. Eerdmans Publishing Company), p. 233.

[7]*Ibid.*

[8]Albert Barnes, *Notes on the OT, Amos* (Grand Rapids: Baker Book House, 1953), p. 233.

[9]Paul T. Butler, *Minor Prophets* (Joplin: College Press, 1968), p. 273.

notes on the text. His residence in a frontier outpost on the edge of the wilderness and the desert suggests that he was an outdoorsman with all the sensitivity to nature and her various moods that usually marks the inhabitants of such desolate and out of the way places.

Date. Many of the dates assigned to eighth century B.C. events are, at best, somewhat tentative and uncertain; but it is possible to affix a definite and approximate time for this prophecy. Amos himself tells us that it was uttered during the reigns of Uzziah, king of Judah, and of Jeroboam, son of Joash, king of Israel, the latter being Jeroboam II. W.J. Deane dated these reigns thus:

> Uzziah . . . 792-740 B.C.
> Jeroboam II . . . 790 to 749 B.C.[10]

If these dates are accurate, then the prophecy was written during the period of 790-749 B.C. Amos added another point of reference in the statement that his prophecy was "two years before the earthquake" (1:1); but unfortunately, the exact date of that earthquake cannot be determined. There were many earthquakes in that part of the world, and even an unusually severe one would not make any permanent intrusion into the records kept by the people. Most of the scholars whose works we have examined establish their respective guesses at 760 B.C., or thereabouts.

The situation. The conditions which prevailed in the generation which received Amos' prophecy were deplorable. (a) Historically, Israel was enjoying her third and last period of great prosperity. Her traditional enemy Damascus which earlier had reduced Israel and subjected them to paying tribute (2 Kings 10:32f, 12:17,18) had itself been subjugated by Assyria in 802 B.C.[11] Assyria's dream of world-conquest, however, was interrupted by internal weakness; and during the joint reigns of Uzziah and Jeroboam II, Israel was left in control of the eastern trade routes (and that meant wealth); and they enjoyed a half century of very great prosperity.

---

[10]W.J. Deane, *Pulpit Commentary,* Vol. 14, Amos (Grand Rapids: Wm. B. Eerdmans Publishing Company, 1950), p. iv.
[11]Hughell E.W. Fosbroke, *Interpreter's Bible,* Vol. VI (New York: Abingdon Press, 1957), p. 764.

(b) Social conditions during this period deteriorated sharply. Wealth and luxury multiplied; and injustice, oppression, and vice were rampant,[12] as indicated by many references in the prophecy itself. The people had interpreted their material prosperity as tokens of divine providence and protection, but they no longer felt any compulsion whatever to be governed by divine law. Unbounded prosperity, throughout history, has almost always resulted in turning away from God; and it was especially true of Israel at this time.

(c) Religiously, the northern kingdom had totally corrupted the true worship, bringing in the vile god of the Canaanites, Baal, at Bethel where the idol calves were enshrined. There was nothing innocent or harmless about this. "The Baal (or 'lord') of each district was worshipped as the giver of its fertility; he was honored accordingly by sexual immorality."[13] The direct result of all this was that the pure worship of Almighty God degenerated into a mere nature cult, being worshipped (!) even through "sacred" prostitutes![14] It is difficult to imagine more depraved and sinful departures from the true knowledge of God.

(d) Morally, sins were about as bad as they could become:

> Drunkenness, sexual license, religious perversion, and idolatry were common. The faithful were scorned, chastised and mocked. The depth to which the people had fallen is characterized by their seeming indifference to their position as a delivered and cared-for nation.[15]

The Scene. How appropriate it is that Amos, the fearless frontiersman, should have gone right to the center of all the immorality and perversions, confronted the wicked pagan priest, and denounced the reprobacy of Israel in the magnificent lines of this tremendous prophecy! He went to Bethel, "where the idol-calves were installed" (Chapter 7:10-13),

[12]G. Campbell Morgan, *op. cit.*, p. 48.
[13]H. Wheeler Robinson, *The Abingdon Bible Commentary* (New York: Abingdon Press, 1929), p. 776.
[14]*Ibid.*
[15]*Wycliffe Bible Encyclopedia* (Chicago: Moody Press, 1975), p. 61.

thus striking the whole degenerate culture at its very center. This, of course, "roused Amaziah the idol priest to accuse him of conspiracy and try to drive him back to Judah."[16] Some have supposed that, "He probably was executed,"[17] after his clash with Amaziah; but this notion would appear to be contradicted by the evident fact that Amos wrote this prophecy some time after the events recorded, most probably from the safety of his residence in Tekoa.

Critical Attacks. The usual strategy of critics of biblical books, when all else fails, is to challenge them with "being far too advanced in theology" actually to belong to the times and the author to which they are credited in the Bible. This type of doctrinaire nonsense is actually an unwilling admission of the authenticity and dependability of the books questioned. Dummelow, for example, went into great detail attempting to show that Amos' concept of God is something very special and advanced; but the truth is that there is absolutely nothing in this prophecy that is not fully in keeping with the understanding of God's nature as it was known by Abraham, Moses, and other sacred writers who preceded him. Even Smart admitted that:

> Amos' theology is not in any way inconsistent with the thought of Amos, and there seems to be no very convincing reason for denying them to him.[18]

As a matter of fact, Amos' prophecy demonstrates a thorough familiarity with the history of Israel, and of God's dealings with the chosen people in times long prior to Amos, with the necessary deduction that the writings of Moses were well known, not merely by Amos, but even by the apostate Israelites to whom he addressed his scathing denunciations. As Keil and many other able and dependable scholars have pointed out, "Amos indicates a close acquaintance on the part of the prophet with Mosaic law, and

---

[16]Jamieson, Faucett, and Brown, *Commentary on the Whole Bible* (Grand Rapids: Zondervan Publishing House, 1961), p. 789.

[17]Vergilius Ferm, *Encyclopedia of Religion* (New York: Philosophical Library, 1945), p. 18.

[18]James D. Smart, *Interpreter's Dictionary of the Bible* (New York: Abingdon Press, 1962), Vol. I, p. 119.

the history of his nation."[19] Barnes gives an extensive analysis of how the perverted worship in Israel was altogether founded upon the basics of the Mosaic system, differing, not in their forms principally, but in the perversions of the ancient rites.

> All the Mosaic festivals, sacrifices, priests, prophets, and a temple were retained in Israel, only perverted to calf-worship. Even the third year tithes they had not bothered to get rid of. They had the same rules in regard to leaven; their altar had horns, as prescribed by the law, etc.[20]

> It is remarkable how many allusions, more or less precise, to antecedent history are found in the compass of this small book; and the significance of them lies not in the actual number of references, but the kind of references and the implications involved in the individual references.[21]

Thus Amos stands as a bold and immovable testimony to the authenticity of the biblical books attributed to Moses, confirming the truth that those books are far antecedent to his own times in point of chronology. Some attention will be given to this truth in the notes.

Purpose of the Prophecy. The purpose of Amos was to denounce wicked perversions, especially of the northern kingdom, but without neglecting Judah, and to warn them of the impending judgment of God, a judgment already confirmed in the sending of the great earthquake some two years following Amos' prophecy of the nation's destruction. As Keil noted, "The idea of the approaching fall or destruction of Israel was, according to human judgment, a very improbable one indeed."[22] Jeroboam had raised and equipped a great army, subjugated the Philistines and the Ammonites, and had even chased the Syrians out of the cities they once possessed (2 Kings 14:25). The great prosperity of the nation, enjoying its greatest territorial expan-

[19]C.F. Keil, *op. cit.*, p. 236.
[20]Albert Barnes, *op. cit.*, p. 230.
[21]James Robertson, *ISBE* (Chicago: Howard-Severance Company, 1915), p. 123.
[22]C.F. Keil, *op. cit.*, p. 234.

sion since Solomon, had made them thoroughly overconfident. They felt perfectly safe in rejecting the dire prophecies of the humble prophet of Tekoa.

In this remarkable overthrow of Israel and the resulting removal of the Ten Tribes, which came to pass exactly as Amos prophesied, there is discernible another purpose of the prophecy, that of setting forth an example of the certainty of God's judgment upon wickedness, no matter how secure the wicked may feel in their disobedience. Thus it may be concluded, as Barnes said, that "The Shepherd has shaken not one country, but the world; not by a passing earthquake, but by the awe of God."[23] The overthrow of Israel as the chosen people of God, their utter removal, and the bringing in of the Gentiles as God's people is implied in Amos, no less than in Jonah and other OT books. "He would pass through his people with a judgment so severe that it would remove them from the face of the earth."[24]

Yet another evident purpose of this great prophecy is that of pointing forward to the coming of the Messiah (8:9), and that "an end" of Israel will occur in that event. Also evident is the rebuilding of "the tabernacle of David," a prophecy of the establishment of Christ's church (Acts 15:16f, and Amos 9:11).

Amos' Style. Two errors are common in this area, (1) that of glorifying the style of this prophet, attributing it to his wealth, education and travel (which are mistaken suppositions), and (2) that of downgrading him as an ignorant peasant with a rough and uncouth message. Both of these views are wrong. While true enough that Amos had not attended any of the accepted schools of his time, he nevertheless demonstrated an eloquence and power equal to anything found elsewhere in the Bible. "The diction of uneducated people has in itself a certain poetic power which raises it to an equality with that of higher social stations."[25] "Both Hosea and Jeremiah seem to have borrowed from this prophet,"[26] and we have already observed that he is

---

[23]Albert Barnes, *op. cit.*, p. 230.
[24]J. Keir Howard, *NLBC* (Grand Rapids: Zondervan Publishing House, 1979), p. 951.
[25]W.J. Deane, *op. cit.*, p. v.
[26]*Ibid.*

directly quoted twice in the book of Acts. "There is considerable rhetorical power, wealth and depth of thought, vivacity and vigour."[27]

The writing of Amos shows that he was not an untutored rustic, but had a deep knowledge of history and of the problems of his day. His language, rich in figures and symbols, stands with the finest literary style in the OT.[28]

Anyone who reads Amos will find him not a whit behind the very chiefest of the prophets; almost equal to the greatest in the loftiness of his sentiments; and not inferior to any in the splendor of his diction and the elegance of his composition.[29]

Outline. A workable outline of the prophecy of Amos is found in the Wycliffe Bible Encyclopedia:[30]

I.   Chapters 1-2, Judgments Against Near Eastern Nations.
     A. Prophecies against heathen neighbors (1:3-2:3).
     B. Wrath upon the two covenant nations (2:4-16).
II. Chapters 3-6, Proclamations Against Israel.
     A. Israel's guilt (3:1-15).
     B. The depravity of Israel (4:1-15).
     C. Israel to be punished (5:1-17).
     D. Israel to go into captivity (5:18-27).
     E. The peril of complacency (6:1-14).
III. Chapters 7:1-9:10, Five Visions Concerning Israel.
     A. Devouring locusts (7:1-3).
     B. Flaming fire (7:4-6).
     C. Plumbline; opposition of Amaziah (7:7-17).
     D. Basket of ripe fruit (8:1-4).
     E. God's judgment to fall on Bethel's altar (9:1-10).
IV. Promise of Restoration (9:1-14).

[27]C.F. Keil, *op. cit.*, p. 236.
[28]Arnold C. Schultz, *WBC* (Chicago: Moody Press, 1962), p. 829.
[29]Adam Clarke, *Commentary on the Whole Bible, Vol. V* (New York: T. Mason & G. Lane, 1837), p. 672.
[30]*WBE* (Chicago: Moody Press, 1975), p. 61.

CHAPTER 1

This chapter actually combines with chapter 2 to form the first division of the prophecy of Amos, in which the prophet thunders the warning of the impending judgment of God upon no less than eight nations, beginning with Israel's surrounding pagan neighbors, then resting for a moment upon Judah, and by way of climax describing the utter ruin and devastation of Israel itself, i.e., the northern kingdom. The awful judgments, "rolling like a storm, in strophe after strophe, over all the surrounding kingdoms,"[1] touched upon three pagan nations that were not related to Israel, and upon three which were related, did not neglect Judah, considered by Amos as one with the northern kingdom, and then rested the fullness of its fury upon the nation of Israel itself.

The following nations were blasted with these eloquent and fierce denunciations: Damascus (1:3-5), Philistia (1:6-8), Tyre (1:9,10), Edom (1:11-12), Ammon (1:13-15), Moab (2:1-3), Judah (2:4,5), and Israel (2:6-16). The skill and power of Amos as a speaker and orator appear in this arrangement of his material:

> The interest and sympathy of the hearers are secured by the fixing of the attention upon the enormities of guilt in their neighbors, and curiosity is kept awake by the uncertainty as to where the next stroke of the prophetic whip will fall.[2]

In this comprehensive pronouncement of God against sin in all these nations, there looms the tremendous fact that God is a God of all nations, and not merely of Israel, and that he will judge and punish sin wherever it exists. Moreover, the sins denounced are not merely those of violence, cruelty, oppression, injustice and social wrongs. Violators of solemn covenants, innovators, and corrupters of the true

---

[1]C.F. Keil, *Commentary on the Whole Bible* (Grand Rapids: Wm. B. Eerdmans Publishing Company), p. 240.

[2]James Robertson, *ISBE* (Chicago: Howard-Severance Company, 1915), p. 122.

worship are likewise guilty and will suffer the judgment of God.

Verse 1, The words of Amos, who was among the herdsmen of Tekoa, which he saw concerning Israel in the days of Uzziah king of Judah, and in the days of Jeroboam the son of Joash king of Israel, two years before the earthquake.

"The words of Amos . . ." Both Ecclesiastes and Jeremiah have similar beginnings; and therefore it is not necessary to attribute these words to "some later editor." Amos was his own editor; and as Coleman observed, "The nature of the text indicates an early recording of the prophet's message."[3] The name of Amos is not to be confused with Amoz the father of Isaiah (2 Kings 19:2,20). Many of the biblical books begin with, "Thus saith the Lord," the very expression which Amos used frequently in this prophecy; and this first clause of verse 1 must not be made the basis of receiving Amos' words here as in any degree other than the very message of God himself, a fact which is categorically affirmed a moment later in the words "which he saw." That this is true "is affirmed by the succeeding clause, 'which he saw.' "[4] Schultz and many others have also discerned this: "The divine origin of the words of the propet is emphasized by . . . 'which he saw.' "[5] In the words of the prophecy of Amos,

> We are in the presence of the miracle of inspiration (Ezekiel 2:8-3:4), that man, without losing individuality or sacrificing personality, should yet speak words which originated not with himself but with his God.[6]

"Among the herdsmen of Tekoa . . ." See introduction for discussion of Amos' occupation and economic status. We reject the notion that he was a wealthy owner of flocks and orchards for he later described himself as "a dresser of sycamore trees" (7:14), in language which, according to Keil indicates that he lived upon this fruit, an article of diet

---

[3] Robert O. Coleman, *WBE*, p. 62.
[4] W.J. Deane, *Pulpit Commentary, Vol. 14, Amos* (Grand Rapids: Wm. B. Eerdmans Publishing Company, 1950), p. 1.
[5] Arnold C. Schultz, *WBC* p. 830.
[6] J.A. Motyer, *NBCR* p. 729.

widely associated with the very poorest people. See under
7:14.

"Tekoa . . ." was a village some six miles south of Bethlehem and about twelve miles southeast of Jerusalem on a
3,000' plateau which affords a beautiful view of the whole
Dead Sea area, and which immediately drops off eastward
and south from Tekoah toward that great desolation.

"Uzziah . . . Jeroboam . . ." See introduction for discussion of the dates of these monarchs. The words "son of
Joash" given in the identification of Jeroboam distinguish
him as Jeroboam II.

"Two years before the earthquake . . ." By Amos' mention of this earthquake's occurrence two years *after* his
prophecy shows that he was not executed in Israel, as some
suppose, but that he lived to return to Tekoah, and to see
the divine confirmation of the truth of his prophecy in the
devastation of the great earthquake. Deane was correct, it
appears, in his opinion that Amos here alluded to it, "as a
token of the judgment which he foretold, such catastrophes
being regarded as signs . . . of God and his vengence upon
sinners."[7]

Some scholars believe that this earthquake was the one
mentioned by Josephus who gave the account of a very
great earthquake in the reign of Uzziah, an earthquake so
great that it was remembered generations afterwards when
Zechariah referred to it (14:5). That earthquake, according
to Josephus, made a breach in the temple, ruined the gardens and palace of the king, and occurred simultaneously
with the smiting of Uzziah with leprosy.[8] It cannot be dated
exactly.

**Verse 2, And he said, Jehovah will roar from Zion, and
utter his voice from Jerusalem; and the pastures of the
shepherds shall mourn, and the top of Carmel shall wither.**

"And Jehovah shall roar from Zion, and utter his voice
from Jerusalem . . ." These exact words are in Joel 3:16; and
if they should be considered as the theme of the book of

[7]W.J. Deane, *op. cit.*, p. 2.
[8]Flavius Josephus, *Antiquities, and Wars of the Jews*, translated by William
Whiston (New York: Holt, Rinehart, and Winston), *Antiquities*, p. 293. (XIV,
10, 4).

Amos, then it may be said that Amos took his text from Joel. Shultz did not hesitate to write, "This verse is the text of the book."[9] It must also be accounted as fact that, "Amos here connects his prophecy with that of his predecessor,"[10] and, hence, with all the scriptures as part of the authentic revelation from the heavenly Father.

This expression is usually cited as proof that Amos was an outdoors man, well acquainted with the roar of the lion attempting to feed upon his flock. This viewpoint seems to be compromised by the existence of the same passage in Joel; and the more pertinent observation would appear to be that Amos knew the scriptures. Still, we cannot deny that the figure, even if he got it out of Joel, would have appealed to one who had heard a lion roar. Adam Clarke has this: "The roaring of the lion in the forest is one of the most terrific sounds in nature; when near, it strikes terror into the heart, both of man and of beast."[11]

"Zion . . . Jerusalem . . ." Amos' message to the northern kingdom thus begins with a stern reminder, "that God was to be worshipped only at Jerusalem."[12] The apostate worship had been installed at Bethel and Samaria. "Zion" is the poetic name for "Jerusalem," and in its extended meaning has an application to the church of Jesus our Lord.

In Joel 3:16, Jehovah is represented as roaring on behalf of Israel, but in the stern denunciations of Amos, he is represented as roaring against Israel. It was calculated to strike terror into the hearts of the wicked and lead them to repentance.

"Pastures of the shepherds shall mourn . . ." All of God's prophets depict him as the God of nature and as one who continually bends the forces of nature in harmony with his larger purpose with reference to humanity. This appears quite early in the Bible, where it is related that God "cursed the ground for Adam's sake" (Genesis 3:17), a curse which has never been repealed and is still in effect. God providentially bends nature itself to provoke man to repentance, and

[9]Arnold C. Schultz, *op. cit.*, p. 831.
[10]C.F. Keil, *op. cit.*, p. 241.
[11]Adam Clarke, *Commentary on the Whole Bible, Vol. V* (New York: T. Mason & G. Lane, 1837), p. 674.
[12]Paul T. Butler, *The Minor Prophets* (Joplin: College Press, 1968), p. 279.

thus the purpose of the primeval curse must be seen as beneficent.

"And the top of Carmel shall wither . . ." Carmel was noted for remaining productive even in times of drouth, the name itself meaning "the orchard, or fertile land."[13] Even the great drouth in the days of Elijah did not wither Carmel; and, thus the meaning of the whole passage here is that utter desolation shall overcome the land, even places like Carmel. Mt. Carmel was the scene of Elijah's contest with the prophets of Baal and consists of a bold mountain forming the terminus of the Samaritan range and dropping off abruptly into the sea. Whatever the ancient excellence of the place, it has long ago disappeared. "It is steep and lofty where it overhangs the Mediterranean above Haifa."[14]

Verse 3, Thus saith Jehovah, for three transgressions of Damascus, yea, for four, I will not turn away the punishment thereof; because they have threshed Gilead with threshing instruments of iron.

"For three transgressions . . . yea, for four . . ." This is a stylized expression, or idiom, having the meaning of, "for many, or for more than enough."[15] As used here, it denotes, "not a small, but a large number of crimes, or ungodliness in its worst form."[16] Of course, "Some critics have taken the terms literally, and have tried to identify that particular number of transgressions in each case; but this is trifling."[17]

"Damascus . . ." This city stands here as a representative of all of Syria, a point to be remembered. It was an outstanding city of the nation of Syria, one of Israel's principal adversaries, "throughout the incessant border wars which ran from the ninth century to the beginning of the eighth."[18]

"They have threshed Gilead with threshing instruments of iron . . ." This happened in the Syrian war against Israel's land east of the Jordan during the reign of Jehu (2

---

[13]J. Keir Howard, *NLBC* (Grand Rapids: Zondervan Publishing House, 1979), p. 953.

[14]W.J. Deane, *op. cit.*, p. 1.

[15]H. Wheeler Robinson, *ABC* (New York: Abingdon Press, 1929), p. 777.

[16]C.F. Keil, *op. cit.*, p. 242.

[17]W.J. Deane, *op. cit.*, p. 1.

[18]J. Keir Howard, *op. cit.*, p. 954.

Kings 10:32,33, 13:7). "They even crushed the prisoners to pieces with iron threshing machines, according to a barbarous war custom that is met with elsewhere (2 Samuel 12:31)."[19]

The grievousness of this sin is seen, not only in the fact of its violation of one of God's most sacred laws, i.e., the sanctity of human life, but also that they "had done despite to the covenant people of God: 'To attack God's people is to attack God.' "[20]

Verse 4, But I will send a fire into the house of Hazael and it shall devour the palaces of Ben-Hadad.

Hazael was the founder of the dynasty that included two or three kings named Ben-Hadad; so this is the equivalent of saying that the royal family would be destroyed. "Ben-Hadad was the title of the dynasty."[21]

These, and the other judgments to follow are truly terrible; and there are always people who cannot understand why God should deal out such awful judgments; but Morgan has a word of explanation, thus:

> No new philosophy will excuse nations that trifle with divine requirements; the walls of doom close slowly, surely, around all those who forget God. These movements of terror are necessary to, and will issue in, the victory of God . . . Out of ruin and wreckage, God will bring again his divine order.[22]

Verse 5, And I will break the bar of Damascus, and cut off the inhabitants from the valley of Aven, and him that holdeth the scepter from the house of Eden; and the people of Syria shall go into captivity unto Kir, saith Jehovah.

"I will break the bar of Damascus . . ." Ancient cities used a bar to lock their gates; and the breaking of the bar was the same as leaving a city defenseless. Keil summarized the meaning of this verse thus:

---

[19]C.F. Keil, *op. cit.*, p. 242.

[20]Paul T. Butler, *op. cit.*, p. 279.

[21]W.J. Deane, *op. cit.*, p. 3.

[22]G. Campbell Morgan, *Minor Prophets* (Old Tappan, N.J.: Fleming H. Revell Company), p. 56.

The breaking of the bar (the bolt of the gate) denotes the conquest of the capital; cutting off the inhabitants of Aven indicates their slaughter (*hikhrith* means to exterminate) and not their deportation; so that captivity in the last clause refers to the remnant of the population not slain in war.[23]

"Captivity unto Kir. . . ." The Kir has been identified with a river (now the Kar), tributary of the Araxes which flows into the Caspian sea on the southwest.[24] The Syrians were thought to have originally emigrated from that same area.

"Saith Jehovah . . ." This is the prophet's solemn affirmation that he is delivering the words of Jehovah and not his own words. This attestation occurs throughout Amos in several variations:

> Thus saith Jehovah
> Saith Jehovah
> Jehovah hath spoken
> The Lord Jehovah hath spoken
> The Lord Jehovah hath sworn by his holiness
> Saith the Lord Jehovah
> Thus saith the Lord Jehovah
> The Lord Jehovah hath sworn by himself saith Jehovah the God of hosts
> Thus the Lord Jehovah showed me
> And Jehovah saith unto me
> Then said the Lord

No less than *fifty times* within the brief compass of this little book, its author solemnly declared his message to be the true word of Almighty God, the very last word in the prophecy being, "saith Jehovah thy God."

Verse 6, Thus saith Jehovah: For three transgressions of Gaza, yea, for four, I will not turn away the punishment thereof; because they carried away captive the whole people, to deliver them up to Edom.

Note that the whole of a nation was represented by one of its principal cities, Syria by Damascus, (1:3), and here,

---

[23]C.F. Keil, *op. cit.*, p. 243.
[24]W.J. Deane, *op. cit.*, p. 3.

Philistia by Gaza. "It is evident that Gaza is simply regarded as a representative of Philistia,"[25] as proved by the fact that in the announcement of the punishment, some of the other great cities of Philistia are also included, all of them, in fact, standing for the entire nation.

"Carried away the whole people . . . to deliver them to Edom . . ." The capture and sale of people as slaves was bad enough, but the deliverance of such captives to their worst enemies was an added touch of cruelty.

Amos has in mind such carrying away of captives as occurred in the events recorded in 2 Chronicles 21:16.

> These Philistines captured whole cities and areas of Hebrew people and sold them to Edomites and Phoenicians. The Phoenicians probably sold them, in turn, to the Greeks, as indicated by Joel 3:6.[26]

Verse 7, But I will send a fire on the wall of Gaza, and it shall devour the palaces thereof.

Although specific punishments are connected here with certain cities, in all probability, "The calamity of each is common to all."[27]

Verse 8, And I will cut off the inhabitants from Ashdod; and him that holdeth the scepter from Ashkelon; and I will turn my hand against Ekron; and the remnant of the Philistines shall perish, saith the Lord Jehovah.

The cities mentioned in this verse were some of the principal cities of Philistia, Gath being the only one omitted of the five provincial capitals; and OT critics, of course, have attempted to make some big thing out of that omission, affirming that, "Gath, destroyed by Sargon of Syria in 711 B.C. (and omitted here) may suggest a date for the oracle subsequent to the time of Amos."[28] Such "suggestions," however, are by no means inherent in this passage. It was not Amos' purpose to list *all* the cities of Philistia; and it is

[25]C.F. Keil, *op. cit.*, p. 245.
[26]Paul T. Butler, *op. cit.*, p. 282.
[27]W.J. Deane, *op. cit.*, p. 3.
[28]Hughell E.W. Fosbroke, *Interpreter's Bible, Vol. VI* (New York: Abingdon Press, 1957), p. 781.

clear enough that the fate of each city mentioned is actually
the fate of all of them. Again, we refer to 1:3, where Damascus *alone* stands for all of Syria. The notion that this
mention of four of the great capitals of Philistia should not
include cities *not mentioned* is ridiculous. The same kind of
reasoning imposed upon the prophecy of the fall of Syria
would mean that the whole nation had already perished
with the sole exception of its capital city!

"And the remnant of the Philistines shall perish ..."
Here too, some scholars allege that all of Philistia had
already perished, with the exception of a small remnant.
This too is a gross error. "The expression 'the remnant of
the Philistines' indicates that a portion of them had already
been destroyed."[29] Such comment only exposes the unwillingness of unbelieving scholars to accept any such thing as
predictive prophecy; and that is a theological position
which we are absolutely unwilling to share. The arguments
in support of it, such as those grounded in these verses, are
weak, unreasonable, and trifling. The awful prophecies of
the destruction of Syria and Philistia, uttered in the solemn
name of God himself, as repeatedly affirmed by Amos,
appeared to the people who received them, not as belated
predictions of events which had already occurred, but as
events impossible of ever happening at all!

Fulfilment of These Prophecies

Regarding Damascus. Tiglath-pileser king of Assyria fulfilled this prophecy when Ahaz applied to him for help. The
Assyrian monarch destroyed the royal family, captured Damascus and carried its people captive into Kir.[30] This fulfilment occurred fifty years after the prophecy of Amos and is
recorded in 2 Kings 16:9.[31]

Regarding Philistia. Sennacherib fulfilled Amos' prophecy regarding Philistia; and his exploits against the very
cities mentioned in these verses is recorded in cuneiform
inscriptions of how he humbled the kings of Ashkelon,

---

[29]J.R. Dummelow, *Commentary on the Holy Bible* (New York: The Macmillan Company, 1937), p. 564.

[30]Robert Jamieson, *JFB* (Grand Rapids: Zondervan Publishing House,
1961), p. 790.

[31]W.J. Deane, *op. cit.*, p. 3.

Ekron, etc.[32] And, significantly, Sennacherib did not ascend the throne until 702 B.C.[33] The destruction of Philistia thus occurred in the seventh century B.C., whereas, Amos prophesied their doom in the eighth century B.C.

In fact, it was the dramatic, startling, and complete fulfilment of these tremendous prophecies that led to the retention of this book among the sacred writings of the Jews, who placed it in their canon of scripture, despite the terrible warnings and predictions it contained with reference to the Jews themselves.

"The remnant of the Philistines," as used by Amos here cannot possibly mean that "all of his *prophecy* (!) had already occurred, and that all of these grim warnings pertained only to a small remnant yet in the land. No! "Remnant," as used here, means, "the rest of Philistia not already specifically mentioned in the prophecy."

Verse 9, Thus saith Jehovah: For three transgressions of Tyre, yea, for four, I will not turn away the punishment thereof; because they delivered up the whole country to Edom, and remembered not the brotherly covenant.

The great sin of Tyre mentioned here is their delivery of Hebrew slaves to their bitterest enemies, the Edomites, and that this was done despite the long record of friendship between Israel and Tyre, dating back to the days of Solomon, and the brotherly covenant of mutual respect and honor which existed between the two peoples. "No king of Israel or Judah had ever made war on Phoenicia."[34] The indifference and cruelty of Phoenicia, the great slave traders of the day, in their dealings with the covenant people of God, ultimately issued in God's destructive judgment against them. The friendliness between Tyre and Israel is mentioned in the OT (2 Samuel 5:11, 1 Kings 5:1, 9:11,14, etc.); and, although there is no mention of any formal treaty existing between them, the relationship, "doubtless had occasionally been cemented by formal

---

[32]*Ibid.*

[33]*Encyclopaedia Britannica* (Chicago: William Benton Publisher, 1961), Vol. 20, p. 327.

[34]C.F. Keil, *op. cit.*, p. 247.

treaty."[35] At any rate, there was a "covenant," as indicated by this verse. The Tyrians had considered themselves bound by no consideration of human rights and free to violate any honor for the sake of their profitable slave trade.

Verse 10, But I will send a fire on the wall of Tyre, and it shall devour the palaces thereof.

Note the similarity with v. 7, both predictions being somewhat stylized prophecies of the destruction of the places indicated. This prophecy was fulfilled, as were all the others.

Fulfilment Regarding Tyre

Within the space of little more than half a century, Tyre was made a vassal city of Assyria, was besieged and captured by "Nebuchadnezzar after a thirteen years siege (585-573 B.C.),[36] and was ultimately wiped off the face of the earth by Alexander the Great in 332 B.C. "The ancient city of Tyre on the mainland has never been rebuilt."[37] Following the destruction of Tyre by Alexander the Great, "Thirty thousand of its people were sold into slavery";[38] and thus, the old slave traders finally received "the just recompense of their deeds."

Verse 11, Thus saith Jehovah: For three transgressions of Edom, yea, for four, I will not turn away the punishment thereof; because he did pursue his brother with the sword, and did cast off all pity, and his anger did tear perpetually, and he kept his wrath forever.

Having dealt with three pagan neighbors of Israel, Amos here moved to address his prophecy of punishment to three pagan relatives of Israel, namely, Edom, Moab, and Ammon. The Edomites were descended from Esau, the brother of Jacob, and were thus blood relatives of the chosen people, being "the seed of Abraham" in a fleshly sense, no less than Israel itself. The great sin of this people was their

---

[35]J.R. Dummelow, *op. cit.*, p. 564.
[36]J.A. Motyer, *op. cit.*, p. 730.
[37]Paul T. Butler, *op. cit.*, p. 283.
[38]H. Wheeler Robinson, *op. cit.*, p. 777.

"perpetual" hatred of Israel, going back to the time when Jacob had cheated their ancestor out of the birthright. Their hatred, anger, and wrath have continued throughout history; and the prophet's charge that "they kept their wrath for ever" has literally come to pass. Note that God disapproved of this vindictive hatred. True, they had grounds for anger at Jacob and his posterity; but God had ratified the covenant in the seed of Jacob, passing Esau for moral and religious reasons, and not because of Jacob's shameful act in cheating his brother. This judgment of God the Edomites never accepted. Perhaps Schultz is right in seeing this verse, not as recounting specific sins of Edom, but as a reference to, "the traditional attitude of Edom toward Israel."[39]

Verse 12, But I will send a fire upon Tenan, and it shall devour the palaces of Bozrah.

"Tenan, according to Jerome, was the capital of Idumaea, and Bozrah was also an important city, likewise supposed by some to have been the capital (Genesis 36:33)."[40] Bozrah was south of the Dead Sea. As in all these denunciations, the land, or nation, then the capital and/or principal city or cities were mentioned as representatives of the entire country, or nation, denounced.

Verse 13, Thus saith Jehovah: For three transgressions of the children of Ammon, yea, for four, I will not turn away the punishment thereof; because they have ripped up the women with child of Gilead, that they may enlarge their border.

The stark effectiveness of the prophet's language here is attested by the fact that "rip off" has passed into a proverb for wicked and wholesale exploitation, an expression that appears to be derivative from Amos' words here. "The occasion when the Ammonites were guilty of such cruelty towards the Israelites as is here condemned is not recorded in the historical books of the OT.[41]

---

[39]Arnold C. Schultz, *op. cit.*, p. 831.
[40]C.F. Keil, *op. cit.*, p. 247.
[41]C.F. Keil, *op. cit.*, p. 249.

The Ammonites were descended from the incestuous union of Lot with one of his daughters; and it would appear that the character of the people thus originated partook in every way of the shameful and unlawful deeds of their ancestors. "What a marvel that Ammon and Moab retained the stamp of their origin, in a sensual and passionate nature? Their choice of idols grew out of this original character and aggravated it."[42] The chief god of this savage people was Milcom (or Malcam), worshipped as the principle of destruction, and appeased, "with sacrifices of living children, given to the fire to devour (1 Kingd 11:7)."[43] They, like the Edomites and the Moabites, despite their being physically related to Israel, exploited every opportunity within their reach for encroaching upon Israel or aiding aggressions against them. "Their nation lay just east of Moab, and northward to the Jabbok river, and southward to the hills of Edom."[44] This area was altogether insufficient to their ambitions, and they were constantly attempting to "enlarge their border" by inroads against Israel.

Verses 14,15, But I will kindle a fire in the wall of Rabbah, and it shall devour the palaces thereof, with shouting in the day of battle, with a tempest in the day of the whirlwind; and their king shall go into captivity, he and his princes together, saith Jehovah.

Note that the announcement of God's judgment is uttered in each instance by formal, stylized pronouncements which are quite effective. "The shouting mentioned here is that of the assailants."[45] The figure of a tempest, or storm, is used to convey the fury and suddenness of their destruction.

"Their king . . ." Some have noted that in some versions, a proper name is used here, signifying "Malcam, or Milcom, the god of the Ammonites."[46] If so, the dramatic meaning is

---

[42]Albert Barnes, *Notes on the OT, Amos* (Grand Rapids: Baker Book House, 1953), p. 252.
[43]Paul T. Butler, *op. cit.*, p. 286.
[44]*Ibid.*, p. 285.
[45]H. Wheeler Robinson, *op. cit.*, p. 778.
[46]*Ibid.*

that the worshippers of the god of destruction, along with their god, shall be destroyed.

Who can deny that it happened exactly as Amos had foretold? The cuneiform inscriptions of Tiglath-pileser, the great Assyrian king, relate how Ahaz of Judah, "Sanipu king of Ammon" both appear in a list of kings who paid tribute to him.[47] Also, some forty years later, "Buduilu of Ammon (along with others) paid Sennacherib tribute and kissed his feet."[48] Both of these destructions of Ammon occurred at substantial time periods subsequent to Amos' prophecy. "Their last stand seems to have been against Judas Maccabeus (1 Macc. 5:6)."[49]

"The wall of Rabbah . . ." Dean has a very interesting account of the strength of the remarkable wall of Rabbah:

> The massive walls, some of which remain in ruins, rise from the precipitous sides of the cliff . . . I bent over them and looked sheer down about three hundred feet into one wady, and four hundred feet into the other. I did not wonder at its having occurred to King David that the leader of a charge against these ramparts would have met with certain death, consequently assigning the position to Uriah![50]

This indicates how unbelievable the prophecy of Amos must have seemed to his first hearers. Nevertheless, the word of the Lord came to pass exactly as the great prophet had declared.

---

[47]Arnold C. Schultz, *op. cit.*, p. 832.
[48]*Ibid.*
[49]Paul T. Butler, *op. cit.*, p. 286.
[50]W.J. Deane, *op. cit.*, p. 5.

CHAPTER 2

The prophecies against eight nations reach their climax in this chapter where the judgments are pronounced against Moab (1-3), against Judah (4,5), and against Israel (1:6-16), in which the principal thrust of Amos' great prophecy reaches its primary object.

It will appear in this chapter that Amos' words were directed against the gross social sins of that era, but also against the sins of apostasy from the true religion of God; and, throughout, the particular sin of fighting God by fighting God's people is repeatedly condemned. By no stretch of the imagination is it true that this prophecy is the "harbinger of the social gospel!" The pronouncements against sins against the poor, the perversion of justice, etc., as found here, are all based upon prior teachings of the Bible, universally known and understood by God's people long before the times of Amos. Frequent references to the Pentateuch are found in this chapter.

Morgan classified the judgments here as being against (1) injustice, (2) avarice, (3) oppression, (4) immorality, (5) profanity, (6) blasphemy, and (7) sacrilege.[1] These violations are specifically related to the portion of the Mosaic law which is applicable in each case. Amos' prophecy should be accepted as sufficient proof of the prior existence of written records of God's law; and the fact that the manifest reference to the Pentateuch, as repeatedly made, along with the evident assumption that the things referred to were well known and universally understood by God's people, encourages the conclusion that, "The written sources in question go back to a much earlier period."[2]

One may only grieve at the gross immorality and irreligion of the northern kingdom:

---

[1]G. Campbell Morgan, *The Minor Prophets* (Old Tappan, N.J.: Fleming H. Revell Company, 1940), p. 50.

[2]James Robertson, *ISBE* (Chicago: Howard-Severance Company, 1915), p. 125.

The depth to which the people had fallen is charactered in their seeming indifference to their position as a delivered and cared-for nation. Repentance and obedience were imperative, the only escape from imminent judgment.[3]

Concerning the Redacter

In this chapter, Amos reached the principal object of his prophecy, i.e., the rebuke of Israel and the prophecy of her destruction. This series of judgments (1:3-2:16) is not a "collection" of separate "oracles," assembled and pieced together by some "editor" or "redacter" from some undetermined period subsequent to the times of Amos; but they constitute a very coherent, logically arranged, and skilfully presented prophecy, the principal import of which was directed against the northern kingdom. In the previous chapter, Amos cried out against the wickedness of Damascus, Philistia, and Tyre (Israel's pagan neighbors), then against Edom and Ammon (two of Israel's pagan relatives). In this chapter, Amos continued the prophecy against Israel's pagan kinsmen, Moab, and then very properly, and of necessity, included the prophetic denunciation of *his own nation*, Judah, including a specific revelation that Jerusalem too would be destroyed for their sins. If Amos had left out this denunciative prophecy of Jerusalem, it would have compromised his whole message. The people would have said, "Ah, we see that this so-called prophet is blind to the spectacular sins of *his* nation at the very moment he is crying out against everyone else!" In the light of this truth which is clearly visible to anyone, how utterly unfounded, unprovable, illogical and arbitrary are the postulations of the malignant critics who would credit verses 4,5 to some nameless "redacter." Further attention to this will be given in the notes on those verses; but let it be said here that the "redacter" of critical fancy is an imaginary person created subjectively by biblical enemies, having no genuine reality

---

[3]Robert O. Coleman, *WBE* (Chicago: Moody Press, 1975), p. 61.

whatever. This ephemeral, shadowy "character" is impossible of any objective identification. He belongs to all races, all centuries, all religions, and all conditions of society. Every conceivable motive is freely ascribed to him, but no one has ever named him! We unhesitatingly declare him to be a fraud and a deceit perpetrated in the interest of destructive criticism. He is the "Piltdown Man" of OT exegesis! If the student is unfamiliar with this universally known hoax, called Piltdown Man, let him consult an encyclopaedia.

Verse 1, Thus saith Jehovah: For three transgressions of Moab, yea, for four, I will not turn away the punishment thereof; because he burned the bones of the king of Edom into lime.

The NEB translation of this place, while being no *translation* whatever, nevertheless gives the true sense of this passage thus:

> For crime after crime of Moab
> I will grant them no reprieve, because they burnt the bones of the king of Edom to ash.

To pursue the dead, even to the point of violating the corpse, is a mark of peculiar hatred and particularly offensive to the common conscience of mankind.[4] Unrestrained hatred will not stop with death. Wycliffe's bones were dug up and burned 44 years after he died.[5]

History reveals nothing whatever regarding this particular crime of Moab, although a Jewish tradition quoted by Jerome says:

> That after this war, the Moabites, in revenge for the assistance which the king of Edom had given to Israel, dug up and dishonored his bones.[6]

---

[4]Henry McKeating, *CBC, The Books of Amos, Hosea, and Micah* (Cambridge: At the University Press, 1971), p. 19.
[5]Ralph A. Smith, *BBC, Vol. 7* (Nashville: Broadman Press, 1972), p. 95.
[6]W.J. Deane, *Pulpit Commentary, Vol. 14, Amos* (Grand Rapids: Wm. B. Eerdmans Publishing Company, 1950), p. 23.

Verse 2, But I will send a fire upon Moab, and it shall devour the palaces of Kerioth; and Moab shall die with tumult, with shouting, and with the sound of the trumpet.

This pronouncement prophesied the overthrow of Moab by military conquest, a forecast actually fulfilled by the Assyrian monarchs Shalmanezer and Sargon. "From then on, a succession of world conquerors subdued, and in the process, annihilated Moab as a nation."[7] Moab is identified with the high plateau, some 3000' high, that lies south of Arnon, north of Edom, and between the Dead Sea on the west and the desert on the east.

"The palaces of Kerioth . . ." Fosbroke identified this place thus:

> Kerioth is perhaps to be identified with Ar, else-where named as a chief city of Moab (Isaiah 15:1). On the Moabite stone, it is named as the site of a sanctu-ary of the Moabite god, Chemosh.[8]

Fosbroke declared that, "This oracle against Moab is beyond doubt an authentic utterance of Amos,"[9] which, of course, is the truth; but we deny the right of biblical critics to decide which portions of God's word are authentic and which are not. Such an admission by the OT critics of the undeniable truth of this oracle, however, actually frustrates their assertions that the so-called "oracle" against Judah is not an authentic part of Amos. As pointed out in the intro-duction, Amos, by thus concluding the prophetic denuncia-tions against surrounding nations, including both the pa-gan neighbors and the pagan relatives of Israel, it would have been absolutely impossible for Amos, in any logical sense, to have proceeded to announce the destruction of Israel, without, at the same time, denouncing the apostasy of *his own country*, Judah. The critics, however, intent on affirming just such a proposition, like to make it out that Amos considered Judah and Israel as a single family! "Therefore, he would not have uttered a special oracle

---

[7]Paul T. Butler, *The Minor Prophets* (Joplin: College Press, 1968), p. 287.

[8]Hughell E.W. Fosbroke, *IB, Vol. VI* (New York: Abingdon Press, 1957), p. 784.

[9]*Ibid.*

against Judah!"[10] What is an argument like that? It is a denial based upon what someone in the 20th century *imagines* that Amos *thought!* There is no evidence whatever that Amos believed Israel and Judah to be a single family; and, in fact there was not any more basis for such a thought than for believing that Israel and Edom were a single family, for both had a common ancestor. We receive the following prophecy against Judah, therefore, as indeed a genuine and dependable portion of the true word of God.

Verse 3, And I will cut off the judge from the midst thereof, and will slay all the princes thereof with him, saith Jehovah.

"The judge ..." This does not mean that Moab was without a king at the time of this prophecy. "It implies the chief magistrate, like the Carthaginian *sufes*, which is the same word."[11] The prophecies of doom for the surrounding nations, "Were fulfilled by the Chaldeans, who conquered all these kingdoms, and carried the people themselves into captivity."[12]

Verses 4,5, Thus saith Jehovah: For three transgressions of Judah, yea, for four, I will not turn away the punishment thereof; becuse they have rejected the law of Jehovah, and have not kept his statutes, and their lies have caused them to err, after which their fathers did walk. But I will send a fire upon Judah, and it shall devour the palaces of Jerusalem.

This is that famous "oracle" against the southern kingdom. See additional comment on this in the introduction and under verse 2, above.

The frantic efforts of critics to get this out of the Bible is based altogether upon a prior bias to the effect that Amos was not all concerned about violations of the Pentateuch (the law of Jehovah), but that he was a prophet like the modern liberals interested only in social reform! In fact some have hailed him as the "father of the social gospel!"

[10]*Ibid.*, p. 485.
[11]W.J. Deane, *op. cit.*, p. 24.
[12]C.F. Keil, *Commentary on the Whole Bible* (Grand Rapids: Wm. B. Eerdmans Publishing Company), p. 251.

To be sure, this pronouncement against Judah categorically refutes such prejudices.

"For three transgressions, yea, for four . . ." This first great strophe is couched in exactly the same language as all the others, being part of a single address, delivered upon a definite occasion, and later written down by the prophet himself. Furthermore, as we have observed, it was the absolutely necessary prelude to pointing the prophetic barrage against Israel herself.

"Because they have rejected the law of Jehovah . . ." Amos could not have formulated a more perfect reference to the Pentateuch, the prior corpus of the divine Law of God, known and received by all the Israelites for generations prior to Amos' times. As Dummelow said, "These offenses are against a law set forth by positive commandments."[13] The word, "Law, here refers to the Torah, the general name for the whole body of precepts and commandments."[14] Thus, Judah is not judged for the wild excesses of the heathen, but for their rejection of the Lord's word. "Judah is not immune to God's judgment because they are God's elect; indeed their judgments are greater because they are his, and being his, they chose to rebel against him."[15] Jamieson was correct in his discernment that this prophecy against Judah was included here, "Lest it should be said that Amos was strenuous in denouncing sins abroad, but connived at those of his own nation."[16] He also positively identified "the law of Jehovah," in this place as, "The Mosaic Code in general."[17] It is difficult to be patient with the type of false definition of "law of Jehovah," as used here, which occurs in so many commentaries of the various liberal persuasions, such as: "Here it must mean religious and moral teaching given in Jehovah's name by priest and prophet."[18] Such a definition, of course, presupposes that

[13]J.R. Dummelow, *Commentary on the Holy Bible* (New York: The Macmillan Company, 1937), p. 565.

[14]W.J. Deane, *op. cit.*, p. 24.

[15]Paul T. Butler, *op. cit.*, p. 250.

[16]Robert Jamieson, *JFB*, (Grand Rapids: Zondervan Publishing House, 1961), p. 791.

[17]*Ibid.*

[18]H. Wheeler Robinson, *ABC* (New York: Abingdon Press, 1929), p. 778.

there actually was no "law of Jehovah" in any definite sense at that time.

"Have not kept his statutes . . ." This is a definite and technical reference to the various ordinances and prohibitions of the law of Moses, as given by God on Mt. Sinai.

"And their lies have caused them to err . . ." This refers to: "The unreal and imaginary deities, the Baalim, and Ashteroth, who have no existence save in the mind of the worshipper, and are therefore sure to disappoint his hopes."[19]

"After which their fathers did walk . . ."

> Their sin is deeply ingrained in them by inheritance from their fathers, a truth which the OT uses, never to excuse the sinner, but always to indicate that he is in the place of mounting guilt.[20]

Judah continued to go after the old idol gods of the Canaanites, despite all that God had done for them; and they were never cured of this shameful idolatry until after the Babylonian captivity, following which, they never again tolerated among them any semblance of idol-worship.

"But I will send a fire upon Judah, and it shall devour the palaces of Jerusalem . . ." The military judgments here prophesied with reference to Judah and Jerusalem were fulfilled by Nebuchadnezzar, and finally a second time in the destruction by Vespasian and Titus in A.D. 70.

It is a pleasure to mention here one of the truly great scholars, Hammershaimb, who has well defended "the genuineness of this passage."[21]

Barnes made a practical application of this passage to the church and the Christians of all ages. God's judgment against sin is certain to be executed:

> It will not the less come, because it is not regarded. Rather, the very condition of all God's judgments is, to

---

[19]J.R. Dummelow, *op. cit.*, p. 565.
[20]J.A. Motyer,*NBCR*, (Grand Rapids: Wm. B. Eerdmans Publishing Company, 1970), p. 731.
[21]J. Keir Howard, *NLBC* (Grand Rapids: Zondervan Publishing House, 1979), p. 956.

be disregarded and to come, and then most to come, when they are most disregarded.[22]

Verse 6, Thus saith Jehovah: For three transgressions of Israel, yea, for four, I will not turn away the punishment thereof; because they have sold the righteous for silver, and the needy for a pair of shoes.

"The righteous for silver, and the needy for a pair of shoes . . ." This expression simply means that, "For mere trifles, they had given debtors over to their creditors as slaves."[23] It appears that efforts to make some big land deal out of the second half of this denunciation are incorrect. Rather than being, as Mays thought, "an idiom for the legal transfer of land,"[24] it is far more probably a statement that the judges in Israel "could be influenced for paltry bribes."[25] "The verb used here is used of selling people into slavery."[26]

Verse 7, They that pant after the dust of the earth on the head of the poor, and turn aside the way of the meek: and a man and his father go unto the same maiden, to profane my holy name.

"Dust of the earth on the head of the poor . . ." "Dust on the head" in ancient Israel was a sign of mourning; and the desire of the oppressors in this passage would appear to be their wish to exploit to the uttermost, and hence bring them to mourning, the poor of the land. This whole clause appears to be merely a figurative expression, "for treading under foot the rights of the poor."[27]

"A man and his father unto the same maiden . . ." Motyer accurately described the sin here as an open defiance of the law of God against adultery (Exodus 20:14), and fornication in the name of religion in particular (Deuteronomy 23:17). The widely supported efforts to eliminate from Amos' writings all except his "social concerns" has led to all kinds of bizarre interpretations of this place, some going so far as to

[22]Albert Barnes, *Notes on the OT* (Grand Rapids: Zondervan Publishing House, 1953), p. 260.
[23]Paul T. Butler, *op. cit.*, p. 291.
[24]James Luther Mays, *Amos* (Philadelphia: Westminster Press, 1969), p. 45.
[25]*Ibid.*, p. 957.
[26]*Ibid.*
[27]*Ibid.*

make an "oppressed domestic servant" out of this girl which Amos mentioned, and then denominating the whole passage as "another expression of the oppression of the poor!"[28] This interpretation of the passage is endlessly parroted, as in, "All the items (here) can be placed under the general rubric of the oppression of the poor."[29] No! Adultery and the frequenting of the sacred prostitutes in such temples as those of Astarte do not come under the classification of oppressing the poor. There can hardly be any doubt that "same maiden" in this place is a reference to idol worship, a conclusion required by the clause immediately following which connects the action with profaning God's name. Jamieson wrote:

> The "damsel" meant is one of the prostitutes attached to the idol of Astarte's temple: the prostitution being part of her filthy worship.[30] The Canaanite religion thought that the performance of the human actions of procreation could be used to remind the god to fertilize the earth. It is this practice which Amos sees and denounces in Israel. The holy Yahweh is being worshiped as a Canaanite Baal.[31]

Some have attempted to deny the obvious connection with idol-worship which surfaces in this verse, basing the denial solely upon Amos' use of an unusual word for "maiden," instead of the word ordinarily used to describe the temple prostitutes; but Keil explained the reason for this thus:

> The meaning is, to one and the same girl, but *'achath* is omitted, to preclude all possible misunderstanding, as though going to *different* prostitutes was allowed. This sin was tantamount to incest, which, according to the law, was to be punished with death (Leviticus 18:7,15 and 20:11).[32]

---

[28]Ralph L. Smith, *op. cit.*, p. 97.
[29]James Luther Mays, *op. cit.*, p. 48.
[30]Robert Jamieson, *op. cit.*, p. 791.
[31]J.A. Motyer, *op. cit.*, p. 731.
[32]C.F. Keil, *Commentary on the Whole Bible* (Grand Rapids: Wm. B. Eerdmans Publishing Company), p. 253.

"To profane my holy name . . ." "The crux of the matter seems to lie in this expression . . . the next lines refer to every altar, and the house of their God, which would indicate that some type of worship is related to these sins."[33]

Verse 8, And they lay themselves down beside every altar upon clothes taken in pledge; and in the house of their God, they drink the wine of such as have been fined.

"Clothes taken in pledge . . ." Jamieson has this:

> *Clothes* refers to the outer garment, which Exodus 25:22-27 ordered to be restored to the poor man before sunset, as being his only covering. It aggravated their crime that they lay on these clothes in an idol temple.[34]

Keil strongly disagreed with the position of Jamieson that these perversions took place in idol temples, affirming that they were being committed in the house of the true God.[35] However, we are compelled to believe that Jamieson is right. God's true house, in the mind of the Jews, was at Jerusalem; and although it was true enough that the apostate Israelites pretended to be worshipping their God, they were nevertheless not doing so, but worshipping idols instead. It is our conviction, then, that it would be better not to capitalize the word God in this verse.

"They drink the wine of such as have been fined . . ." Drinking liquor, however procured, and lying down on clothes taken in pledge (in order to commit fornication) in connection with worship are sufficient clues to determine *who* was being worshipped by such actions; and we do not think it was the God of heaven. It was, of course, an aggravation of guilt that the pledged garments were illegally retained; and there would also seem to be something reprehensible in their possession of the wine mentioned here. This, of course, is speculative; but Fosbroke supposed that this may have reference to, "wine pawned and forfeited to creditors who lost no time in foreclosing."[36] However, since Amos certainly did not mention anything illegal about their

[33]Ralph L. Smith, *op. cit.*, p. 97.
[34]Robert Jamieson, *op. cit.*, p. 791.
[35]C.F. Keil, *op. cit.*, p. 254.
[36]Hughell E.W. Fosbroke, *op. cit.*, p. 788.

possessing wine, it appears that it is the desecration of worship that is primarily condemned. Certainly, we cannot find any way to agree with the opinion that, "Amos had only one standard by which a society is judged . . . by the way it treats the poor."[37] Such a view is sternly rebuked by this very passage where, adultery, incest, fornication, and getting drunk in the worship are the sins primarily in focus, although oppression of the poor is also cited, but not as the one and only mistake of that society.

Verse 9, Yet destroyed I the Amorite before them, whose height was like the height of the cedars, and he was strong as the oaks; yet I destroyed his fruit from above, and his roots from beneath.

In this through verse 12, Amos turned his attention to the great redemptive acts of God's love for Israel wherein he had delivered them from bondage, dispossessed the nations of Canaan, and done many other marvelous works upon their behalf. The remarkable nation of the Amorites was one of the dispossessed peoples, being noted particularly for their remarkable physical prowess and their great size (Numbers 13:32). He had been wiped out of existence by the divine decree, due to their idolatries and gross sins. This singular mention of the Amorites does not mean that they *alone* were displaced to make way for Israel; but here "The Amorite, the most powerful of all the Canaanite nations is put for them all."[38]

Verse 10, Also I brought you up out of the land of Egypt, and led you forty years in the wilderness, to possess the land of the Amorite.

"Why does Amos list the conquest of Canaan before the exodus from Egypt?"[39] Some commentators seem quite troubled by that question since chronologically the exodus came first; but it appears to be a climactic arrangement of God's wonders, reserving the greatest act of his mercy to the last. "From the many allusions in this section, we see

---

[37]Henry McKeating, *op. cit.*, p. 23.
[38]Robert Jamieson, *op. cit.*, p. 791.
[39]Ralph L. Smith, *op. cit.*, p. 98.

how familiar Amos and his hearers were with the history and the law of the Pentateuch."[40]

Verse 11, And I raised up of your sons prophets, and of your young men for Nazarites, is it not even thus, O ye children of Israel? saith Jehovah.

The next verse will recount the shameful manner in which Israel had responded to the wealth of spiritual leaders which God had raised up from among them to teach them and to lead them in the right way. Some of the prophets God had raised up out of Israel were: Ahijah of Shiloh, Jehu, Elijah, Elisha, Hosea and Jonah! The Nazarites were a class of spiritual leaders who used neither wine nor strong drink and never allowed the use of a razor. There were two classes of these: (1) the Nazarite of days, whose vows were for a stated season only, and (2) the Nazarite for life, of whom there are three mentioned in the Bible: Samson, Samuel, and John the Baptist.

Verse 12, But ye gave the Nazarites wine to drink, and commanded the prophets, saying, Prophesy not.

This indicates that God's word and the spiritual leaders who taught it and advocated it were alike hated by the Israelites. They despised the Nazarites and tempted them to drink, in violation of their sacred vows. The prophets also were silenced, if not by one device, then by another; and even the Saviour referred to the dishonorable and even fatal treatment of God's prophets that was heaped upon them by Israel and by Judah. (Matthew 23:29-36). Much of the OT is a history of the brutal and inhumane treatment of the prophets by God's chosen people. It will be noted that this section pertains almost exclusively to those matters which are strictly religious.

Verse 13, Behold, I will press you in your place, as a cart presseth that is full of sheaves.

The overthrow of Israel is given in different words from that of the other nations, but the meaning is the same, i.e.,

---

[40]W.J. Deane, *op. cit.*, p. 25.

military defeat and destruction. This verse is as if he had said:

> Behold, I will run over you with a loaded wagon!

Scholars tell us that the translation of the Hebrew here is uncertain; and the sense of the English version is that the load of Israel's sin and guilt is a burden that presses God down; but the figure of being run over by a wagon (or wain) "is very natural in the mouth of the shepherd Amos."[41] "Whatever meaning is given to the verb, it is clear that the ultimate action of God would be catastrophic upon the nation.[42] The divine judgment against Israel in these four verses (13-16) will be such that, "Neither natural ability (v. 14), military equipment (v. 15), nor outstanding courage (v. 16) will avail."[43]

Verses 14-16, "And flight shall perish from the swift; and the strong shall not strengthen his force; neither shall the mighty deliver himself; neither shall he stand that handleth the bow; and he that is swift of foot shall not deliver himself; neither shall he that rideth the horse deliver himself; and he that is courageous among the mighty shall flee away naked in that day, saith Jehovah.

See under verse 13 above for further comment on these verses. The complete and irreversible overthrow of Israel is solemnly prophesied in this climactic denunciation.

"Naked . . ." This word, "upon which the description ends, sums up effectively the pitiful helplessness of a man stripped of all the resources on which he had counted to maintain himself when he faces the final catastrophe."[44]

"In that day . . ." The day of the Lord refers to that day when, "God's judgment would fall upon Israel."[45] Although the immediate application of these words is thus accurately indicated, there is a more extended and ultimate sense in which they refer to the Great and Final Day of Judgment,

---

[41]W.J. Deane, *op. cit.*, p. 26.
[42]J. Keir Howard, *op. cit.*, p. 958.
[43]J.A. Motyer, *op. cit.*, p. 731.
[44]Hughell E.W. Fosbroke, *op. cit.*, p. 790.
[45]Arnold C. Schultz, *WBC* (Chicago: Moody Press, 1962), p. 830.

when the entire human race shall confront the judgment of
God upon human rebellion and wickedness.

All of the predictions here made against Israel, as is also
the case in all the other judgments cited in these two chapters, were most accurately and circumstantially fulfilled.
We conclude this chapter with the following discerning paragraph from McKeating:

> (The predictions of Amos) were fulfilled to the letter,
> and within the prophet's own lifetime or shortly after-
> wards. They were fulfilled while there were still plenty
> of people around who could remember what they said.
> Their words were therefore treated with respect and
> eventually written down.[46]

---

[46]Henry McKeating, *op. cit.*, p. 6.

CHAPTER 3

The nature of chapters 3-6 has been disputed; but it appears that Keil's analysis is correct:

> The contents of these chapters show that they do not contain three separate addresses delivered to the people by Amos at different times, but that they group together the leading thoughts of appeals delivered by word of mouth, so as to form one long admonition to repentance.[1]

Amos had just concluded the great prophecy looking to the utter destruction of eight nations; and, as regarded the six pagan nations included, the Israelites were indeed delighted to have it so; but much to their consternation and disappointment, the prophet had included *them*, both Judah and Israel, in the doom foretold; therefore, Amos dealt with the *reasons why* the favored and chosen people, "the whole family" which God brought up out of Egypt, would also be destroyed, and why that destruction was fully deserved. The children of Israel had long disregarded the words of comfort, instruction, and discipline which God, through many prophets, had spoken to them; "And now they shall be made to hear the word of reproof and threatening that the Lord has spoken against them; for he will act as he has spoken."[2] Beginning with chapter three, this word of denunciation and warning continues through chapter six.

The divisions of this chapter usually noted are:

An introductory justification of his message (1-8).
Samaria as an oppressor (9-10).
Doom of Samaria foretold (11-12).
Doom of Bethel foretold (13-15).

Thus, it is evident that the particular subject of this chapter is the northern kingdom, especially the capital of

---

[1]C.F. Keil, *Commentary on the Bible* (Grand Rapids: Wm. B. Eerdmans Publishing Company), p. 258.

[2]Matthew Henry, *MHC, Vol. IV* (Old Tappan, N.J.: Fleming H. Revell Company), p. 1233.

Samaria, and also the center of the nation's religious life at
Bethel.

Introductory Authentication

**Verse 1, Hear this word which Jehovah hath spoken
against you. O children of Israel, against the whole family
which I brought up out of the land of Egypt.**

"Against the whole family. . ." The indictment is against
the entire covenant people, both Judah and Israel. Judah
had already been warned of impending doom (2:4); and, as
the principal thrust of the whole prophecy is against Israel,
the prophet turned immediately to the business in hand.

"Which I brought up out of Egypt . . ." The thing which
Amos was called to do lay totally beyond the thought-
pattern of God's "chosen people," who had assumed that
their unusual privileges endowed upon them a status of
exemption from any unusual requirements. It was inconceivable to them that their God would punish them for
wickedness, no matter how great it was; God was thought
to be their tower of strength always, no matter what they
did. It was surely a difficult task which Amos discharged in
"getting through" to the people with that attitude. It was
this difficulty which led him to authentication of his message in verses 3-8. This is also probably the reason why, in
these chapters, "The prophet shows in greater detail the
depth to which Israel had fallen and the inevitability of
God's righteous judgment upon them as a result."[3]

**Verse 2, You only have I known of all the families of the
earth: therefore I will visit upon you all your iniquities.**

"You only have I known . . ." "The word 'known' in this
context is a covenant word, used to describe a relationship
instead of cognition."[4] It means, "Jehovah chose Israel
alone to be his people."[5] To infer from this that God had no
information of other nations, or that, in any sense, he was

---

[3]J. Keir Howard, *NLBC* (Grand Rapids: Zondervan Publishing House, 1979),
p. 958.
[4]Ralph L. Smith, *BBC, Vol. VI* (Nashville: Broadman Press, 1972), p. 99.
[5]J.R. Dummelow, *Commentary on the Holy Bible* (New York: The Macmillan
Company, 1937), p. 565.

unaware of them, "would be a limitation upon God's nature,"[6] and also a notion utterly confounded by the stern judgments against other nations appearing in this very prophecy. In short, the doctrine of the election of Israel is the thing in view; but Amos revealed an altogether shocking corollary of it, i.e., responsibility and conformity to the will of God, a corollary that Israel had overlooked. Instead of reading their election as:

> Now that we are God's, he will help and bless us no matter what we do.

Amos gave them the true version of it:

> Now that we are God's, he will surely punish us for all of our iniquities.

It is amazing how this ancient delusion of Israel persists even today in millions of people who think they are "saved by faith alone." God's election, God's grace, God's covenant with his people has from the beginning, continually, and always rested upon the contingency that the recipients of his mercy would continue to love God, and to the best of their ability, obey him.

Christians today should also read the true version of their salvation by the grace of God:

> We are God's, and therefore we are under the uttermost obligation to love him and obey him.

Verses 3-6, Shall two walk together except they have agreed? Will a lion roar in the forest, when he hath no prey? will a young lion cry out of his den, if he have taken nothing? Can a bird fall in a snare upon the earth, where no gin is set for him? shall a snare spring from the ground, and have taken nothing at all? Shall the trumpet be blown in a city, and the people not be afraid? Shall evil befall a city, and Jehovah hath not done it?

These verses are the prelude to verses 7,8, below; and they consist of a series of questions, each of which demands

---

[6]James Luther Mays, *Amos, A Commentary* (Philadelphia: The Westminster Press, 1969), p. 56.

a negative answer from the hearers, an answer that is not awaited, for it is considered obvious.

"Shall two walk together . . ." Israel's having forsaken God's way means that they are no longer "agreed" with God. "Can they continue together? The law of cause and effect operates to separate them."[7] As Butler noted, "This verse is often quoted in treatises on 'Unity,' but verse 3 has nothing to do with the subject of 'Unity.' "[8] There is a sin and consequence relationship in all of the statements here. They all mean the same thing: "No calamities or judgments can fall upon any people, but by the express will of God, on account of their iniquities."[9] All of these sayings likewise have a cause and effect connection. "They illustrate the truth that all effects have causes, and that from the cause you can infer the effect."[10]

God in History

One of the big things in this whole passage is Amos' view of history, not as the accidental and opportunistic deployment of peoples upon the earth, but as a "controlled" entity, subject, absolutely to the will of God. Nations rise and fall by God's will only, wicked nations being used for a season to punish the righteous, but themselves being quickly liquidated when their sins have gone beyond that hidden boundary that separates God's mercy from his wrath.

No matter how men resent and oppose this view of history, it is nevertheless the truth. Nebuchadnezzar was compelled to eat grass with the beasts of the earth for seven years in order that he might know that, "The Most High ruleth in the kingdom of men, and giveth it to whomsoever he will" (Daniel 4:25). Paul affirmed that, "God made of one every nation of men . . . and determined their appointed seasons, and the bounds of their habitation, *that they*

[7]J.A. Motyer, *NBCR* (Grand Rapids: Wm. B. Eerdmans Publishing Company, 1979), p. 732.

[8]Paul T. Butler, *The Minor Prophets* (Joplin: College Press, 1968), p. 301.

[9]Adam Clarke, *Commentary on the Whole Bible, Vol. V* (New York: T. Mason & G. Lane, 1837), p. 678.

[10]W.J. Deane, *Pulpit Commentary, Vol. 14, Amos* (Grand Rapids: Wm. B. Eerdmans Publishing Company, 1950), p. 40.

should seek God" (Acts 17:26,27). The reason that one nation is blessed is that they might seek God and lead others to know him; and the reason that another nation is oppressed is that they may be punished for their iniquities and know repentance.

So-called "modern man" rejects a premise such as this, as effectively stated by McKeating:

> They (the Israelites) did not think of themselves as wicked. Most modern men would deny the logic of the conclusion. It would be reassuring if history could be shown to exhibit a consistent moral purpose, but such a pattern is difficult to demonstrate convincingly.[11]

Aside from the viewpoint of basic humanism regarding the oppression of the poor, most "modern men" find nothing at all wrong with the conduct of the Israelites. Such vices as drunkenness, adultery, fornication, idol-worship, neglect of religious duty, etc., are merely "doing what comes naturally." Despite the unawareness of the terrible sinfulness of sin which characterizes our own generation to a degree rivalling, we fear, that of ancient Israel itself, God still rules in the kingdom of men; offenses against God will be severely punished; and nations that forget God shall be turned to destruction, regardless of whether or not "modern man" believes it. Ancient Israel did not believe, nor did any other of the eight nations confronted by the judgments of Amos' prophecy; but where are any of those nations now?

"Will a lion . . . will a young lion . . ." These two similies have the same meaning. Just as the roar of the lion, or the growl of the young lion, means that the prey is before them, the roaring of the prophet against Israel means that, "God not only has before him the nation that is ripe for judgment, but that he has it in his power."[12]

"Can a bird fall into a snare . . . etc." The two previous similes were from the standpoint of the predator; in these two (v. 5) the standpoint is that of the prey. "The snare"

---

[11]Henry McKeating, *Amos, Hosea, and Micah* (Cambridge: At the University Press, 1971), p. 28.
[12]C.F. Keil, *op. cit.*, p. 261.

which God has set for sinners is "the consequence" inevitably connected with evil doing. The very consequences of evil indicate that the Infinite Intelligence wills it so. He indeed has "set the snare." The springing up of the trap is always the consequence of the trigger having been set off by the trespasser. None of the judgments, therefore, which have already been declared by Amos against Israel, and which he is here attempting to explain to the unbelieving people, are in any sense capricious or undeserved. Israel has tripped the trigger of the wrath of God; and the trap would not have sprung had this not been so. Keil quoted a passage from Jeremiah to explain what is said here: "Can destruction possibly overtake you, unless your sin draw you into it? (Jeremiah 2:35)."[13]

"Gin . . ." as used in verse 5, "is an old English contraction of 'engine.' referring to the mechanism that releases the trap."[14]

"Shall the trumpet be blown in a city and the people not be afraid . . ." Here is "the application of the two sets of illustrations,"[15] namely, that the prey hear the voice of the predator and are afraid. Israel has heard the roar of the lion in the prophetic warnings of Amos, and they should be afraid. Motyer pointed out here that:

> The only view of history that the Bible espouses is that the Lord is the Great Agent. Behind every event stands a cause; behind all history stands the Lord (Isaiah 45:5-7). Maybe thus they will prepare themselves for his future acts of judgment.[16]

Keil likewise discerned this as the import of this passage:

> As the trumpet when blown frightens the people out of their self-security, so will the voice of the prophet . . . The calamity which is bursting upon them comes from Jehovah, and is sent by him for punishment.[17]

[13]*Ibid.*
[14]Arnold C. Schultz, *WBC* (Chicago: Moody Press, 1961), p. 833.
[15]J.A. Motyer, *op. cit.*, p. 732.
[16]*Ibid.*
[17]C.F. Keil, *op. cit.*, p. 260.

Verses 7,8, Surely the Lord Jehovah will do nothing, except he reveal his secret unto his servants the prophets. The lion hath roared, who will not fear? The Lord Jehovah hath spoken; who can but prophecy?

The logic of this verse requires its placement exactly where it is. The foolish arguments of some to the effect that "this is a later insertion,"[18] are effectually denied and refuted by the sheer necessity of this thought in relation to what has preceded it. The whole passage gives the prophetic view of history as a drama in which sin is punished and righteousness rewarded; omitting vv. 7,8 would have been subject to the objection in Amos' hearers that such calamities as those foretold would have been "unfair without adequate warning." Very well, Amos here affirmed the validity of such a forensic objection, but set it aside by the fact that his great prophecy was itself the adequate warning, indicating also that thus it had ever been with God's dealings with the human race. Howard commented on the unity and skilful arrangement of this passage thus:

> The whole saying (verses 1-8) is a very skilful linkage of cause and effect, developed as a series of questions leading up to the final statement (v. 8), that in the same way as natural events are linked in such a causal chain, so too there is a causal relationship behind his own words to Israel.[19]

Samaria as an Oppressor (9-10)

Verse 9, Publish ye in the palaces at Ashdod, and in the palaces in the land of Egypt, and say, Assemble yourselves upon the mountains of Samaria, and behold what great tumults are therein, and what oppressions in the midst thereof.

"In the palaces of Ashdod . . ." The desire of some scholars to translate this "Assyria" instead of Ashdod should be rejected. There is no other mention of Assyria in this prophecy (although it is evident enough that Assyria

---

[18]James Luther Mays, *op. cit.*, p. 59.
[19]J. Keir Howard, *op. cit.*, p. 959.

was clearly the enemy Amos had in mind); but the proposition here seems geared to the ancient fear of Israel that their wickedness and calamities should be known to their traditional enemies. Following the death of Saul, the lament took this form:

> Tell it not in Gath,
> Publish it not in the streets of Ashkelon;
> Lest the daughters of the Philistines rejoice,
> Lest the daughters of the uncircumcised rejoice
> —2 Samuel 1:20.

There is definitely an echo of this in the verse before us. "Ashdod" also carries a more pointed meaning for Israel than would "Assyria" in this verse. "It is a more stinging implication that the Philistines (Ashdod) and the Egyptians, the two hated ancestral enemies were morally superior to Israel."[20] "It was to the eternal disgrace of Israel that there were doings in her cities which the very heathen would condemn."[21]

"Assemble yourselves upon the mountains of Samaria . . ." The imagery is that of a court of world-judgment summoned to take places of advantage overlooking Samaria and to view the terrible wickedness that was perpetuated there. "The mountains are Ebal and Gerizim, from which one could look down upon Samaria."[22]

Verse 10, For they know not to do right, saith Jehovah, who store up robbery and violence in their palaces.

"Know not to do right . . ." Butler paraphrased this, "Israel does not even know how to do right."[23] This charge is perhaps the worst of all:

> It speaks of a state of depravity in which the conscience ceases to function properly and the sinner is unable to distinguish between right and wrong . . . When people do not do right, the time comes when they cannot do right.[24]

[20]J.A. Motyer, *op. cit.*, p. 733.
[21]W.J. Deane, *op. cit.*, p. 41.
[22]Arnold C. Schultz, *op. cit.*, p. 833.
[23]Paul T. Butler, *op. cit.*, p. 304.
[24]Ralph L. Smith, *op. cit.*, p. 103.

"Store up robbery and violence . . ." The most of the commentators interpret this to mean that the ill-gotten gains of those who lived in palaces were stored in their strongholds; but it could very well mean that the people trusting in their wealth were merely storing up plunder for the forthcoming invader. Smith agreed that, "Society was only storing up or postponing the day of violence . . . a foreign invasion or internal disruption."[25] However interpreted, it simply means that the day of judgment upon their wickedness is promptly coming.

Doom of Samaria Foretold (11-12)

Verse 11, Therefore thus saith the Lord Jehovah: an adversary there shall be, even round about the land; and he shall bring down thy strength from thee, and thy palaces shall be plundered.

It will be noted that there are multiple references to: "saith Jehovah, thus saith the Lord Jehovah, etc." in this section, and, in fact, throughout Amos; but the conclusion of critical scholars that, "The multiplicity of introductory formulae shows that here we have a collection of three or four fragmentary sayings,"[26] should be rejected as unfounded and unproved. The repetition of such expressions is merely characteristic of Amos' style, a fact that cannot be denied. Look at the repeated questions that are propounded in verses 3-6. Repetition was also a characteristic of the teachings of Jesus our Lord.

"There shall be . . ." It will be noted that these words are italicized in the ASV and in the AV, but they should nevertheless be retained. "The KJV here makes sense of the awkward Hebrew text by introducing *there shall be.*"[27]

The three measures of the line (v. 11) sketch in terse staccato sentences the stages of a military campaign: invasion, siege, and looting. The foe is not identified;

---

[25]*Ibid.*, p. 102.
[26]Henry McKeating, *op. cit.*, p. 29.
[27]Hughell E.W. Fosbroke, *IB, Vol. VI* (New York: Abingdon Press, 1957), p. 797.

but it is generally assumed that the Assyrians are in mind.[28]

Verse 12, Thus saith Jehovah: As the shepherd rescueth out of the mouth of the lion two legs, or a piece of an ear, so shall the children of Israel be rescued that sit in Samaria in the corner of a couch, and on the silken cushions of a bed.

This and the preceding verse relate the doom of Samaria; and this verse is addressed to the possible hope that they would be rescued. Rescued? Yes, but it will be like the gory remains when a shepherd picked up a part of the carcass which had been devoured by a lion, nothing worth rescuing! To the query of the present that might be expected today as to why the shepherd would pick up such worthless pieces of a carcass, it was due to the law of God (Exodus 22:13). "A shepherd was accountable to the sheep-owner for any animal lost, unless he could prove it was lost owing to circumstances beyond his contol."[29] Note that this indirect reference to the Pentateuch together with the implied assumption that all of Israel knew it shows beyond question that the Pentateuch was not merely in existence, but that it had been known for a long, long time prior to the days of Amos. Thus, the rescue which is mentioned in this verse is a "rescue" of that which is worthless. Of Israel, "Nothing will be saved that is worth saving."[30] It implies that, the Divine Shepherd (Psalm 23), on whose protection they presumed, now only wanted the evidence of their death."[31]

The translation of this verse, which is very difficult due to uncertainties in the text, is given thus in NEB:

> As a shepherd rescues out of the jaws of a lion
>   two shin bones or the tip of an ear,
> So shall the Israelites who live in Samaria be rescued
>   like the corner of a couch or a chip from the leg of
>   a bed.

---

[28]James Luther Mays, *op. cit.*, p. 65.
[29]Henry McKeating, *op. cit.*, p. 30.
[30]*Ibid.*
[31]James Luther Mays, *op. cit.*, p. 68.

This translation has the merit of rounding out the simile more perfectly. Furthermore, this rendition is known to have been fulfilled literally when excavations at Samaria uncovered broken pieces of furniture and remnants of the ivory house of Ahab. "These fragments must be what was left when the city was sacked by the Assyrians in 722 B.C."[32] Despite the attractiveness of the NEB rendition, however, Fosbroke defended the "silken cushions" of the ASV as being "satisfactory as any."[33] In that rendition, the meaning is the same, but not as dramatically stated, the focus shifting to the luxurious lives of the Samaritans.

Doom of Bethel Foretold (13-15)

Verse 13, Hear ye, and testify against the house of Jacob, saith the Lord Jehovah, the God of hosts.

This is a reference to the ten northern tribes, as indicated in the next verses by the mention of the altars of Bethel.

"The Lord Jehovah, the God of hosts . . ." "This full title appears nowhere else in the book,"[34] indeed nowhere else in the entire Bible. "It emphasizes in a special way the omnipotence of God for the purpose of magnifying the effect of the predicted judgment."[35] "In Hebrew the name is *adonai yahweh Elohim tsba'oth*."[36] It is from the last member of this quadruple designation that our word "Sabaoth" is derived. The Lord of Sabaoth means the Lord of Hosts and is found some 300 times in the OT. The imagery of "Lord of Sabaoth, i.e., Lord of Hosts" is that of the ruler over an organized host, such as a great army, or all of the angels of heaven.

Verse 14, For in the day that I shall visit the transgressions of Israel upon him, I will also visit the altars of Bethel; and the horns of the altar shall be cut off, and fall to the ground.

The singling out of the polluted shrine at Bethel is significant, as this was the seat of the religion of Israel. It will be

---

[32]Ralph L. Smith, *op. cit.*, p. 31.
[33]Hughell E.W. Fosbroke, *op. cit.*, p. 798.
[34]James Luther Mays, *op. cit.*, p. 68.
[35]Arnold C. Schultz, *op. cit.*, p. 833.
[36]Ralph L. Smith, *op. cit.*, p. 102.

recalled that when Jeroboam led the ten tribes in their secession from "the house of David," he was alarmed that the people returning to Jerusalem to worship God might eventually defect from his authority; he perpetuated a most contemptible and daring perversion of the worship of God:

> Whereupon the king took counsel, and made two calves of gold; and he said unto them (the people), It is too much for you to go up to Jerusalem: Behold thy gods, O Israel which brought thee up out of the land of Egypt. And he set the one in Bethel, and the other he put in Dan (1 Kings 12:28,29).

"It has commonly been assumed that the golden calves were direct representtions of Yahweh as bull-god,"[37] and some commentators claim that the true God was thus worshipped in Israel; but the very making of those golden calves was a flagrant violation of the law of God as known for centuries prior to Jeroboam. Aaron, it will be remembered, had done such a thing in the wilderness of wanderings while Moses was absent to receive the tables of the law, an event quite early in Israel's history; and that sinful episode had resulted in unqualified disaster for the Israelites. This action, therefore, on the part of Jeroboam was actually a repudiation of the worship of God, no matter how he had dressed it up and attempted to make it look like a "new form" of genuine worship. "The bull affiliations of Baal were too closely connected with the more degrading aspects of pagan cults to be safe, and there is every indication that the Northern Kingdom fell a prey to idolatrous pollution as a result."[38] The stinging words of this prophecy also indicate that the people were lying down upon pledged garments "beside every altar" (2:8), a plain reference to the fornication that was openly practiced in "the house of god!" Israel had forsaken the true God and had gone back to the gross idolatry of the old Canaanites, even adoring their filthy old "bull god." It is no wonder that God promised to "visit" those altars in Bethel, with the purpose of their total destruction. "The punishment of these altars

---

[37]Merrill F. Unger, *Archeology and the OT* (Grand Rapids: Zondervan Publishing House, 1954), p. 236.

[38]*Ibid.*, p. 237.

suggests that false religion is the root of social deca-
dence."³⁹ In fact, false religion was the root of all Israel's
sorrow.

Together with verse 15, below, we have in this denunciation of Bethel God's emphatic "cease and desist" in regard
to all that Israel held dear. The word "house" as repeatedly
used in the passage shows the completeness of this stop
order which was hurled against them from heaven. Note the
following from Mays:

> House of Jacob, house of God (Beth-El), winter
> house, summer house, ivory house, and great house.
> What Israel had built stands as the manifestation of
> the nation's rebellions. The devastation of these
> houses is the actualization of Yahweh's "No" to Is-
> rael's cult and culture.⁴⁰

The claim of the Israelites, of course, was that they were
indeed worshipping the true God, a farce which they encouraged by observing many of the rituals and commandments of the law of Moses. Burnt offerings, thank offerings,
and meal offerings were presented there (5:22); but as Dummelow wrote:

> All this was vitiated by two faults: (1) The god whom
> the worshippers adored was not the Holy One, who
> alone is worthy, but a mere nature god, and (2) the
> worship was not of a kind to make men better; but it
> was closely associated with immorality and with luxu-
> rious eating and drinking.⁴¹

**Verse 15, And I will smite the winter house with the
summer house; and the houses of ivory shall perish, and the
great houses shall have an end, saith Jehovah.**

The heartless affluence, luxury and self-satisfied uncon-
cern of the ruling classes in Israel were the sins of the
people who owned and lived in the houses described in this
passage; and their rich and easy lives had been made possible through all kinds of corruption and deceit as outlined in

³⁹J.A. Motyer, *op. cit.*, p. 733.
⁴⁰James Luther Mays, *op. cit.*, p. 69.
⁴¹J.R. Dummelow, *op. cit.*, p. 565.

Amos' prophecy. They would sell a man into slavery for a pair of shoes. God announced that he was putting an end to that kind of culture, an end which came within the lifetime of those who heard Amos' words. We cannot highly regard the words of McKeating who criticised Amos as a nomad who was merely hostile to the refinements of city life, saying that his "was the uncomprehending indignation of what he sees as the vices of city life."[42] This is totally wrong. It was not Amos' indignation that is poured out in Amos, but the indignation of the infinite God. Mays more clearly understood the words of this remarkable prophecy thus:

> The judgment which Amos announces is no ascetic primitivism, growing out of simple hostility against a commercial culture and its influence. The houses were built beam by beam, and stone by stone, from a store of crimes.[43]

"Houses of ivory. . ." The import of this is not likely to be that houses were built entirely out of this substance, but rather that they were extensively decorated with it. The Bible mentions the "ivory house which Ahab built" (1 Kings 22:39).

"Winter houses and summer houses . . ." Plural houses were provided for some who could afford them with elevations that were designed to provide comfort in diverse seasons.

That ancient culture, founded upon the heartless oppression of the poor, is not the only such society that God has destroyed, as a trip through the palaces of Europe will quickly demonstrate. Maria Theresa's bedroom was decorated with over three million dollars worth of gold and precious stones. Wherever such selfishness is enshrined and honored, the wrath of God abides there for ever.

"The horns of the altar shall be cut off . . ." The horns of the altar were supposed to be its most sacred part; and, in pagan societies, a criminal could claim refuge by taking hold of the horns of the altar; but this was not allowed in Israel. Joab attempted to do this but was executed in spite

---

[42]Henry McKeating, *op. cit.*, p. 31.
[43]James Luther Mays, *op. cit.*, p. 70.

of his doing so (1 Kings 2:28ff). The meaning is simply that
the whole religious apparatus at Bethel shall perish, along
with the rest of Israel.

CHAPTER 4

There is a continuation in this chapter of the general thought and movement of the last, consisting of denunciations and exhortations of Israel. First, there is a powerful blast against the idle, sinful and oppressive rich "in the mountain of Samaria" (1-3), then, a sarcastic and ironical "call to worship" at Bethel and Gilgal (4,5), and next, a dramatic reminder by the prophet of the seven disasters God had sent upon Israel with the benign purpose of leading them to repentance (6-12). Some have considered these disasters as progressive in intensity and severity. "Amos has arranged them in climactic form."[1] Mays, however, wrote that:

> There is no perceptible development in the sections, no heightening of the disasters' intensity. Each is terrible in its own right, no worse than the previous one. The sequence gains its effect from repetition, the recollection of one disaster after another as though the narrative meant to exhaust the catalogue of human misery.[2]

Of particular interest is May's reference to "repetition," which we have already cited as one of the principal characteristics of this remarkable prophet; and the recurrence of a number of different names for God, the recurrence of identical phrases in his denunciations of the nations (chs. 1-2), and the dramatic repetitions of this section (vv. 5-12) are all alike genuine and inseparable from the authentic words of this prophecy. Of this chapter, Mays said:

> The sequence is not the work of a collector assembling units of similar form. The individual sections have no point as isolated sayings. The art of repetition is a feature of Amos' own style.[3]

---

[1]Paul T. Butler, *The Minor Prophets* (Joplin: College Press, 1968), p. 311.
[2]James Luther Mays, *Amos, A Commentary* (Philadelphia: The Westminster Press, 1961), p. 78.
[3]*Ibid.*

Finally, there is a beautiful but brief doxology in verse 13, a logically placed exclamation, concluding the terrible indictment and announced punishment of Israel.

Verse 1, Hear this, ye kine of Bashan, that are in the mountain of Samaria, that oppress the poor, that crush the needy, that say unto their lords, Bring, and let us drink.

"Ye kine of Bashan . . ." By far the majority of modern translators and commentators render this. "Ye cows of Bashan," making it a reference exclusively to the "fat cat" women of Samaria. We shall accept this, but it should be noted that most of the older commentators did not go along with that view. Clarke wrote, "I think the prophet means men of effeminate and idle lives."[4] The word here is "cows," the feminine form of "kine" having no other meaning; but the uncertainty with regard to the meaning derives from the fact that the Hebrew text in this place uses a mixture of feminine and masculine gender words with some inevitable confusion as to what exactly is meant. The best explanation of this we have seen is this:

> "Kine of Bashan . . ." is figurative for those luxurious nobles mentioned in chapter 3:9, etc. The feminine *kine*, or *cows*, not *bulls*, expresses their effeminacy. This accounts for masculine forms in the Hebrew being intermixed with feminine; the latter being figurative, the former the real persons meant.[5]

The fact which overrules the view thus expressed by Jamison derives from the last clause in which they say to "their lords":

"Bring, and let us drink . . ." giving a situation which answers most properly to the assumption that the sinners condemned here are those wicked, dissolute and voluptuous women of Samaria who had only one imperative for their "lords," or "husbands," and that was, *Bring!* This means, "Get it; we don't care how!" The only thing that mattered

[4]Adam Clarke, *Commentary on the Whole Bible* (New York: T. Mason & G. Lane, 1837), p. 680.
[5]Robert Jamieson, *JFB* (Grand Rapids: Zondervan Publishing House, 1961), p. 793.

to them was the procurement of the means to carry forward
their luxurious parties.

"Cows of Bashan . . ." Hammershaimb thought that such
an expression could have been used in a complimentary
fashion, saying that, "Oriental writers use the comparison
with thoroughbred cows as a compliment to the women's
beauty and opulence."[6] We dare not accept this view, however, as that of the prophet. If he had been giving a compliment, it seems incredible that he would have chosen a sleek
fat beast as an appropriate comparison.

"And let us drink . . ." Butler's terse paraphrase of this
is, "You debauched women who nag your husbands to supply you with intoxicants."[7] Thus, the husbands of those
women, "are induced to deal oppressively with the poor
that they may procure the viands needed for their wives'
debaucheries."[8] Due to the general character of the language employed here, their *drinking*, "may be understood
to have included drinking, feasting, and wanton luxury of
every kind."[9] Why was Amos so concerned with the actions
of these idle and wicked women? McFadden was right in his
declaration that:

> All of the Hebrew prophets knew that for the temper
> and quality of a civilization the women are greatly
> responsible. A country is largely what its women make
> it; if they are cruel or careless or unwomanly, the coun-
> try is on the road to ruin.[10]

But these particular women so vigorously condemned by
God's prophet had done what no animal could do, "They
had made coarse pleasure the deliberate end of life."[11]

The great ladies of Samaria! What were they, really?
Intent only upon pleasure, cruel and oppressive to subordi-
nates, dominating and demanding of their husbands, com-

---

[6]Erling Hammershaimb, *The Book of Amos, translated by John Sturdy*
(New York: Schocken Books, 1970), p. 65.

[7]Paul T. Butler, *op. cit.*, p. 307.

[8]William Rainey Harper, *Amos and Hosea* (New York: Charles Scribner's
Sons, 1910), p. 86.

[9]*Ibid.*

[10]John Edgar McFadden, *A Cry for Justice* (New York: Charles Scribner's
Sons, 1912), p. 36.

[11]*Ibid.*

peting endlessly with their contemporaries for preeminence in staging one debauchery after another, with never a thought of God, or of any fellow-human, what were they? Just, "so many prime beasts from Bashan, sunk in a purely animal existence."[12]

"Bashan . . ." Before leaving this verse, it should be remembered that Bashan was proverbially the home of fine pastures and fat cattle. "The bulls of Bashan" were mentioned by the Psalmist (22:12). It was the land lying eastward from the sea of Galilee and somewhat to the north.

One other thing of interest is the way some have tried to downgrade Amos' denunciation of these sensual women with the assertion that:

> There is something about fashionable upper-class women that brings out the venom in a puritan. They epitomize for him the most offensive vices of society. Isaiah reacts to them much as Amos does (Isaiah 3:16-4:1).[13]

How blind are they who can get nothing out of this passage of the word of God except what they call "the venom" of a humble prophet! What a low concept such so-called "scholars" have of the word of the Lord, and how clearly their prejudice in favor of the "upper-class" appears in words which suggest approval of their wicked and dissolute conduct. Given such a glimpse of the writer's "soul" as afforded by the above quotation, one need not be troubled at all regarding his allegations against the Bible. It would be impossible for them to be otherwise than opposed to the truth.

Verses 2,3, The Lord Jehovah hath sworn by his holiness, that, lo, the days shall come upon you, that they shall take you away with hooks, and your residue with fish-hooks. And ye shall go out at the breaches, every one straight before her; and ye shall cast yourselves into Harmon, saith Jehovah.

[12]J.A. Motyer, *NBCR* (Grand Rapids: Wm. B. Eerdmans Publishing Company, 1970), p. 733.
[13]Henry McKeating, *CBC, Amos* (Cambridge: At the University Press, 1971), p. 32.

The exact meaning of this passage is very difficult to determine, due to the damaged nature of the Hebrew text from which it is translated. Some widely different translations have come down to us. Wolfe translated it thus:

> You shall be dragged by the nose with hooks,
> And by your buttocks with fish spears;
> Even as dung you shall be hauled out, one by one,
> To be cast forth on the dump heap naked.[14]

The Septuagint and Vatican renditions of this place have, "And fiery destroyers shall cast those with you into boiling cauldrons."[15] Such uncertainties are due to the fact that the words translated "hooks," "fish-hooks" and "Harmon" are not exactly known, as to their meanings. Such difficulties, however, do not in any sense obscure the meaning of the prophet in this passage, that being that a terrible fate is in store for the sensual profligates called the "kine of Bashan." The leading of captives by "hooks" which is certainly one of the possible meanings here was no unlikely event, for:

> The Assyrian illutrations depict such scenes with captives being led with hooks through their noses or mouths, and Amos was no doubt familiar with this barbaric practice.[16]

"The breaches ..." mentioned here indicate that the city will be overthrown by military action and that its citizens shall be removed through the breaches made in the walls.

"Harmon ..." is sometime construed as "naked" and sometimes as a place-name; but if it is the latter, no such place has ever been identified.

Verses 4,5, Come to Bethel, and transgress; to Gilgal, and multiply transgressions; and bring your sacrifices every morning, and your tithes every three days; and offer a

---

[14]Rolland Emerson Wolfe, *Meet Amos and Hosea* (New York: Harper & Brothers Publishers, 1945), p. 24.

[15]W.J. Deane, *Pulpit Commentary, Vol. 14, Amos* (Grand Rapids: Wm. B. Eerdmans Publishing Company, 1950), p. 61.

[16]J. Keir Howard, *NLBC* (Grand Rapids: Zondervan Publishing House, 1979), p. 960.

sacrifice of thanksgiving of that which is leavened, and proclaim freewill offerings and publish them: for this pleaseth you, O ye children of Israel, saith the Lord Jehovah.

False religion is the root of all social ills, and here the prophet poured out God's wrath upon the polluted, innovative, and unauthorized worship that marked the religious culture of Israel.

"Come to Bethel, and transgress . . ." Of course, they called it "worship"; but it was no such thing. It was, first of all, conducted at an unauthorized place, Jerusalem only being the appropriate place for the Jews to worship God. They pretended, of course, that it was the true God whom they adored there, but it was not true. The "god" they really worshipped was the filthy "Baal," the old god of the Canaanites, and with all the drunkenness, fornication and other debaucheries practiced by the pagans for centuries prior to God's placing Israel in their land. The identification of such human lust with the worship of Almighty God was at the very seat of all Israel's troubles. We have no desire at all to accommodate with that school of expositors who are willing to declare that the only thing wrong in Israel was social injustice as manifested in the oppression of the poor. That was only the froth that had risen to the top of the barrel of rotten irreligion that characterized Israel's culture at that time. What do such exegetes suppose was the utility of those "garments of the poor" spread out around "every altar" in Israel?

"Your sacrifices every morning, and your tithes every three days . . ." To interpret this as it stands in our version, "Amos exaggerates in order to emphasize the beloved fallacy"[17] that the "more" they served "god" (!) the better things would be for them. The tithes were due once a year, but in this place Amos seems to say, "If you tithed your possessions every three days" it would be only an increase in your sins! Why? nothing connected with that worship at either Gilgal or Bethel had any genuine connection whatever with the true worship of the Lord. The NEB, of course, translates this:

---

[17]J.A. Motyer, *op. cit.*, p. 733.

Bring your sacrifices for the morning,
And your tithes within three days.

We believe that our own version is better and that Amos used hyperbole. Amos utterly rejected the worship of Israel because it was not offered to the true God, but to Baal, because the idolatrous images of the calf were adored there, because the so-called "worship" consisted of drunkenness, fornication, gluttonous feasting, and other low forms of debauchery, because they were violating the clear rules of the Pentateuch regarding freewill offerings, by publishing the names of the donors, and by offering *leavened bread*, which was contrary to the law of God, and because their oppression of the poor indicated their heartless and disobedient disregard for the entirety of God's law.

"Offer a sacrifice of thanksgiving which is leavened . . ." Here is a clear, forceful, and undeniable denunciation by the prophet Amos of a violation regarding one of the rituals in the service of God. The Mosaic law has this:

Thou shalt not offer the blood of my sacrifice with leavened bread (Exodus 23:18).

However, some expositors of God's message in Amos are very unwilling to let this go unchallenged, because it contradicts their major premise that only the social ills were of any concern to Amos. Well, there's no social ill involved here, however it may be sought; and that is the mountain truth that set off a series of comments like this:

Amos does not here refer to the transgression of any law in existence.[18] It is not, however, likely that Amos is sarcastically charging Israelites with a breach of ritual regulations.[19] Amos is not condemning the offering of sacrifice with leaven because it was forbidden in the law, but because the presence of leaven was simply another sign of their affluence.[20]

Despite postulations such as those, it is quite clear that the Law of Moses was indeed in existence when Amos

---

[18]William Rainey Harper, *op. cit.*, p. 91.
[19]James Luther Mays, *op. cit.*, p. 75.
[20]Ralph L. Smith, *BBC, Vol. 7* (Nashville: The Broadman Press, 1972), p. 104.

wrote, and it was known wherever Jews lived; and this prohibition in that law would never have been mentioned in the context here unless that is the way it was. As for Smith's notion that "leaven" was the sign of anyone's *affluence* (!), one would be hard-pressed indeed to come up with anything more ridiculous. The children of Israel, *while in slavery*, had plenty of leaven, hence the prohibition that the Passover should be celebrated with "unleavened" bread.

Note also another violation of the Mosaic law in the matter of publishing the names of donors of "freewill offerings."

"And proclaim freewill offerings, and publish them . . ." The violation here is two-fold. Freewill-offerings were not supposed to be motivated by any specific regulation, but the people of Amos' day had "proclaimed" freewill-offerings, that is, exhorting the people to give them. They were supposed to be absolutely spontaneous; and these proclamations were a violation of that intention. Furthermore, as an added incentive, they were "publishing" the freewill-offerings, that is, they were publishing the names of the donors! This, of course, was a good fund-raising device, but it was contrary to God's will.

Now, in the light of these very specific, yet incidental, references to the Law of Moses, it is impossible logically to support the notion that no such law existed when Amos wrote. If no such law had been in existence, it would have been necessary for him to explain why the things mentioned were sinful; and the fact of no explanation being offered *proves* the prior existence of the Mosaic law which included those prohibitions. The mere denials of scholars who wish to think otherwise are worthless in such a clear-cut demonstration as is found here.

"For this pleaseth you . . ." The ancient Israelites had fallen into the error of supposing that whatever was pleasing and acceptable to themselves was allowable in the worship of God. Many moderns are blinded by the same delusion. The determinative factor regarding what is, or is not, acceptable to God in his worship is the fact of whether or not God has commanded whatever actions, sacrifices, etc., are offered. The proposition that God has no concern with regard to "how" he is worshipped by men is refuted on every page of the Bible. Cain was condemned for violating God's prescription for worship; and, both in that instance, and here, there is no way to limit God's displeasure to prior social injustice on the part of the worshipper. And why do men do otherwise than what God has commanded in their worship? The answer is right here. As in this case with ancient Israel, "they do what pleases them" and not what pleases God.

Disasters God had sent Upon Israel

In verses 6-12, are listed no less than seven calamities which the Lord had visited upon Israel in the hope of inducing them to repentance and wooing them to return unto the Lord. The lesson to be derived from such events is one which has proved to be very difficult for the human race to learn; and yet it is one of the oldest admonitions in the holy scriptures:

> And unto Adam he said, because thou hast hearkened unto the voice of thy wife, and has eaten of the tree of which I commanded thee, saying, Thou shalt not eat of it: cursed is the ground for thy sake; in toil shalt thou eat of it all the days of thy life; thorns and thistles shall it bring forth to thee; and thou shalt eat the herb of the field; in the sweat of thy face shalt thou eat bread, till thou return unto the ground; for out of it wast thou taken, and unto dust shalt thou return (Genesis 3:17-19).

The simple and obvious meaning of this passage is that man's environment shall exhibit a certain hostility to him throughout man's pilgrimage upon earth. Also, the opposition which shall arise from the environment itself has a benign purpose, not the mere punishment of man, but "for his sake," in order that he might not forget God. This principle, from the very first book in the Bible is carried forward in the last book of the Bible, in Revelation, chapters 8,9. in which is related the story of the seven trumpets sounding over the human environment; and significantly, the disasters foretold there are part and parcel with the disasters visible in this section regarding God's dealings with ancient Israel.

Amos' view of these calamities is clearly that of emphasis upon their relationship to the long-standing covenant with God. If the Pentateuch did not exist, if there had been no solemn covenant with God, then this portion of Amos makes no sense at all; but, of course, *they did exist*, and had long existed when Amos wrote. Speaking of Amos' view of these events, Howard said, "Such an interpretation of history can only possess significance within the covenant situation."[21]

Regarding the disasters mentioned here, Motyer enumerated them as follows:

> God sent his people seven warning chastisements: famine (v. 6), drought (vv. 7,8), mildew (v. 9a), locusts (v. 9b), epidemic (v. 10a), war (v. 10b), and earthquake (v. 11), before the great threat of direct confrontation.[22]

The ancients regarded "seven" as a round, perfect number, and the appearance of this number of disasters in this list proves that this denunciation is not "a fragment," or that any of it is missing; it is all here. It is the cumulative weight of these calamities which was supposed to have its effect upon Israel. Time after time, God had sent punishments upon them, but in every instance, he had received only obstinate and stubborn rebellion from his people. This situation clearly called for redress, and Amos here proclaimed God's intention to destroy the Northern Kingdom, showing by these repeated opportunities Israel had had for repentance, that despite the ultimate severity of God's judgment, his final destruction was nevertheless one that bore testimony to his longsuffering, as well as to his justice and holiness.

Verse 6, And I also have given you cleanness of teeth in all your cities, and want of bread in all your places; yet have ye not returned unto me, saith Jehovah.

"Cleanness of teeth . . ." If there is nothing to eat, one has no difficulty keeping his teeth clean; they stay clean! As Jamieson put it, "Where there is no food to masticate, the

---

[21]J. Keir Howard, *op. cit.*, p. 961.
[22]J.A. Motyer, *op. cit.*, p. 733.

teeth are free of uncleanness."[23] This is not the only place in the Bible where cleanness is made to stand for something else. "Where no oxen are, the crib is clean" (Proverbs 14:4).This is the first of the seven disasters that had fallen upon Israel.

"Yet have ye not returned unto me . . ." Note the purpose of human disasters which, in their aggregate, are due to the displeasure of heaven with a fallen and rebellious race of men, that purpose being benign. God's purpose had been that difficulties would turn the hearts of his people towards himself; but, in the case of Israel, nothing like that had occurred.

Verse 7, And I also have withholden the rain from you, when there were yet three months to the harvest; and I caused it to rain upon one city, and caused it not to rain upon another city: one piece was rained upon, and the piece whereupon it rained not withered.

The disaster in view here is that of drought. The ultimate authority and power for sending either rain or drought is resident not in men but in God. Man finds it absolutely impossible to predict weather even for periods that lie immediately in the future; and all over the earth are startling evidences that areas once favored with abundant rains are now arid and barren. Look at the ancient rain forests of Arizona. Its huge trees are now almost as hard as diamonds; and they lie glistening in the desert sun, startling adornments of an environment which now provides hardly enough rain to grow a cactus. God is the author of such changes, despite the eagerness of some men to deny it.

The perversity, if we may call it that, of man's natural environment is a condition ordered and directed by God himself as a response to the human race which is in open rebellion against God, a situation that has existed ever since God cursed the ground for Adam's sake (Genesis 3:17-19), and a condition that should not be expected to change. Despite the sorrows and inconveniences that come as a result of environmental woes, God's purpose in it is surely

---

[23]Robert Jamieson, *op. cit.*, p. 794.

that of leading men to repentance, and not merely that of
punishing men.

"When there were yet three months to the harvest . . ."
This was drouth at the most critical part of the crop-year,
with the result of almost certain crop failure.

"Rain upon one city . . . not to rain on another . . ." This
merely describes the capricious and indiscriminate aspect
of the drouth; but there is no thought here that cities
blessed with rain were any more righteous than the ones
without it. Jesus taught quite clearly that the "rain falls on
the just and unjust," and God sends the sunshine upon the
good and bad alike. It is the over-all condition that is sent
by God, the controlling pattern which produces failures and
blessings indiscriminately mingled. Men proved to be unde-
pendable in their responses to the will of God; and therefore, God has sent them an environment in which to live
which is also not dependable. Men should get the message
and repent and turn to God.

**Verse 8, So two or three cities wandered unto one city to
drink water, and were not satisfied: yet have ye not returned unto me, saith Jehovah.**

The efforts of scholars to reduce this chapter to the
status of a poem are frustrated by Amos' inclusion here of
material which defies such a classification; and, as should
be expected, the liberal critics cry, "Interpolation!"[24] However, as many scholars have testified, the Hebrew text of
Amos is one of the best preserved of all OT texts; and there
is no evidence whatever of any interpolation here, the "alleged evidence" being nothing more than the ephemeral
and uncertain *imagination* of men seeking to overthrow
portions of the holy scriptures.

"Yet have ye not returned unto me . . ." "After each
visitation, she (Israel) seemed to plunge deeper into immorality and crime. Instead of being brought to a reflective
mood, the national conscience had become increasingly
dulled."[25]

---

[24]William Rainey Harper, *op. cit.*, p. 98.
[25]Rolland Emerson Wolfe, *op. cit.*, p. 34.

Verse 9, I have smitten you with blasting and mildew: the multitude of your gardens and your vineyards and your fig-trees and your olive-trees hath the palmer-worm devoured: yet have ye not returned unto me, saith Jehovah.

The two disasters recorded here are (1) the blasting and mildew, and (2) the invasion of the palmer-worm, or locust (as in some versions). Some doubt persists as to which insect, exactly, is mentioned; but, whatever it was, the effect of it was totally ruinous.

"Blasting and mildew . . ." Barnes noted that:

> Both words are doubly intensive. They stand together in the prophecy of Moses (Deuteronomy 28:22), among the other scourges of disobedience; and the mention of these would awaken in those who would hear, the memory of a long train of other warnings and other judgments.[26]

Verse 10, I have sent among you the pestilence after the manner of Egypt: your young men have I slain with the sword, and have carried away your horses; and I have made the stench of your camp to come up even into your nostrils: yet have ye not returned unto me, saith Jehovah.

Two more disasters are recounted here, (1) pestilence, and (2) military disaster. The NEB renders "plagues of Egypt" instead of "pestilence after the manner of Egypt"; but despite this there remains some doubt of what, exactly, is meant. All of the disasters mentioned in these verses were known to the Israelites, either as experiences through which they themselves had passed, or as experiences of their ancestors known by tradition. Amos had no need to explain any of them. Thorogood also believed that Amos has in mind here the plagues of Egypt, and also:

> There is some likeness to the terrible series of warnings (28:15-57): "All these curses shall come upon you . . . because you did not obey the voice of the Lord your God."[27]

---

[26]Albert Barnes, *Notes on the OT, Vol. 1, The Minor Prophets* (Grand Rapids: Baker Book House, 1953), p. 285.

[27]Bernard Thorogood, *A Guide to the Book of Amos* (Valley Forge: Judson Press, 1971), p. 44.

"Yet have ye not returned unto me, saith Jehovah . . ."
This dire lament is dramatically repeated five times (vv.
6,8,9,10,12), somewhat like a refrain. It has the utility of
constant emphasis upon the truth that the disasters were
not mere punishments, but solicitations for the chosen people to repent and return to the Lord, the purpose of the
Father being benign throughout.

**Verse 11, I have overthrown cities among you, as when
God overthrew Sodom and Gomorrah, and ye were as a
brand plucked out of the burning: yet have ye not returned
unto me, saith Jehovah.**

In a sense, Sodom and Gomorrah were surely "cities
among" the Israelites; and yet, despite the fact that Israel
was actually "more corrupt than they (Sodom and Gomorrah)" (Ezekiel 16:47f), God had nevertheless spared them.
This truth, that Israel was worse than Sodom and Gomorrah is seldom stressed, but it is profoundly evident in the
Bible; and the only reason that God spared Israel, as far as
we are able to discern, was that the promise of the Messiah
to come through Israel had not yet been realized; and, in a
sense, God was "stuck" with the chosen people till that
promise should become a reality. Instead of being humbled
by the judgment of other nations around them, Israel only
presumed upon God's unlimited tolerance of their wickedness, a presumption that nerved them to the murder of the
Son of God himself when he finally arrived.

"I have overthrown cities among you . . ." "This is generally taken to refer to an earthquake of extreme severity,"[28]
an opinion followed by Barnes,[29] Smith,[30] and many others;
but it appears to us that a specific reference to the judgment of Sodom and Gomorrah is made. Of course, that
event was accompanied by a great earthquake also.

McFadden's quotation from Lecky is:

[28]Hughell E.W. Fosbroke, *IB, Vol. VI* (New York: Abingdon Press, 1957), p. 807.
[29]Albert Barnes, *op. cit.*, p. 286.
[30]Ralph L. Smith, *op. cit.*, p. 106.

The theological habit of interpreting the catastrophes of nature as Divine warnings or punishments or discipline, is a baseless and pernicious superstition.[31]

This is a fair representation of so-called "scientific" or "modern man"; and, while true enough, that each individual disaster might not be attributed to the immediate sin of the victim (John 9:1-10), there is nevertheless a direct and pertinent connection between the disasters of earth and the rebellion of Adam's race.

To the sensitive heart, every disaster speaks an urgent message. We have no right to interpret it as the punishment of others, but we have every right to regard it as a call to ourselves, a call to reflection and repentance.[32]

Verses 6 through 11 have recounted the seven great disasters through which Israel had passed, ending in the same plaintive cry every time. "Yet have ye not returned unto me, saith Jehovah."

Some critics make a big thing out of God being referred to in this verse (11) in the third person, whereas, the first person is otherwise prominent throughout; but this is not due to any interpolation, and only signifies that Amos unconsciously reverted to quotations from the Pentateuch in mentioning Sodom and Gomorrah, as any one familiar with the Bible would have done.

It should be noted, as Smith pointed out, that:

The oracles in chapters 1 and 2 were addressed to seven nations before reaching Israel. Here seven calamities strike before the final act of judgment is experienced.[33]

That final judgment upon the Northern Kingdom will be uttered in the very next verse.

Verse 12, Therefore, thus will I do unto thee, O Israel; and because I will do this unto thee, prepare to meet thy God, O Israel.

---

[31]John Edgar McFadden, *op. cit.*, p. 46.
[32]*Ibid.*
[33]Ralph L. Smith, *op. cit.*, p. 107.

"Thus will I do unto thee . . ." Nothing specific is mentioned in this verse, for it was unnecessary. The carrying away of the people from Samaria, the Northern capital, had been factually and dramatically prophecied in vv. 1-5, above; and this is a terse reference to what was already prohesied. This arrangement proves the unity of the whole passage, in fact, the whole prophecy; because all that the prophet says in any portion of this book is evidently in the mind of the author throughout all of it.

"Prepare to meet thy God . . ." Howard saw in this a summons for Israel, "to meet her God in the final judgment";[34] and although true in a typical, or ultimate, sense, something much more immediate was in store for Israel. The people were to be carried away captive with "hooks," a prophecy which the Assyrians fulfilled in the customary habit of taking away the captives of the lands they ravaged with hooks in their lips, or noses, and fastened together in chains. There was still time for Israel to repent and turn to the Lord in order to avert the impending judgment; but they never heeded it. They simply overlooked the truth that God will not indefinitely warn and threaten; for the incorrigibly wicked, there remains the final and ultimate confrontation of God; and, for Israel, the time was growing short indeed.

Verse 13, For lo, he that formeth the mountains, and createth the wind, and declareth unto man what is his thought; that maketh the morning darkness, and treadeth upon the high places of the earth—Jehovah, the God of hosts is his name.

We should begin the study of this verse with the words of Smith who wrote:

> There is very little agreement among scholars as to the origin of this verse and the reason for its being placed where it is . . . Of course, if one accepts the tradition that Amos wrote all of this book, just as we have it, there can be no problem here except a difficulty in understanding why he put a hymn of praise

---

[34]J. Keir Howard, *op. cit.*, p. 962.

immediately after an announcement of terrible judgment.[35]

We are happy indeed to be placed among those who indeed accept the view that Amos wrote this whole book, just as we have it; for that is our deep and abiding conviction. Furthermore, the book itself carries the unmistakable imprimature of the Holy Spirit, not the least of which is observable in this very verse. In placing this hymn of praise in close juxtaposition with the announcement of judgment, Amos was writing in the tradition later followed by the holy apostles of Christ who did exactly the same thing. In the book of Revelation, the apostle John frequently inserted, immediately following the announcements of great and terrible judgments, a proleptic vision of the saints rejoicing in heaven, that being, in fact, one of the outstanding characteristics of that prophecy; and it is a very similar thing which Amos has done here. The truth is that any mind fully attuned to the will of God should have *expected* this doxology precisely where it is located. As Hammershaimb said:

> This concluding doxology which describes the might of Jehovah serves to assure the hearers that he will also be able to carry out what he threatens. It is therefore a complete misunderstanding that many commentators have wanted to explain this doxology and the two in 5:8f and 9:5f as secondary because they do not fit the style of the context.[36]

The beautiful doxology with which this chapter closes has another valid utility:

> Some have claimed that Israel did not have a developed doctrine of creation until the postexilic period. Such claims are no longer valid. Amos 4:13 has five phrases describing Yahweh as the Lord of creation.[37]

Motyer's summary of this verse is:

> God is sovereign over things *visible* (the mountains), things *invisible* (the wind), and things *rational* (man

---

[35]Ralph L. Smith, *op. cit.*, p. 107.
[36]Erling Hammershaimb, *op. cit.*, p. 74.
[37]Ralph L. Smith, *op. cit.*, p. 107.

and his thought). He is in direct executive control of the world, as is evident when he makes the morning darkness, i.e., brings about the sequence of day and night. No place is beyond his reach, even the heights of the earth being beneath his feet.[38]

"Jehovah, the God of hosts, is his name . . ." This means that the eternal God has every conceivable power and ability to do as he wills. Blessed be his name for ever.

---

[38]J.A. Motyer, *op. cit.*, p. 733.

CHAPTER 5

There are suggestions in this chapter of the method of the apostle Paul, as when he used the diatribe so effectively in Romans. There are apparent interruptions of Amos' line of thought, such as might have occurred when members of his audience objected to his preaching, or attempted to refute his arguments. The discernment of this completely refutes the allegations of critical scholars who laboriously postulate a paste and scissors job that some later editor is alleged to have done on this chapter, the great weakness of such postulations being that they are believed by no one except the postulators! Also, the postulators exhibit no agreement regarding any of their alleged "solutions." The entire chapter is a continuation of Amos' prophecy against Israel, elaborating and expanding the condemnation and overthrow of Israel already announced in chapter 3.

Verse 1, Hear ye this word which I take up for a lamentation over you, O house of Israel.

The impact of this upon Amos' hearers was essentially that of his crying, "Listen, Israel, while I preach your funeral!" The whole chapter has no other purpose than, "to impress upon the people of God the impossibility of averting the threatened destruction, and to take away from the self-secure sinners the false foundations of their trust."[1] To make his message still more powerful, Amos actually uttered it in the tone and meter of the traditional funeral service known by all the people; and Hammershaimb, along with others, supposes that the occasion was that of a popular feast at Bethel:

> We can picture him appearing during the feast at Bethel and suddenly tearing the participants away from their revelry by starting the mournful tones of the lament, so that when they listen to him they are seized with terror and perhaps also with indignation

[1]C.F. Keil, *Commentary on the Whole Bible* (Grand Rapids: Wm. B. Eerdmans Publishing Company), p. 277.

when they hear that it is the death of Israel that he is lamenting.[2]

"Amos to this point has spoken of the fall of Israel as being still in the future. Here he speaks as if it had already happened. He sings a funeral song (a dirge) for Israel."[3]

The dirge which Amos chanted for Israel was the real thing, a traditional and highly stylized lament, "cast in 3 + 2 metre."[4] It was probably spoken in a very loud and wailing voice, calculated to stun and shock everyone who heard it.

Verse 2, The virgin of Israel is fallen; she shall no more rise: she is cast down upon her land; there is none to raise her up.

It is a mistake to make this whole chapter into a "poem," for it is no such thing. The lament was certainly cast into poetic form; but this was merely an attention-getting device used by the prophet as the background for the shocking and devastating words of God's prophecy which he was delivering to Israel.

"The virgin of Israel is fallen . . ." The use of the present tense here is prophetic, indicating that the projected overthrow of the kingdom was as certain as if it had already occurred. This device called "the prophetic tense" was widely used throughout the Hebrew scriptures. Likewise, in the NT, the final overthrow of Babylon the great is given in words very similar to these (Revelation 18:2), "Fallen, fallen is Babylon the great." The fact that the figure employed here is that of a virgin "does not indicate that this is (or will be) the first time that Israel is defeated,"[5] nor that the nation is in any sense righteous. "It is a feature related to the representation of Israel as a beautiful young

---

[2]Erling Hammershaimb, *The Book of Amos, translated by John Sturdy* (New York: Shocken Books, 1970), p. 76.

[3]Ralph L. Smith, *BBC, Vol. 7* (Nashville: Broadman Press, 1972), pp. 107, 108.

[4]James Luther Mays, *Amos, A Commentary* (Philadelphia: The Westminster Press, 1969), p. 85.

[5]Erling Hammershaimb, *op. cit.*, p. 76.

woman."[6] "The death of a virgin, or of a man who had no children, was regarded as peculiarly sad."[7]

This outburst of Amos against Israel came at the very apex of Israel's pride and prosperity, the better part of a century having elapsed since Jeroboam II had restored the borders of the kingdom and seized control of the lucrative trade routes to the east. Israel had never had it so good; and a message like that so dramatically delivered by Amos would have been just about as unpopular as any that could be imagined.

> But the very fact that Amos' message has been preserved for us shows that some people listened and remembered. There were some who honored the prophet and his message, and who gave service to God.[8]

Verse 3, For thus saith the Lord, Jehovah: The city that went forth a thousand shall have a hundred left, and that which went forth a hundred shall have ten left, to the house of Israel.

Military defeat and the near-total destruction of Israel's reservoir of fighting men are sternly indicated by this. This portion of Amos' lament continues in the stylized $3+2$ metre; and, "Some scholars have imagined that Amos actually put on the garb of a professional mourner and sang this song in Samaria and Bethel."[9]

Verse 4, For thus saith Jehovah unto the house of Israel, seek ye me, and ye shall live.

"Seek ye me . . ." "This does not mean, 'inquire about,' or 'search for' something or someone lost or inaccessible. When *Yahweh* is the object, the meaning is, 'turn to Yahweh,' and 'hold to Yahweh' as a way of life."[10] Many have noted that this passage does not in any sense mean that the

---

[6]*Ibid.*
[7]Henry McKeating, *CBC, The Books of Amos, Hosea, and Micah* (Cambridge: At the University Press, 1971), p. 39.
[8]Bernard Thorogood, *A Guide to the Book of Amos* (Valley Forge: Judson Press, 1971), p. 55.
[9]Ralph L. Smith, *op. cit.*, p. 108.
[10]James Luther Mays, *op. cit.*, p. 87.

Lord is hiding from Israel, or even that he is not available
to them. "It must be understood as meaning, to seek out
and observe God's commandments."[11] W. R. Harper noted
the audience-response type of thing which we mentioned in
the chapter introduction; these words, "suggest at once the
question, 'Are we not zealouly engaged in the worship of
Yahweh? Why are we then to suffer?' "[12] Very well, Amos
will respond to such a question, whether or not it was
actually raised by any of his hearers. The answer is simple,
and simply devastating: "Their religion is false!" We deplore the apparent blindness of so many who do not see in
Amos' prophecy anything except the social injustice and
oppression of the poor. Of course, those aspects of Israel's
sins are courageously denounced in Amos, but no more so
than are condemned the vanities of their religious system.
To deny that God was also gravely concerned about *that* is
to miss the principal relevance of this prophecy for modern
man. Thorogood accurately observed the intention of this
section of Amos when he declared that: "The chief theme in
chapters 5 and 6 is the contrast between true religion and
false religion."[13]

This is a good place to mention the scholarly superstition
to the effect that, "The *editors* who put together the book
of Amos, divided his sayings into sections; but the divisions are not very clear, etc."[14] Of course, no "editors" or
"redactors" had anything to do with Amos. The so-called
"evidence" of any such thing is usually pointed out in this
fashion:

> (This chapter has): a funeral song (vv. 1-3); a call to
> repent (vv. 4-7); part of a song of praise (vv. 8-9); a
> warning about injustice (vv. 10-13); a further call to
> repent (vv. 14-15); and a further funeral song, or vision
> of death (vv. 16-17).[15]

With all due deference to the intelligence and understanding of those scribes who take the piece-meal nature of this

[11]Erling Hammershaimb, *op. cit.*, p. 77.
[12]William Rainey Harper, *Amos and Hosea* (New York: Charles Scribner's Sons, 1910), p. 110.
[13]Bernard Thorogood, *op. cit.*, p. 55.
[14]*Ibid.*
[15]*Ibid.*

chapter as the work of some "editor," they are simply mistaken, the mistake being due to an apparent total ignorance of the art of preaching. What we really have here is a typical "shotgun type" of sermon; and this writer is free to confess that he has preached a hundred just as strangely put together as Amos' words in this chapter. One need look no further than the prophet himself to account for the motley arrangement which confronts us here. Of course, such a thing would seem inconceivable to a seminarian! Amos was no seminarian, but a shepherd! To fasten this hodge-podge chapter upon some later "editor" or "redactor" must be to suppose that the one or ones doing the scissors and paste job here were phenomenally stupid. Any "editor" worthy of the name would have put the elements of the dirge together and also those of the hymn of praise. By far the most logical and reasonable explanation of the piece-meal, intermittent style which is seen in these chapters is that they are the result of an extemporaneous, give and take, free-for-all confrontation between Amos and Israel, with many interruptions to answer questions, either actually propounded by the audience, or astutely discerned by the speaker before they were propounded. Instead of criticising the style of these chapters, the really discerning student will recognize them as the impassioned outflow of a soul in tune with God, burning with righteous indignation against the gross abuses of Israel's social order, overburdened by the tragic weight of the message of destruction he was commissioned to deliver, and yet motivated by a passionate patriotism and love of God's "chosen people," and an unspeakable grief at the tragic words he faithfully delivered. The message of such a man with such a burden of his soul and spirit could never have taken the form of neat little tidy messages such as many so-called sermons of the present day. No indeed! The impassioned words flow forth without any particular organization, tumbling over each other like red-hot rocks out of a volcano. Behold here the truly magnificent structure of genuine prophecy!

Verse 5, But seek not Bethel, nor enter into Gilgal, and pass not to Beersheba: for Gilgal shall go into captivity, and Bethel shall come to naught.

The people no doubt supposed that their frequenting the shrines at such places as Bethel, Beersheba and Gilgal would enable them to know God; but in this they were totally wrong. "God can only be sought and found through his revelation."[16] It was impossible to find God at such places.

> Those were centers of idolatry, false teaching, false worship; they would find there only ruin, destruction and captivity, for that is what God had planned for those places.[17]

The high places mentioned in this verse had never been a proper place for seeking God; and what we have here is the total repudiation of an entire system of false religion. Many commentators seem to be unaware of this. Some seem to have forgotten that the golden calf-idols installed by Jeroboam were the principal features of the so-called worship at Bethel; and that all of the shrines here mentioned were notorious for the debaucheries and immoralities that were carried on there.

"Gilgal shall go into captivity, and Bethel shall come to naught . . ." The scholars tell us that there is a play upon the words Gilgal and Bethel in the Hebrew text, incapable of being translated into English; but many approximations of it have been given. One of the most interesting is that of Wellhausen, as cited by Hammershaimb: "Gilgal will go to the gallows, and Bethel will become the devil's."[18]

"Beersheba . . ." It is a little surprising to find this place mentioned as one of the shrines frequented by the Israelites, since it was in the extreme southern part of Judah and quite a long distance from the Northern Kingdom. Barnes observed that:

> Jeroboam I pretended that it was too much for Israel to go up to Jerusalem; and yet Israel thought it not too much to go to the extremest point of Judah

---

[16]Paul T. Butler, *The Minor Prophets* (Joplin: College Press, 1968), p. 319.
[17]*Ibid.*
[18]Erling Hammershaimb, *op. cit.*, p. 79.

towards Idumaea, perhaps four times as far south of Jerusalem, as Jerusalem lay from Bethel![19]

Verse 6, Seek Jehovah, and ye shall live; lest he break out like fire in the house of Joseph, and it devour, and there be none to quench it in Bethel.

"The house of Joseph ..." here means the Northern Kingdom, of which the tribes of Ephraim and Manasseh (the sons of Joseph) constituted the most powerful component of the kingdom. This led to the "House of Joseph" being a kind of title for the Northern Kingdom.

The great contrast in these verses is between "Seek Jehovah" and "Seek not Bethel," or any other of the false shrines. The limitation which Almighty God has placed upon those who would truly seek him should never be overlooked. People who are merely doing what pleases them religiously are just as hopeless as were those ancient Israelites condemned in this chapter. As Keil put it: "God can only be sought, however, in his revelation, or in the manner in which he wishes to be sought, or worshipped."[20] Jamieson's comment on this verse is:

> "Break out like fire in the house of Joseph ..." means bursting through everything in his way. God is a consuming fire (Deuteronomy 4:24, Isaiah 10:17, and Lamentations 2:3).[21]

Verse 7, Ye who turn justice to wormwood, and cast down righteousness to the earth.

As already indicated in this prophecy, and as will appear also in later passages, the whole system of justice had failed in Israel, even the judiciary being corrupted, leaving the poor and the humble with no protection whatever against the avarice and oppression of heartless ruling classes.

"Justice to wormwood ..." Wormwood was the name of a plant having an exceedingly bitter taste; and this is a very

---

[19]Albert Barnes, *Notes on the OT, Minor Prophets, Vol. 1* (Grand Rapids: Baker Book House, 1953), p. 290.

[20]C.F. Keil, *op. cit.*, p. 279.

[21]Robert Jamieson, *JFB Commentary on the Whole Bible* (Grand Rapids: Zondervan Publishing House, 1961), p. 795.

effective figure for the perversion of justice. Any honest man seeking redress of his wrongs in the Israel of that day would have found "justice" turned into a very "bitter pill" for him. Righteousness is represented as fallen and prostrate on the ground with no one to raise it up and support it. Those were horrible times indeed; and it seems incredible that the very people responsible for such gross wickedness should have fancied themselves to be the favored children of God! How blind is the worshipper of false gods!

Verse 8, Seek him that maketh the Pleiades and Orion, and turneth the shadow of death into the morning, and maketh the day dark with night; that calleth for the waters of the sea, and poureth them out upon the face of the earth (Jehovah is his name).

We have exactly the same theme here that was visible in verse 13 of the previous chapter; it is just Amos' way of emphasizing that the God who threatens such awful consequences upon Israel is fully able to bring them to pass just as he has promised.

"Pleaides and Orion . . ." These great constellations, the first dominating the spring and summer months, and the second the months of fall and winter, were known to the ancients; and, "They are referred to in the OT (Job 9:9, 38:31) as demonstrations of God's creative power."[22]

The changing of day and night, and the sending of rain upon the earth are usually thought to be what is indicated by the balance of this verse; and certainly there is good reason for so construing it; but Keil was of the opinion that a reference to the deluge which came upon sinful men in the time of the Genesis flood is involved. This may well be, for it would have been a most appropriate reminder in the context of Amos' prophecy of a similar doom upon Israel, and for exactly the same reasons, unbridled wickedness and rebellion against God. He wrote:

> We should not understand this as a reference to the moisture that rises from the sea and then falls upon the earth as rain. The words suggest the thought of

---

[22]Arnold C. Schultz, *WBC* (Chicago: Moody Press, 1962), p. 834.

terrible inundations of the earth by the swelling sea, and the allusion to the judgment of the flood can hardly be overlooked.[23]

If this is merely a reference to the mysterious power of God in sending the rain upon the earth, it would still have a very potent and appropriate meaning for the people of that day who attributed the rain to certain of their false gods:

> They had a god of rain and storm; in some places he was called Baal, and in others Hadad. Amos here asserts that it is Yahweh who sends the rain.[24]

Verse 9, That bringeth sudden destruction upon the strong, so that destruction cometh upon the fortress.

McKeating and other critical scholars mention this and the preceding verse as "the second of the hymn fragments, or doxologies," favoring the theory (a subjective imaginative "guess") that they were not "composed or inserted by the prophet, but put in, almost at random, by an editor."[25] See under verse 4, above, for our refutation of the "editor" theory. No responsible, intelligent "editor" could possibly have arranged a chapter in the form of this one. Only a preacher like Amos could have produced such a "shotgun sermon" as this; and, with that view of it, it becomes a classic of power and effectiveness.

On this and the preceding verses, Deane has this:

> Here is an allusion to the flood and similar catastrophes, which are proofs of God's judicial government of the universe, when, "he maketh his creature his weapon for the revenge of his enemies" . . .God doeth all these marvelous things, and men presume to scout his law and think to be unpunished.[26]

Verse 10, They hate him that reproveth in the gate, and they abhor him that speaketh uprightly.

---

[23]C.F. Keil, *op. cit.*, p. 281.
[24]Ralph L. Smith, *op. cit.*, p. 111.
[25]Henry McKeating, *op. cit.*, p. 40.
[26]W.J. Deane, *Pulpit Commentary, Vol. 14, Amos* (Grand Rapids: Wm. B. Eerdmans Publishing Company, 1950), p. 84.

A picture of the rotten judicial system of Israel is in this. The "court" was a type of open forum conducted in the gate of the city, where the wall was expanded to enclose a considerable area where important city business was conducted and affording an outdoor theater large enough for a considerable gathering of people. In the ancient system of justice, men of good will were expected to appear before the city fathers in court proceedings and speak the truth on behalf of the poor or oppressed; but anyone performing such a function in that society was "hated" and "abhored." The indifference and corruption of the whole society were the result.

Smith makes a big "to do" over the fact that "verse 10 is in the third person, and verse 7 is in the second person!"[27] What do the critics expect? That this shepherd should have kept all of his *persons* in the proper focus? Some of the changes from one person to another are evidently due to Amos' reference to God's law in the Pentateuch, the person of the passage cited, naturally appearing in his address here, whether it matched the person he was using or not. One of the Proverbs (15:12) could have been in Amos' mind here, accounting for the third person. Such quibbles are unimportant, and are certainly no proper basis for postulations about "editors" and "redacters!" The entire concept of "the redacter" so vital to current biblical criticism is in reality a kind of scholarly Piltdown Man, in short, a hoax widely received and honored, but a hoax nevertheless. This is a second reference we have made to this in this commentary, but it is necessitated by the incessant and reitereated appeal to this monstrosity by the commentaries which we are reading.

Verse 11, Forasmuch therefore as ye trample upon the poor, and take exactions from him of wheat: ye have built houses of hewn stone, but ye shall not dwell in them; ye have planted pleasant vineyards, but ye shall not drink the wine thereof.

In this verse again, Amos goes back to the great covenant passages of the Pentateuch where almost the identical

[27]Ralph L. Smith, *op. cit.*, p. 112.

language of this verse is used, making it likely, as we indicated above, that this pattern of his thinking was habitual. By thus appealing to the great covenant words of the Mosaic law, Amos is declaring the justice of God's forthcoming judgment against Israel:

> When Amos uses these formulations, he is saying in effect, that Yahweh will invoke the sanctions of his covenant with Israel against these perverters of Israel's social order . . . The maintenance of that order, especially justice and righteousness in the courts is a requirement of God's covenant; and for those who violate his will, the salvation-history will become a judgment-history.[28]

Verse 12, For I know how manifold are your transgressions, and how mighty your sins, ye that afflict the just, that take a bribe, and turn aside the needy in the gate from their right.

What is evident in this verse is not merely oppression of the poor, despite that's being an invariable result of it, but the absolute corruption of Israel's judiciary. The courts of law are always the last vestiges of justice in a decadent society; and when that is gone, there is nothing else left to go. It is *that* awful condition that is uppermost in this prophecy. Wolfe further commented on this very thing:

> Usually, the last stand of respectability in a declining nation is found in her judiciary. With the degeneration of Israel's legal machinery, the fate of the nation seemed certain.[29]

To be sure, the results of such a corrupt system were particularly devastating to the poor and weak of the nation, who were mercilessly exploited, their exploiters apparently having no conscience whatever. The cries of the poor for justice were not heard in the gates of Israel, but they were heard in the gates of heaven; and God moved immediately and effectively to destroy that whole wretched society.

---

[28]James Luther Mays, *op. cit.*, p. 94.
[29]Rolland Emerson Wolfe, *Meet Amos and Hosea* (New York: Harper and Brothers, Publishers, 1945), p. 38.

Human personality cannot be abused for personal gain without Divine retribution. Let us pray that our own generation learns this lesson from God's book before it has to experience God's judgment.[30]

Verse 13, Therefore, he that is prudent shall keep silence in such a time; for it is an evil time.

This verse has posed a problem for some commentators. It is admitted by all that the viewpoint expressed in this verse could not possibly be that of Amos; for he was then in the act of daring to speak out vehemently against the evil of that society, without regard to any "prudent" concern either for his own safety, or his own life. The best explanation of this verse is that it is merely a sarcastic statement of Amos of the sinful view that had led to the perversion of justice in the Northern Kingdom. The prophet is here putting in the mouths of his audience their lazy, indifferent, and selfish philosophy which was the underlying cause of the judiciary's corruption. The words stand here at this dramatic point in Amos' address like Banquo's ghost at the feast; and we may well hope that some of Amos' hearers were shamed and corrected by it. Whatever this verse is, the above explanation of it satisfies all the requirements of the text. Certainly, it is not "a bit of advice added to the book"[31] by some later editor, a view which would denominate such an editor as a very foolish and unspiritual person! We therefore reject out of hand the groundless speculation to the effect that verse 13, "is a manifestly later insertion."[32] What "editor" could have been so perverse and unspiritual as to inject a "sour note" like this into Amos' beautiful prophecy? Such a conception of how these words happened to be in it is not supported by any reasonable thesis or any evidence whatever. As we have interpreted it, it makes good and wholesome sense.

Verse 14, Seek good, and not evil, that ye may live; and so Jehovah, the God of hosts, will be with you, as ye say.

---

[30]Paul T. Butler, *op. cit.*, p. 324.
[31]Ralph L. Smith, *op. cit.*, p. 113.
[32]Henry McKeating, *op. cit.*, p. 43.

The very fact that Amos here definitely quotes from what his hearers were in the habit of saying surely supports what was just said regarding his having done so sarcastically in the preceding verse. Amos here strikes at the fundamental *cause* of all of Israel's transgressions and sorrows: they *loved* the wrong things. That, of course, is exactly the way it still is with the world. As McFadden said:

> The root of the social problem, as some one has said, is not defective social arrangement, but sin; and no fundamental improvement can be effected by a change in the environment, but only by a change in the men.[33]

Much of the present-day preoccupation of churches with such things as "better housing," "improved standards of living," etc., has resulted from the failure to behold this truth. No matter what social planners and environmentalists may say, there is no escaping the fact that all of man's problems originated in Eden; and there was nothing at all wrong with that environment. The entry of sin was the destructive factor that drowned the whole world in woe.

Regarding the probable reason for Israel's confidence that the Lord was with them, Hammershaimb explained it thus: "It arose from the people's conviction of the unfailing good fortune which they thought they had evidence of in the external successes of Jeroboam II."[34] It is also a fact that the whole nation had blindly trusted in their boasted fleshly descent from the patriarch Abraham, claiming to be "the seed of Abraham," despite their spiritual rejection of the obedient faith which marked the life of Abraham.

Verse 15, Hate the evil, and love the good, and establish justice in the gate: it may be that Jehovah, the God of hosts, will be gracious unto the remnant of Joseph.

The slender thread of hope which marks this verse is recurrent throughout the prophecy; but the uncertainty which is indicated as to whether or not mercy would be extended did not derive from any unwillingness on God's

---

[33]John Edgar McFadden, *A Cry for Justice* (New York: Charles Scribner's Sons, 1912), p. 60.

[34]Erling Hammershaimb, *op. cit.*, p. 85.

part. "The prophet regarded it as dubious whether they would really repent."[35]

"Love the good . . ." or "seek good," as in v. 14 was not considered by Amos as one and the same thing as seeking God.

> When he said in one place, "Seek the Lord," and in another "Seek good," he was not making them synonymous. Amos was not preaching just an ethical religion. The seeker of Yahweh was more than "a do-gooder." He was emphasizing the two dimensions of true religion: the vertical, Seek Yahweh, and the horizontal, Seek good.[36]

Verse 16, Therefore, thus saith Jehovah, the God of hosts, the Lord: Wailing shall be in all the broad ways; and they shall say in all the streets, Alas! alas! and they shall call the husbandman to mourning, and such as are skilful in lamentation to wailing.

"They shall call the husbandman . . ." This means that:

> The citizens shall call the inexperienced husbandmen to act the part usually performed by professional mourners, as there will not be enough of the latter for the universal mourning which will prevail.[37]

"Alas! alas! . . ." "This renders the wail of the mourners rather than actual words. Wailing and mourning with loud public lamentations mark the funeral rite throughout the east."[38] One meets with this also in the NT, as, for example, when the paid mourners were lamenting the death of Jairus' daughter whom Jesus raised from the dead.

To paraphrase this verse, it means that the mourning over the deceased shall be so widespread and universal that there will be not enough personnel to observe properly the funeral rites.

[35]*Ibid.*
[36]Ralph L. Smith, *op. cit.*, p. 114.
[37]Robert Jamieson, *op. cit.*, p. 796.
[38]J. Kier Howard, *NLBC* (Grand Rapids: Zondervan Publishing House, 1979), p. 964.

Verse 17, And in all vineyards shall be wailing; for I will pass through the midst of thee, saith Jehovah.

"I will pass through . . ." For ages, at the time Amos wrote, Israel had observed the Passover Feast which celebrated the "passing over" of Israel in the visitation of the death of the firstborn upon the land of Egypt; and the terrible contrast evident in this verse is that God, instead of "passing over" Israel in the forthcoming judgment will instead "pass through the midst" of them, indicating that there would be no mitigation of the penalty for their wickedness.

> Amos was reminding Israel that God had been passing by in judgment, as he did that night in Egypt. But now, he would not pass by them any more. He would pass through their midst and leave a trail of tears as he had in the homes of the Egyptians.[39]

This sobering thought with reference to these stern words is that there is not a line of exaggeration anywhere in them. All that is foretold here *happened* exactly as God had promised; and that proud, arrogant and rebellious people were led away to their doom, never more to appear as an organized entity upon the earth! What a tragedy that none of them, or at the most, very few of them, believed the impassioned warning of the shepherd prophet.

The Day of the Lord

Verse 18, Woe unto you that desire the day of Jehovah! Wherefore would ye have the day of Jehovah! It is darkness and not light.

This, and through verse 20, presents a remarkable view of the Day of the Lord, that is, the Day of Judgment, first as it would be in the case of Israel when God judged and destroyed her for her sins, and secondly, as it will be at the end of time for the great majority of the rebellious race of mankind. This has been cited as the very earliest reference to the Judgment Day in scripture; but regardless of whether that is actually the case or not, the knowledge of it

---

[39]Ralph L. Smith, *op. cit.*, p. 115.

had existed for generations in Israel, as attested by the widespread, but untaught, desire for that day to come, mentioned in this very verse.

Some of the Bible critics are very sensitive about such a doctrine as "The Day of the Lord," going out of their way to deny that even Amos approved of any such doctrine. "Amos did not deny or refute the doctrine"[40] was the way Smith viewed it; but in the viewpoint here, it must be affirmed that Amos did far more than refrain from denying the popular theology regarding the judgment day. "Yes," these words mean, "there is to be a judgment day, but it will not be the type of judgment day you people are longing for, but a day of terror and destruction."

Regarding the source of the prevalent conviction regarding the judgment day, or "the day of the Lord," it came into being at least a very long, long way prior to the times of Israel. "This idea had a central place in the religious expectation of the people."[41]

The true origin of the theology of the day of the Lord must be looked for in the revelation of God himself to his people; and our inability at the present time to pinpoint the time and place and name of the particular prophet who *first* revealed the mind of God with reference to it does not at all diminish the truth and authenticity of the doctrine itself. Amos was inspired of God, and his acknowledgment of the popular belief in the day of the Lord is proof enough of the validity of the doctrine. What Amos condemned in the words of these verses (18-20) was not the public confidence in the coming of the day of the Lord, but Israel's perversion of the doctrine, lowering the conception of it to that of a military victory for the Israelites. Israel's view of that day has been described thus:

> They looked for a new era in which the deity himself would be their special champion, miraculously intervening in history, subduing Israel's enemies permanently, ushering in an age of world dominion and grandeur for her people.[42] When the heathen should be

[40]*Ibid.*
[41]Erling Hammershaimb, *op. cit.*, p. 87.
[42]Rolland Emerson Wolfe, *op. cit.*, p. 41.

judged, all the enemies of Israel defeated, and when Israel herself would be exalted to the highest pitch of prosperity and dominion, and without any regard to the moral condition.[43]

Regarding our own confidence in the doctrine of the Day of the Lord, or the Final Judgment of all men, it is anchored firmly in the teachings of the Son of God himself who brought to mankind, through his own words, and those of his apostles, a very definite and extensive corpus of teaching related to this very thing, the words of the NT, therefore, providing an inexhaustible reservoir of truth regarding this *fundamental* doctrine of Christianity (Hebrews 6:2). All OT references to the day of the Lord are illuminated by the NT.

Verse 19,20, As if a man did flee from a lion, and a bear met him; or went into the house and leaned his hand on the wall, and a serpent bit him. Shall not the day of Jehovah be darkness and not light? even very dark, and no brightness in it?

The word "or" in the above could likewise be translated "and," according to McKeating, thus making all of the actions consecutive, thus:

> Running from a lion, he meets a bear. In even greater panic, he reaches the shelter of his house. A snake strikes him from a crevice in the wall.[44]

However it may be translated, the passage clearly teaches that there shall be no possibility of escape from the adverse judgment of God upon human wickedness.

It must not be thought that Israel was totally wrong about the judgment day, for they were profoundly correct about two things: (1) there would indeed be such a day, and (2) it would also be a time of deliverance, joy and utmost felicity for the *true Israel*. Whatever their sources of this information, they were accurate in these important elements of the doctrine; and we have no alternative except to conclude that one or more of their prophets had conveyed to

[43]W.J. Deane, *op. cit.*, p. 85.
[44]Henry McKeating, *op. cit.*, p. 46.

them the mind of God regarding such matters. There was only one flaw in the people's thinking; they had made a mistake about who were the *true Israel*, that not being themselves at all with their stubborn and impenitent wickedness, but the *spiritual seed* of Abraham, those of Abraham's obedient faith and righteous disposition! Butler is correct in viewing Amos' words here as typical and prophetic of the final Day, the Great Assize, at which time God through Jesus Christ shall judge the whole word in righteousness.

> The truth of the matter was, the Day of the Lord would be a day of deliverence, but only for the true Israel, those who were Jews inwardly and not Jews only outwardly; for the Day of the Lord of which Amos speaks is typical and prophetic of the climactic Day of the Lord, the coming of the Messiah.[45]

The illustration of the man fleeing from the lion and the bear and finally gaining the shelter of his home, only to be bitten to death by a serpent in the very place of his imagined security is one of the most forceful in the Bible. Howard commented that:

> The death he thought he would escape awaited him at his own house. Thus it was to be for Israel, there would be no escape; the day of Yahweh would be a day of gloom and darkness in which there would be no relieving feature for the rebellious house of Israel.[46]

Our own summary of these three verses is simply that the "day of the Lord" was to be bad news for Israel; and the great corollary of that is that it will be likewise "bad news" for the entire race of sinful and rebellious men. The entire book of Revelation might be interpreted as an extended commentary and revelation regarding this very passage in Amos. The theme of Revelation is "the judgment" of the great Day; and all of the figures that describe the onset of that occasion (of which there are seven) are those depicting

[45]Paul T. Butler, *op. cit.*, p. 328.
[46]J. Kier Howard, *NLBC* (Grand Rapids: Zondervan Publishing House, 1979), p. 965.

unalloyed terror, slaughter, destruction and sorrow for the near-total family of Adam who may live at the time it occurs. Just one passage from Revelation is sufficient (of thirty that might be cited) to show how it will be for humanity at the judgment, i.e., 6:12-17.

One other thing should be noted. Those in Israel who longed for the day of the Lord were apparently sincere, but sincerely mistaken; but Barnes pointed out another class who pretend to long for the coming of the Lord. They are today professed Christians, hypocrites:

> Who in order to appear righteous before men, are wont to long for the Judgment Day, and to say, "Would that the Lord would come; would that we might be dissolved and be with Christ," imitating the Pharisee who said, "God, I thank thee that I am not as other men are!"[47]

Verse 21, I hate, I despise your feasts, and I will take not delight in your solemn assemblies.

God's repudiation of their worship was based upon several things: (1) it was not really the worship of God at all, but the worship of the old pagan gods they had always adored, even in the wilderness; (2) the formal services which were patterned after the commandments laid down in the Mosaic Law had been conspicuously altered and perverted by such things as (a) the omission of the sin-offering, and (b) the mingling of leavened bread with the burnt offerings, and (c) sacred images in the form of such things as the golden calves, adored at the shrines, (d) instruments of music such as had always marked pagan worship which they added to the worship, etc.; (3) all ethical and moral requirements of God having been forgotten and rejected in the practice of all kinds of immorality, drunkenness, and gluttonous feasting in the very worship itself; (4) the very shrines of Bethel, Gilgal, and Beersheba, where they worshipped, were illegal and contrary to the will of God, having been set up in their inception as supports for the throne of Jeroboam I. These are but a few of the outstanding features

---

[47]Albert Barnes, *op. cit.*, p. 29.

of an entire system of religion which was totally unacceptable to God.

"I despise your feasts . . ." As Hammershaimb noted: "The three great pilgrimage feasts (were): The Feast of Unleavened Bread, the Feast of Weeks, and the Feast of Tabernacles."[48] These correspond to Passover, Pentecost and Tabernacles. The prior existence of the Mosaic Law, as well as the radical drift away from it, on the part of Israel are in clear focus in this picture which emerges from Amos.

The words in this verse carry the thought expressed in AV, that "I will not smell in your solemn assemblies," reminding Israel of that threat in the law (Leviticus 26:31). Although the outward forms of the worship in Israel carried many distinctive likenesses to the true Mosaic Law from which much of it had been originally derived and later perverted, there were also radical and presumptious departures from it. "So secure were they that the only sacrifice which they *did not offer* was the sin or trespass offering."[49] "Amos stripped away all of Israel's false hopes."[50] Here it was their trust in an inadequate, incomplete, unauthorized, perverted, and innovated worship. In chapter 3, he took away their vain trust in the doctrine of election. In chapter 4, he took away their trust in tithes and offerings; and also in this chapter (18-20), he took away their trust in the future destruction of their enemies by God himself.

Verse 22, Yea, though ye offer me your burnt-offerings and meal offerings, I will not accept them; neither will I regard the peace-offerings of your fat beasts.

Conspicuous by their absence were the sin-offerings, the Israelites being conscious of no sin whatever and feeling no need of forgiveness. This accounts for their longing, without fear, for the "day of the Lord." As Barnes wrote, "The very fact that they desired but did not fear 'The Day of the Lord' shows that they were worthy of punishment, since no man is without sin!"[51] Butler observed that the same principles taught in this verse hold good today for, "those who

---

[48]Erling Hammershaimb, *op. cit.*, p. 89.
[49]Albert Barnes, *op. cit.*, p. 299.
[50]Ralph L. Smith, *op. cit.*, p. 116.
[51]Albert Barnes, *op. cit.*, p. 298.

claim to be covenant people of God."[52] Men need to take a look at their worship. Is some conspicuous part of it missing, such as the weekly observance of the Lord's Supper? Have instruments of music been added to the singing? Are the solemn ethical, moral and personal virtues of God's kingdom no longer stressed or particularly honored? Has so-called Christian worship become a parade of what men like, what they like to do, what they like to hear? Is the word of God, the Bible, received, honored, respected, quoted, read, believed and obeyed? Let everyone who prays not to be disappointed when "the day of the Lord" finally comes, answer such questions for himself.

Verse 23, Take thou away from me the noise of thy songs; for I will not hear the melody of thy viols.

There are two things God condemned in this verse: (1) the noise of the songs of their worship, and (2) the mechanical instruments used in their worship. Commentators generally have (1) either skipped the questions raised by this verse as did McKeating,[53] (2) dismissed the verse on the grounds that the only thing God had against anything at Bethel was the worshipper's violation of the rights of the poor, (3) suggested that instruments of music were a part of the regularly established Hebrew worship, or (4) affirmed that, "There is no hint that the ritual was irregular."[54] (5) Barnes thought that the thing God condemned here was the fact that, "Their melody, like much church-music was for itself and ended in itself."[55] Thorogood summed up the generally accepted opinions on this verse as, "What God really desired was that the Israelites should show justice and righteousness in their personal and national lives."[56] Of course, such an opinion regarding justice and righteousness being desired by God is correct, the Lord having thundered that message very clearly a half dozen times already in the scope of this prophecy; but *it is something else which God*

[52]Paul T. Butler, *op. cit.*, p. 331.
[53]Henry McKeating, *op. cit.*, p. 46.
[54]James Luther Mays, *op. cit.*, p. 107.
[55]Albert Barnes, *op. cit.*, p. 300.
[56]Bernard Thorogood, *op. cit.*, p. 65.

condemns here. Regarding that specific problem of what is condemned in this passage, note this:

God Here Condemned:

Their feast days (v. 21), not the great festivals which God himself instituted, but the idolatry, drunkenness, immorality, etc. which *they had added.*

Their solemn assemblies; the sweet smell (AV) induced by the burning of leavened bread (condemned in 4:5) had rendered even their assemblies unholy.

Their burnt-offerings and meal offerings (v. 22), rendered absolutely unacceptable to God by the drunkenness, immorality, the omission of any sin-offering, and the adoration of the gold image of a calf installed by Jereboam I.

Their peace-offerings of fat beasts, pretending that peace with the Lord had been established without a sin-offering, and with no regard at all for their sins.

Their *noise* of what were supposed to be songs! This word *noise* removes all thought of anything holy or spiritual. The singing had likely degenerated into that same kind of screaming cacophany one hears today.

Their instruments of music.

Now, the undeniable fact is that the Lord was condemning and crying out, through his prophet, against *all of the things* here mentioned; and there is no way to remove the instruments of music from that condemnation; for, unlike the case of the songs, it was not their *melody* which was lacking; it was not their *noise* which was condemned; and the only thing visible that could have been condemned here was the use of such unauthorized devices in God's worship.

Instrumental Music

This subject is still a current and pertinent one to those who really wish to serve and honor God. Many religious communions, Jewish, Protestant, and Catholic reject instruments of music in God's worship, including: The Orthodox Hebrew, the Armenian Catholic, the minor sects of both Baptist and Methodist communions, and churches of

Christ all over the world. The reasons for this rejection are weighty, impressive and convincing:

I. The NT has no record of mechanical instruments of music being used in Christian worship, the mention of harps in Revelation being absolutely figurative. The significance of this truth is enhanced by the fact of their being instruments of music all over the pagan Roman empire during the period when Christianity began.

II. This ban against mechanical instruments, and there was a ban, was continued for centuries afterwards in the early Christian communion, as any good encyclopaedia of religious knowledge will show. Their use in Christian worship came centuries too late to identify them with genuine Christianity. Our Puritan ancestors in Plymouth Colony received the gift of an organ from England, but conscientiously rejected it and left it uninstalled for two generations. It was later put in.

III. Many of the great reformers cried out against their use, including John Wesley, Alexander Campbell, and many others. Some of the great scholars of the 19th century adamantly opposed them, including the great Methodist scholar Adam Clarke. The arguments such men offered in support of their rejection were accurate, convincing, and clearly evident.

IV. All NT references to music in the NT churches carry the words, singing, sing, or songs, with no mention of mechanical instruments. In context, such passages mean "don't play." Colossians 3:16, Ephesians 5:19, etc.

V. Even the communions which introduced them were usually far from being whole-hearted in their departure, either restricting the kinds of instruments that could be used, or, as in the case of the Catholic church, forbidding them altogether in such services as the High Mass.

VI. Mechanical instruments are not *spiritual*. The only musical instrument that God ever made is the human voice; and nothing that man ever invented is worthy of comparison with it.

VII. Their use in Christian-related communions has been and is widely noted for developments which follow, such as the building of relatively small choirs of paid singers and musicians, and the greater and greater deemphasis upon the singing which God commanded. Any big city pastor knows that the most unspiritual part of his church is the choir!

VIII. Arguments which are skilfully advocated as justification for this historical departure from NT Christianity are false; and we shall note some of these a moment later.

IX. When instruments of music are introduced into the worship of God through Christ, such an action constitutes the entering point of a wedge leading to further and further departures from God's word, the reason for this being that the same arguments that will justify instruments of music in Christian worship will also justify the use of holy water, the burning of sacred incense, the lighting of religious lamps and blessed candles, the sign of the cross, the rosary of the Virgin Mary, or any one or all of many other innovations which have perverted Christianity, such as changes in the action that constitutes NT baptism, etc.

X. Those who are committed to abiding "in the doctrine of Christ" (2 John 9) will inevitably behold in any such thing as the introduction of mechanical instruments a "going onward" and a failure to respect that apostolical admonition.

XI. There are only two ways to worship God: (1) after the manner of Christ and the apostles of the NT, or (2) after the manner of men who are doing what pleases them, instead of what the NT commanded and sanctions. Of course, the latter is false worship.

XII. The introduction of mechanical instruments into the worhip of God, even in the OT, was unauthorized and condemned as in the very passage we are studying.

XIII. From time immemorial, even for long centuries prior to Christianity, instruments of music were notoriously and invariably associated with pagan worship, as, for example, in Daniel 3:4,5. That pagan association alone is enough to make instruments of music inappropriate in the worship of the Son of God.

XIV. Even if it could be proved, which is unlikely enough, that mechanical instruments of music were authorized by the Lord in the worship of the Hebrews (in the OT), that would in no way open up approval for their use by Christians, as there were many of the legitimate actions of Jewish worship which are inappropriate and sinful in the worship of Christ.

Objection Refuted

Despite the facts cited above, many learned, skilful, and, it may be presumed, sincere men have labored diligently to prove the acceptability of mechanical instruments in the worship of Christ, usually by *proving* a point that has no connection with it, namely, that God authorized them under the old covenant. What if he did? That would not authorize them in the worship of Christ. But a fair sample of such arguments is the following from the great scholar C. F. Kiel:

> Singing and playing on harps formed part of the temple worship of God (1 Chronicles 16:40, 23:5, & 25).[57]

Keil did not proceed from this with any kind of argument, except by leaving off any condemnation of the practice as observed in Christianity. The passages cited do indeed indicate that David placed instruments of music in the temple worship, which is undeniable; but what is inferred is that this was authorized by the Lord. David was guilty of many gross sins, not merely in the moral sector, as in the case of the wife of Uriah, but also in the very conception that led to the erection of the Jewish temple, a thing that God never authorized, and which was manifestly contrary to the will of God from the very moment when David dreamed up the idea. See II Samuel 7:1-17, where David's error in proposing a temple is clearly set forth. It is a great mistake to suppose that whatever David did was the will of God. See a full discussion of the Jewish Temple in CJ, pp. 192-196.

In addition to this, there is genuine doubt of whether or not God authorized David's introduction of instruments even into the Jewish temple. The principal passage supposed to teach this is I Chronicles 16:40, concerning which Adam Clarke noted that:

> The Syriac version of this place has this: "These were upright men who did not sing unto God with instruments of music, nor with drums, nor with listra,

---

[57]C.F. Keil, *op. cit.*, p. 288.

> nor with straight nor crooked pipes, nor with cymbals;
> but they sang before the Lord Almighty with a joyous
> mouth, and with a pure and holy prayer, and with
> innocence and integrity.[58]

Clarke went on to mention the Vulgate, the Septuagint, and
the Arabic, affirming that, none of the versions implied
that the instruments of music were "of God," but that they
were used to worship him.[59] Their sanction was clearly upon
the authority of David, and not of the Lord. We shall note
this question further in the notes on 6:5, below.

In his discussion of I Chronicles 16:40, Clarke propounded the following series of questions, each of which
requires a negative answer:

> Did God ever ordain instruments of music to be used
> in his worship?
> Can they be used in Christian assembles according
> to the spirit of Christianity?
> Has Jesus Christ, or his apostles, ever commanded
> or sanctioned the use of them?
> Were they ever used anywhere in the apostolical
> church?
> Does the use of them at present ever increase the
> spirit of devotion?
> Does it ever appear that bands of musicians, either
> in their collective or individual capacity, are more
> spiritual, or as spiritual, as the other parts of the
> Church of Christ?
> Is it ever remarked or known that musicians in the
> house of God have attained to any depth of piety, or
> superior soundness of understanding, in the things
> of God?
> Is it ever found that Christian societies which use
> them are more holy, or as holy, as those societies
> which do not use them?
> Is it ever found that the ministers who recommend
> their use are the most spiritual?

[58]Adam Clarke, *Commentary on the Whole Bible, Vol. II* (New York: T.
Mason & G. Lane, 1837), p. 610.
[59]*Ibid.*

> Can mere sounds, no matter how melodious, where
> no word or sentiment is or can be uttered, be consid-
> ered as giving praise to God?
> Is it possible that pipes or strings of any kind can
> give God praise?
> Can God be pleased with sound emitted by no senti-
> ent being, and can have no meaning?

It is our humble opinion that the instruments of music at
Bethel were in exactly the same category as the golden calf,
the drunken priests, the immoral worshippers, the burning
of the leavened bread, and all the other things here condemned by Amos in the name of Almighty God. To conclude the observations on this verse, "Arguments for instruments of music from their use in the Jewish church is
futile in the extreme when applied to Christianity."[60]

**Verse 24, But let justice roll down as waters, and right-
eousness as a mighty stream.**

There are two things commanded here: (1) let justice be
done, and (2) return to the commandments and *ordinances*
of God. It was not merely the proper regard for the poor
and needy that God wanted, as in (1); but it was also a
return to true worship which was required by the admonition in (2). Most of the commentators have failed to recognize what is implied by the biblical usage of the word
righteousness. It has no reference at all to a proper regard
for the poor and oppressed, that having been covered in the
previous clause; but it means "have the proper regard for
the commandments and ordinances" of God, as indicated in
Luke 1:6, and in Psalm 119:172.

**Verse 25, Did ye bring unto me sacrifices and offerings in
the wilderness forty years, O house of Israel?**

Amazingly, this verse is made the grounds for denying
that the Pentateuch had been written at the time this
prophecy was given, or that the custom of offering sacrifices had been instituted in Israel at all prior to the days of

---

[60]*Ibid.*, p. 611.

Amos. Such a viewpoint is in error. It is alleged, of course, that a negative answer to the question propounded is implied; but what is meant is that that portion of the whole nation of the Jews, namely, those who ultimately made up the Northern Kingdom, had *never* kept those commandments. The very next verse tells what they did *instead* of obeying God's commandments. It should be remembered of practically the whole Jewish nation in the wilderness that they repeatedly rebelled against God and that they were ultimately denied entry into Canaan for that specific reason. Furthermore, there is not a denial of any kind here that offerings and sacrifices were offered by Israel in the forty years wanderings; for as Jamieson said, "This is not a denial, for they *did* offer in the wilderness sacrifices to Jehovah of the cattle which they brought out of Egypt. It is not a denial, but an affirmation."[61]

No matter how this passage is interpreted, whether by assuming that the answer is affirmative, as did Jamieson, above, or whether by insisting that a negative answer is implied, as do Mays, Harper and many others, there can certainly not be any contradiction of the Pentateuch as in the notion that, "There is no way to reconcile this view (of Amos) with the extant Pentateuchal tradition."[62] If Amos said here that the Israelites had *not* offered sacrifices in the wilderness, the meaning would then be that as stated by Keil, to the effect that:

> The denial that they had offered sacrifices applied to the nation as a whole, or the great mass of the people, individual exceptions being passed by... During that forty years, not even the rite of circumcision was practiced (See Joshua 5:5-7); and the sacrificial worship prescribed by the law fell more and more into disuse, so that the generation that was sentenced to die in the wilderness for their rebellion offered no more sacrifices.[63]

---

[61]Robert Jamieson, *op. cit.*, p. 796.
[62]James Luther Mays, *op. cit.*, p. 111.
[63]C.F. Keil, *op. cit.*, p. 290.

Furthermore, it is doubtless true that, "Israel during this period must have restricted their sacrifices very considerably because of circumstances.,"[64] which would have more than justified what is implied here by Amos' question. That prophetic question was also justified by the fact that, although the people did offer sacrifices, they did not truly offer them to Jehovah, but to those favorite gods which they secretly adored during the forty years wanderings, a truth attested by the fact that after they entered Canaan, it was still necessary for Joshua to order them to "put away the strange gods from among them" (Joshua 24:33). One gets the proper idea by emphasis upon *me*. "Did you bring unto *me*, etc.?" No! They did not, but while pretending to worship God, they were actually worshipping idols. The great Christian martyr quoted this very passage in affirming this very thing (Acts 7:42). This has the meaning of:

> You have always been idolators, corrupters of pure worship. Your service in the wilderness, when you were little exposed to external influences, was no more true and faithful than that which you offer now.[65]

Thus it was altogether true of the Northern Kingdom, as stated by Barnes, that: "The idolatry of the ten tribes was the revival of the idolatry in the wilderness. The ten tribes owned as the forefathers of their worship those first idolators."[66] All of these considerations, therefore, are more than sufficient reason for rejecting allegations to the effect that, "The point Amos was trying to make was that sacrifice is not essential to a right relationship with God."[67] The NT affirms, of that period, that "without the shedding of blood, there is no remission of sins" (Hebrews 9:22); and, therefore, there can be no acceptance of such a view as that just quoted. With equal authority, we also set aside as erroneous all such affirmations as this: "Amos was disputing the divine origin of the institution of sacrifice as it existed in his day."[68] Such erroneous misconceptions are actually

---

[64]Erling Hammershaimb, *op. cit.*, p. 92.
[65]W.J. Deane, *op. cit.*, p. 86.
[66]Albert Barnes, *op. cit.*, p. 300.
[67]Ralph L. Smith, *op. cit.*, p. 118.
[68]Henry McKeating, *op. cit.*, p. 47.

founded in a failure to read the sacred text. Everything that
is either stated or implied in this verse is fully explained by
the observation that:

> The generation of Amos' day, in mixing idolatry
> with sacrifices done in the name of Jehovah, was just
> like the contemporaries of Moses, practicing idolatry
> and all the while claiming to be worshippers of Jeho-
> vah.[69]

**Verse 26, Yea, ye have borne the tabernacle of your king
and the shrine of your images, the star of your god, which
ye made to yourselves.**

This verse is accounted to be very difficult by scholars
who have difficulty with any agreement as to the way it
should be translated; but, for us, the solution is easy, because this is one of only two verses in Amos quoted in the
NT; and we are perfectly safe in taking the NT rendition of
it:

> Did ye offer unto me slain beasts and sacrifices
> Forty years in the wilderness, O house of Israel?
> And ye took up the tabernacle of Moloch,
> And the star of the god Rephan,
> The figures which ye made to worship them: and I
> will carry you away beyond Babylon (Acts 7:42,43).

What is plainly indicated from Stephen's interpretation
of this place is that the Israelites in the wilderness, instead
of worshipping the true god, were privately passing around
the images of Moloch and Rephan, which they made themselves, and perhaps even hiding these forbidden and idolatrous objects in the very tabernacle itself in such a manner
as to conceal them from Moses. This is uncertain, to be
sure; and scholars have even questioned the rendition in the
NT; but the meaning expressed there was accepted by the
Sanhedrin as such a sufficient indictment of themselves
that they murdered Stephen for making it. Thus we are
surely safe in declaring that something along this line of
thought is most surely included in the meaning.

---

[69]Paul T. Butler, *op. cit.*, p. 333.

Verse 27, Therefore, will I cause you to go into captivity beyond Damascus, saith Jehovah, whose name is the God of hosts.

"Beyond Damascus . . ." Strangely, this is altered in the NT quotation of it to read, "Beyond Babylon"; but the meaning is the same either way. Amos has in mind Assyria, and his hearers all know it. According to some renditions of these difficult verses, they carry this thought: "The idolators will have to carry their idols into exile beyond Damascus, i.e., Assyria, which is thus vaguely indicated."[70]
Did this captivity occur? Indeed yes . . .

The terrible consequences of rebellion against God grew steadily worse. Injustice, crime, and immorality of all degrees soon led to complete anarchy in the land. In 722-721 B.C., the ten tribes of the Northern Kingdom were subjugated by the Assyrian king; and the people were deported to Assyria never to return as a nation.[71]

What ever became of them? Nothing may be affirmed with any certainty; but in all probability, the whole generation of them were reduced to slavery, worked mercilessly in fields, quarries, brick plants, and domestic service until death mercifully released them from their hopeless and tragic estate. Such was the ultimate reward of their turning against their God.

[70]J.R. Dummelow, *Commentary on the Holy Bible* (New York: The Macmillan Company, 1937), p. 568.
[71]Paul T. Butler, *op. cit.*, p. 333.

CHAPTER 6

This chapter continues the further elaboration of the prophetic doom pronounced upon Israel at the conclusion of chapter 2. First, he uttered the second woe over the careless and indulgent leaders of the nation, sunk in their revellings and indifference (1-6). For them, he pronounced their destruction and the overthrow of their nation (7-11), emphasizing that they had acted perversely, trusting in their own power (12-14). The blunt reiteration of their doom in v. 14 concludes this section of the prophecy.

In the first sub-section of the chapter (1-6), "The link word is *first*."[1] They considered themselves first among the nations (v. 1); they only used the finest oils (literally, *first*)[2] (v. 6); and then in the first line of the second section is revealed the fact that they shall also be *first* into captivity (v. 7). The whole chapter is pointed squarely at the overconfidence and conceit of the nation, as exhibited in its evil leaders.

Verse 1, Woe to them that are at ease in Zion, and them that are secure in the mountain of Samaria, the notable men of the chief of the nations, to whom the house of Israel come.

God's gospel of dealing with mankind is a gospel of grace; but in Amos the emphasis is not upon grace but upon law and obedience, an emphasis which should certainly be observed in our own times; because as McFadden put it:

> It is the gospel of law, for that, too, is gospel. To understand and obey the laws by which God governs his world is the way of peace; to ignore or defy them is the way to destruction.[3]

---

[1]J.A. Motyer, *NBCR* (Grand Rapids: Wm. B. Eerdmans Publishing Company, 1979), p. 736.

[2]*Ibid.*

[3]John Edgar McFadden, *A Cry for Justice* (New York: Charles Scribner's Sons, 1912), p. 71.

"Woe to them that are at ease in Zion . . ." This is the second great woe, the first being in 5:18, where it is written. "Woe unto you that desire the day of Jehovah!" Zion here is the poetic name of Jerusalem, and some of the commentators would like to get it out of the text on the basis that, "It would seem out of keeping with his habit of concentration upon the immediate situation for him";[4] but such a view ignores one of the outstanding features of Amos, i.e., the fact that Judah is by no means left out of these prophecies of destruction, as in 2:4,5, 3:1, 5:1,5, etc. To be sure Amos was sent particularly to the Northern Kingdom; but Judah is always in the back of his mind; for it is not the Northern Kingdom only, but, "The whole family which I brought up out of the land of Egypt" (3:1) which is under the judgment of God for their sins. Hammbershaimb has brilliantly refuted the allegations of those intent upon disturbing the validity of the text here as it has come down to us. "We must nevertheless keep the MT, which must be understood as showing the threat worked out with poetic parallelism against the two capital cities."[5]

The over-confidence of the entire nation of the Jews was founded in their regard for Zion (Jerusalem) as the place where the name of God was recorded, and considered by them invulnerable to any disaster of whatever nature, and (especially in the Northern Kingdom) upon the strength and military fortifications of the "mountain of Samaria." The confidence they had in Samaria, although destined to be frustrated, was nevertheless justified to a certain extent by the unusual strength of the place. When it finally fell, some three years were required to subdue it. The great error lay in the people's having forgotten that, "Unless the Lord keep the city, the watchman waketh but in vain" (Psalm 127:1).

> These people misunderstood the terms of the covenant, thinking that God would spare Jerusalem regardless of what they did; they were at ease in Zion . . .

---

[4]Hughell E.W. Fosbroke, *IB, Vol. VI* (New York: Abingdon Press, 1957), p. 823.

[5]Erling Hammershaimb, *The Book of Amos, translated by John Sturdy* (New York: Shocken Books, 1970), p. 96.

(in Samaria) they were trusting in the mountain of Samaria, a natural fortress which Israel's leaders must have thought impregnable.[6]

"At ease in Zion ..." has entered all languages as an idiom for self-indulgent complacency, indifference and over-confidence.

Verse 2, Pass ye unto Calneh, and see; and from thence go ye to Hamath the great; then go down to Gath of the Philistines: are they better than these kingdoms? or is their border greater than your border?

This verse again follows a pattern already observed in Amos' words, that of putting words or arguments into the mouths of his hearers in order to prove his point, much as the apostle Paul used the diatribe in the book of Romans. Some scholars have mistakenly tried to take these words as a threat from Amos based upon the premise that since other great cities of the neighboring kingdoms have fallen, Israel herself should not be over-confident; but this is not the case at all. It is a quotation from those proud leaders boasting that they were "Number 1." As Smith pointed out, it could hardly be a threat, "Since it is fairly certain that Calneh and Hamath did not fall until after Amos' ministry."[7] The mention of Gath in this place also proves that the omission of that city from the list of those enumerated in 1:6-8, could not be interpreted as proof that Gath no longer existed when Amos wrote. See note on those passages.

The writers who insist upon the other interpretation, which is manifestly false, are evidently doing so in order to use the passage as an assualt upon the integrity of the verse. McKeating said, "If this interpretation is correct (the false one), the verse must have been inserted after Amos' time."[8] This is an excellent example of one of the favorite devices of destructive critics, namely, that of giving a verse a false interpretation, and then using it as an

---

[6]Ralph L. Smith, *BBC* (Nashville: Broadman Press, 1972), p. 119.
[7]*Ibid.*, p. 120.
[8]Henry McKeating, *CBC, The Books of Amos, Hosea, and Micah* (Cambridge: At the University Press, 1971), p. 49.

argument against the validity of biblical texts. The true interpretation of this place was accurately discerned by Motyer, thus:

> Amos is ironically repeating the propaganda handout of the rulers who kept up the morale of their people by drawing advantageous comparisons with reasonably distant and clearly inferior places.[9]

"Are they better than these kingdoms . . ." This obviously requires a negative answer. "These kingdoms" are Judah and Israel. As Keil said, "Amos names three great and flourishing capitals, because he is speaking to the great men of the capitals of the two kingdoms of Israel."[10]

Before leaving this verse, it should be noted that Mays also defended the correct interpretation of this verse by noting that the other one is "embarrassed by the uncertainty whether Hamath and Calneh had been captured by the Assyrians in the mid-eighth century."[11] He also observed that the MT (as followed in our version) makes excellent sense as a quotation. "The boast articulates a pride that is nurtured by the success of Jeroboam's reign, and a belief in their manifest destiny as the people of Yahweh."[12]

Verse 3, Ye that put far away the evil day, and cause the seat of violence to come near.

"Put far away the evil day . . ." This does not mean, of course, that they actually moved the evil day. They did not really put it off. The passage means "to regard as far off."[13] They were indifferent to the eventual consequences of their wickedness and regarded their sure and certain punishment as a thing that could be relegated to the remote future, and as something for which they needed not to have any apprehension at all.

[9]J.A. Motyer, *op. cit.*, p. 736.
[10]C.F. Keil, *Commentary on the Whole Bible* (Grand Rapids: Wm. B. Eerdmans Publishing Company), p. 298.
[11]James Luther Mays, *Amos, A Commentary* (Philadelphia: The Westminster Press, 1969), p. 115.
[12]*Ibid.*, p. 116.
[13]C.F. Keil, *op. cit.*, p. 299.

"And cause the seat of violence to come near . . ." A society that tolerates violence and corruption is hastening the day when violence and corruption will be enthroned among them. As Motyer commented:

> They were hastening the day when lawlessness would reign, "the reign of terror." So it must have been in the final years of the kingdom of Israel when, after Jeroboam II, only one king passed the throne on to his son, and the rest ended their reigns by assassination.[14]

Verse 4, That lie upon beds of ivory, and stretch themselves upon their couches, and eat the lambs out of the flock, and the calves out of the midst of the stall.

"Beds of ivory . . ." The idle rich were using inlays of ivory to decorate their beds, indifferently ignoring the gross poverty around them, and living as extravagantly as possible.

"Lambs out of the flock . . . calves out of the . . . stall . . ." This was a custom severely frowned upon by God's prophet, because it was an extravagant and unnecessary waste. The result was that the flocks and herds were diminished. The current society is guilty of a similar waste in their extravagant taste for caviar, which has practically destroyed the whole species of the sturgeon from which the fish-eggs are derived. It would appear that Amos was particularly outraged by their eating of the lambs!

There is a great deal in Amos that might induce a superficial criticism to the effect that he was merely a country bumpkin who was opposed to the aristocracy, affluence and culture of city life; "But it is unjust to regard him so."[15] It is the rebellion of the people against God and his word which is the primary concern of Amos:

> His message is primarily a religious one, and only inferentially social. Hate the evil, and love the good — that is a motto as applicable to the city as to the country, and as capable of realization.[16]

---

[14]J.A. Motyer, *op. cit.*, p. 736.
[15]John Edgar McFadden, *op. cit.*, p. 71.
[16]*Ibid.*

Verse 5, That sing idle songs to the sound of the viol; that invent for themselves instruments of music, like David.

"That sing idle songs to the sound of the viol . . ." One is amused at a comment which finds nothing more here than the fact (?) that, "Amos does not like the contemporary fashion in music! We might translate, 'who wail to the accompaniment of the lute.' "[17] Not much is known about this singing; but Barnes is probably correct:

> The word which Amos alone uses in this place describes probably a hurried flow of unmeaning, unconsidered words, in which the rhythym of words and music was everything, the sense, nothing.[18]

"That invent to themselves instruments of music, like David . . ." Whatever was reprehensible in those who were condemned in this clause, it was compared to a similar reprehensible action on the part of David. Much more is known with reference to David's sinful action than is known about the sinful actions of the class Amos rebuked with these words; and a little further attention to what David did, and particularly to the action mentioned here, should give the clue to what the lords of Samaria were guilty of. Some things can be ruled out at once. It is not a sin to invent instruments of music, or anything else, so *that* could not be the thing in focus here. However, it was sinful for David to introduce, organize, and maintain the use of mechanical instruments in the worship of God, a fact clearly discernible in 5:23. The explanation usually offered on this interesting verse is given thus by Keil:

> As David invented stringed instruments in honour of his God in heaven, so do these princes invent playing and singing for their god, the belly.[19]

This, of course, is ingenious; and many have followed it in their own interpretations, almost verbatim, as, for example, Butler:

---

[17]Henry McKeating, *op. cit.*, p. 50.
[18]Albert Barnes, *Notes on the OT, The Minor Prophets, Vol. 1* (Grand Rapids: Baker Book House, 1953), p. 307.
[19]C.F. Keil, *op. cit.*, p. 300.

As David invented instruments of music to worship his God, you invent musical instruments to worship your god, your belly.[20]

Clever as this interpretation appears, however, it cannot be correct; the key element being overlooked in it is that the passage makes it quite clear that what David did was wrong. If, as this interpretation suggests, the action of the nobles was *sinful*, that being clear enough from the text, how was it "as" or "like" what David did? The incredible, fanciful view that their worshipping their belly was in any way comparable to David's "honouring his God" is too fantastic to be accepted. On the other hand, if the passage is viewed as the sinful action of David in introducing instruments into God's worship, and the action of the nobles (also sinful) who were likewise introducing the intruments of music into the alleged worship of "God" at Bethel, then the comparison is perfect; and that is exactly what we believe to be taught here. It is clearly and uniquely a "religious thing" that is evident, not only in this verse, but in verse 6, immediately following, where the "sacrificial bowls" were being profaned by these gluttonous and drinking nobles. See notes on v. 6, below.

Note also that it is not the "invention" of musical instruments which is primarily in focus here, that having no element of sin in any way connected with it; but it is the sin of "inventing for or *unto themselves*," a clear echo of "Thou shalt not make *unto thee* a graven image" (Exodus 20:4), the thing forbidden there not being merely the making of any kind of image, but the making "unto themselves" of graven images, i.e., the making of religious images! The similarity of the language here shows that the innovative nobles of Samaria had further corrupted their own perverted worship at Bethel by following the sinful example set by David in his introduction of the musical instruments into God's worship in Jerusalem. There is no good reason for setting aside this obvious meaning of the passage. Some astute scholars have discerned this and, accordingly, have invoked their rule of last resort, i.e., screaming "Interpola-

[20]Paul T. Butler, *The Minor Prophets* (Joplin: College Press, 1968), p. 335.

tion,"[21] when there's no other way to support the popular
prejudice that freely allows the use of mechanical instruments in the worship of the Author of Christianity.

The great leaders of the Reformation practically all understood the obvious teaching of this place, including Wesley and many others. There is no need to multiply the
witnesses from that era as to what these verses most certainly mean; but we shall quote a few lines from Adam
Clarke:

> I believe that David was not authorized by the Lord
> to introduce that multitude of musical instruments
> into the Divine worship of which we read; and I am
> satisfied that his conduct in this respect is most sol-
> emnly reprehended by this prophet; and I further be-
> lieve that the use of such instruments of music in the
> Christian Church is without the sanction and against
> the will of God.[22]

We have included this quotation because it is not widely
known, the great scholar's words having long ago been
edited out of his commentaries by those who did not agree
with his conclusions, the same not appearing in any of the
recent abridged editions.

One other word regarding this passage. The orthodox
Hebrew church, who understand the Hebrew text of the OT
better than any Gentile commentator could ever expect to
know it, have never allowed instruments of music in their
worship of God, their conviction of the sinfulness of it being
due in part to the teaching of these very passages in Amos;
and the Jews, at least a very considerable percentage of
them, have consistently maintained this conviction for
some twenty-seven centuries! The view of this passage advocated here is then, by no means, a Johnny-come-lately
opinion.

If David's action in introducing mechanical instruments
into God's worship was *honorable*; and if the Samaritan
leaders were using instruments *dishonorably* in the worship
of "their belly," how could the Holy Spirit possibly have

[21]James Luther Mays, *op. cit.*, p. 113.
[22]Adam Clarke *Commentary on the Whole Bible* (New York: T. Mason & G.
Lane, 1837), Vol. IV, p. 686.

equated these actions or referred to one of them as "like" the other?

Verse 6, That drink wine in bowls, and anoint themselves with the chief oils; but they are not grieved for the affliction of Joseph.

"That drink wine in bowls . . ." The sin indicated here is not merely that of "funnelling." Something far different is indicated:

> One view is that their offence consists in not being satisfied with drinking wine in small quantities, but drinking it from the bowl; but the meaning is certainly that they have committed an offence by using sacrificial bowls, which it was not permissible to drink from.[23]

> The Hebrew word for "bowl" in this place actually means "the great bowl" and is mentioned elsewhere in the OT only in connection with ritual procedures.[24]

The sin which Amos condemned here is therefore a religious violation, and not merely excessive drinking, further pointing up the truth that this whole passage deals *primarily* with perversion of God's worship, the particular thing here, being desecration of holy vessels. The ancient people of God viewed this latter thing with extraordinary abhorrence. It will be recalled that for a similar offence of drinking from the sacred vessels robbed from the temple in Jerusalem, Belshazzar was punished by a summary judgment from God; and the kingdom was torn away from him in the same night (Daniel 5:1-25).

"And anoint themselves with the chief oils . . ." Hammershaimb assures us that the word for chief oils (or *first* oils) could also "be taken with the meaning of *firstfruits*; their sin would then be that they have anointed themselves with the firstfruits which belong to God."[25] Thus it is seen that the religious factor is the dominating thought throughout these verses. Understanding the transgression in this

---

[23]Erling Hammershaimb, *op. cit.*, p. 101.
[24]James Luther Mays, *op. cit.*, p. 116.
[25]Erling Hammershaimb, *op. cit.*, p. 101.

light certainly clears up the problem with the other view, which would make it appear that Almighty God was concerned about the "size" of a wine-guzzler's goblet, bottle, or bowl. It was not "drinking," as such, which was condemned here, but their drinking from "bowls," evidently the consecrated vessels which had been dedicated to God. Here also is strong presumptive evidence that it is a similar religious violation in verse 5.

An additional facet of the sin mentioned in these verses with regard to their anointing themselves with the "first" oils is seen in the fact that all anointing was suspended in time of mourning (1 Samuel 14:2); and, the sad state of Israel's rebellion against God should have led to widespread mourning and prayer, instead of the drinking and anointing evident here. That Amos probably had this in mind also, is manifest in the next clause which mentions "the affliction of Joseph."

Verse 7, Therefore shall they now go captive with the first that go captive; and the revelry of them that stretched themselves shall pass away.

Motyer's summary of the balance of this chapter is thus:

> The fact of pride (v. 8), its moral indifference (v. 12), and its self-centeredness (v. 13) are brought before us; but now we see the divine reaction to them. Vv 1-7 tell us in so many words that pride goes before a fall; vv. 8-14 tell us why this is. The divine reactions are hatred (v. 8), alienation (vv.9,10), and enmity (vv. 11-14).[26]

"Go captive with the first that go captive . . ." Here is a glimpse of eternal justice. These gross sinners who were hailed as the "first" among the "first" of nations, and used up the "first" fruits (or oils) for their own pampering instead of giving them to God, as was their duty, shall now be "first" to go into captivity! Keil added this: "You that are first in riches will be the first to bear the yoke of captivity."[27]

However, they do Amos an injustice who suppose that he

---

[26]J.A. Motyer, *op. cit.*, p. 736.
[27]C.F. Keil, *op. cit.*, p. 301.

was opposed to the rich merely because of their riches. "His message is, by no manner of means, 'Down with the aristocracy!'; but 'Return unto God' (4:6), 'Seek good and not evil!' "[28] As verses 1-6 of this chapter sternly reveal, the thing that was wrong with the leaders of Israel was that they had lost all regard for their status as a God-rescued, God-redeemed, and God-chosen community and had corrupted his worship, prostrated themselves before idols, desecrated his sacred vessels, introduced pagan mechanical instruments into his worship "like David," and had violated with impunity the sacred ordinances of the Pentateuchal covenant, except in those cases where the observance of them was in some manner pleasing to themselves!

Verse 8, The Lord Jehovah hath sworn by himself, saith Jehovah, the God of hosts: I abhor the excellency of Jacob, and hate his palaces; therefore will I deliver up the city with all that is therein.

"Jehovah hath sworn by himself ..." It may not be allowed that God's oath is any more binding, or more true, than his word; but, inasmuch as the opposite is true among men, the Holy Spirit here, wishing to emphasize the dependability and certainty of God's words, uses this anthropomorphic accommodation to the prejudices of men in order to achieve that purpose.

"I abhor the excellency of Jacob ..." This expression shows that Amos never has Judah very far out of mind; for Jacob was the ancestor of Judah, as well as of Israel. Writers who try to make out that these various references to Judah, Jacob, and the whole house of Israel which came up out of Egypt, etc. are added to the prophecy by later writers are totally wrong. Despite the principal burden of Amos' commission having been to cry out against the Northern Kingdom, unless he had kept before them continually the reminder that God was also displeased with similar sins in Judah, he would have lost his effectiveness through the appearance that he was merely crying out against the sins of his neighbor, and not against the sins of his own nation.

---

[28]John Edgar McFadden, *op. cit.*, p. 81.

Verses 9,10, And it shall come to pass, if there remain ten men in one house, that they shall die. And when a man's uncle shall take him up, even he that burneth him, to bring out the bones out of the house, and shall say to him that is in the innermost parts of the house, Is there yet any with thee? and he shall say, No; then shall he say, Hold thy peace; for we may not make mention of the name of Jehovah.

The situation envisioned by these verses presupposes the possible survival of "ten men in one house," evidently one of the "great houses" which normally had a hundred or more inhabitants, as the remnant after a devastating military defeat; and the prophecy is that they (these few survivors) will all die of the plague. The plague is evidenced by the burning of the bodies, contrary to the usual Hebrew custom.

"A man's uncle . . ." An alternate reading here is "kinsman," in any case, the person who came to burn the bodies.

"Is there any yet with thee? . . ." The picture is that of the very last of the survivors who answered the inquiry negatively.

"Hold thy peace, for we may not make mention of the name of Jehovah . . ." A number of somewhat fanciful interpretations have been given to this, but it seems merely to indicate that all of the people at that late stage of their sorrow had at last recognized that their punishment was of God, and that it was God's judgment that was upon them. The solicitation, therefore, not to invoke the name of God would have come from the fear that if God were aware of "any" survivor, he also would have been destroyed. That such a conception does not take account of the omniscience of God does not nullify it, for the very fault that led to Israel's destruction was their total failure to develop any adequate conception of the true nature of God.

Verse 11, For behold, Jehovah commandeth, and the great house shall be smitten with breaches, and the little house with clefts.

"The great house . . ." does not mean any particular "great house," but all of the great houses, the same being true of the "small house." The mention of "great house" first in this verse, immediately after vv. 9,10, strongly supports the probability that the "ten men left in one house" in those verses has reference to one of those great palatial establishments for which Samaria was famous, each having an occupancy of a hundred or so, including domestics, servants and retainers. Although the great houses shall all be carried away by the destruction, the small houses also will not escape. Why? God has commanded it! "Rich and poor alike have been guilty of turning away from Jehovah to serve their appetites."[29]

Verse 12, Shall horses run upon the rock? will one plow there with oxen? that ye have turned justice into gall, and the fruit of righteousness into wormwood.

The meaning of this verse was thus summarized by Schultz:

> There is a spiritual and moral order in the universe that is just as impossible to ignore as the natural order. It is as senseless to pervert justice as it is to expect horses to run on the rocks, or for oxen to plow on rock.[30]

Translators have difficulty with this verse, some of them rendering it "horses to run up a cliff . . . or plow in the sea with oxen"; but such renditions, even if allowed, would not change the essential meaning of the passage.

> It is easier to change the course of nature, or the use of things of nature, than the course of God's providence or the laws of his just retribution.[31]

As Keil said, "These verses show the moral perversity of the unrighteous conduct of the wicked."[32]

Verses 13,14, Ye that rejoice in a thing of naught, that say, Have we not taken to us horns by our own strength? For, behold, I will raise up against you a nation, O house of

---

[29]Paul T. Butler, *op. cit.*, p. 341.
[30]Arnold C. Schultz, *WBC* (Chicago: Moody Press, 1962), p. 835.
[31]W.J. Deane, *Pulpit Commentary, Vol. 14, Amos* (Grand Rapids: Wm. B. Eerdmans Publishing Company, 1950), p. 113.
[32]C.F. Keil, *op. cit.*, p. 303.

Israel, saith Jehovah, the God of hosts; and they shall afflict you from the entrance of Hamath, unto the brook of the Arabah.

"Things of naught . . . horns . . ." Recent scholarly studies on these words indicate that, "*a thing of naught is* actually a mistranslation for *Lodebar*, which has the same sound in Hebrew, and that *horns* is the same as the proper name *Karnaim*, which means *horns* in Hebrew."[33] In this light, most recent translations render verse 13, as follows:

> You brag about capturing the town of Lodebar. You boast, We were strong enough to take Karnaim.

"The verse is a sarcastic allusion to the conquests of Jeroboam II in Transjordan, which are narrated in 2 Kings 14:25, two towns that he captured being mentioned here."[34] Amos here made a play upon the meaning of the names of the towns, Lodebar, for example, meaning "a thing of naught." Nevertheless, the people were very arrogant and boastful about their successes. "The reiterated emphasis on 'our . . . we . . . ourselves' mocks the boasting assessment which the people made of Jeroboam's successes."[35]

"I will raise up against you a nation, O house of Israel . . ." It should always be remembered in studying this prophecy that it was exactly and terribly fulfilled just as God had promised. Both the sacred scriptures and the testimony of the archeologist testify to the overwhelming destruction of Israel within some thirty years after Amos wrote this prophecy.

> The kingdom of Israel was destroyed in the year 722 by Sargon in the first month of his reign when Samaria was taken after a siege which was begun by his predecessor, Shalmanezer IV, and had lasted three years.[36]

Excavations made about 1843 revealed the old palace of Sargon II and the so-called "Display Inscription" at Khor-

---

[33]*Good News Bible* (New York: American Bible Society, 1976), p. 996.
[34]Erling Hammershaimb, *op. cit.*, p. 105.
[35]James Luther Mays, *op. cit.*, p. 122.
[36]J.R. Dummelow, *Commentary on the Holy Bible* (New York: The Macmillan Company, 1937), p. 569.

sabad, in which Sargon II described the humiliation of Samaria in his own words:

> I besieged and captured Samaria, carrying off 27,290 of the people who dwelt therein. 50 chariots I gathered from among them. I caused others to take their portion (of the deported inhabitants). I set my officers over them and imposed upon them the tribute of the former king.[37]

"From the entrance of Hamath, unto the brook of Arabah . . ."

"This expression stands for the northern boundary of the kingdom and the southern boundary of Canaan,"[38] thus including the southern kingdom of Judah also, a recurring theme in Amos.

"Hamath is the pass between Lebanon and Anti-Lebanon, the northern limit of Israelite territory. The Arabah is the deep valley in which the Dead Sea lies."[39] The most extended borders of Jewish dominion in the days of Solomon were encompassed in these limits; and, although they had for a brief season been restored under Jeroboam II, it was but for a little time. All was swept away by the Assyrian invasion, except that Jerusalem and the southern kingdom remained about 150 years till they were carried away to Babylon.

The relevance of this prophecy for our own times should never be overlooked. As Butler said:

> The message of Amos is still quite relevant and contemporary. Our society is almost a sister to that one in its ingratitude, irresponsibility, arrogance, and sensuality. Amos was not able to call men back to God in his day; but he was willing to lay down his life if necessary to give God's call to repentance. Can prophets of today succeed where Amos did not? Time alone will tell.[40]

---

[37]Merrill F. Unger, *Archeology and the Bible* (Grand Rapids: Zondervan Publishing House, 1954), p. 200.
[38]C.F. Keil, *op. cit.*, p. 304.
[39]Henry McKeating, *op. cit.*, p. 52.
[40]Paul T. Butler, *op. cit.*, p. 342.

CHAPTER 7

Here begins the final major section of Amos, consisting principally of five visions, three of which are found in this chapter: (1) that of the locusts (1-3), (2) that of the fire (4-6), and (3) that of the plumb-line (7-9). The balance of the chapter (10-14) has an exceedingly interesting and instructive narrative of the confrontation between God's Prophet (Amos) and Jeroboam's Priest. The appearance of this historical narrative in the midst of these visions has been seized upon by biblical critics anxious to use it in some way as a basis for their attacks upon the validity of the prophecy. However, this last section of the chapter (10-14) belongs exactly where it is. The pagan priest Amaziah quoted from the third vision in his report of Amos's words to the king (vv. 9-11), and also referred to Amos as a "seer," literally, one who *sees* visions (v. 12), a word which McFadden discerningly translated "visionary."[1] Thus it is impossible to deny that the first three of these visions actually provoked and led up to the dramatic confrontation between Amos and Amaziah. When this is discerned, the reason for the narrative's appearance here (where and when it occurred) is evident.

The form of the narrative is designated by some as a terse prose, contrasting with what they call the poetry of the rest of the chapter; and the RSV has followed this false allegation of incompatibility between the narrative and the rest of the chapter, printing the narrative in prose form and the rest as poetry. However, the truth is that the narrative is just as poetic as anything else in Amos. W. R. Harper discussed this extensively, giving six reasons why this narrative *is* poetry, noting especially, "the logical division into two parts (vv. 10-13, and 14-17), and the use of regular trimeter in the first, and regular tetrameter in the second."[2] His conclusion was that:

---

[1] John Edgar McFadden, *A Cry for Justice* (New York: Charles Scribner's Sons, 1912), p. 100.

[2] William Rainey Harper, *Amos and Hosea* (New York: Charles Scribner's Sons, 1910), p. 168.

The artistic skill which put the accusation (vv. 10-13) in a trimeter movement, and the strong and terrible reply (14-17) in the heavier and statelier tetrameter is characteristic of Amos. The symmetry is throughout extraordinary.[3]

In the light of this, which can hardly be denied, it is deplorable that the RSV accommodated the critics by printing this chapter as a poem into which a prose narrative had been inserted. As a matter of obvious truth, the chapter is a unit, being composed by one of Amos' extended public sermons at the shrine of Bethel, a sermon long enough for Amaziah to send a message to the king, and then attempt upon his own authority to expel the prophet. And what was the result of this interruption? *Amos finished his sermon*, including a special prophecy for Amaziah! The wild speculations to the effect that Amos was arrested and executed, or that, "He left under protest, for Judah,"[4] or that, "Amos appeared no more as a prophet in the Northern Kingdom,"[5] are unsupported by any evidence. The known sequel to this confrontation between God's Prophet and the King's Priest is that Amos went right on and gave the other two of the five visions that composed his sermon.

Verse 1, Thus the Lord Jehovah showed me: and, behold, he formed locusts in the beginning of the shooting up of the latter growth; and lo it was the latter growth after the king's mowings.

The thing to remember about the first two of the visions of threatened disasters against Israel is that they did not occur, but were averted through the prophet's intercession. The evident reason why Amos included these first two visions in his sermon was that of showing to all the people that he in no manner desired the evil things to come to pass which it was his duty to prophecy, but that he actually stood before God as an advocate of the people and as a

---

[3]*Ibid.*

[4]Henry McKeating, *Amos, Hosea and Micah, CBC* (Cambridge: At the University Press, 1971), p. 59.

[5]Erling Hammershaimb, *The Book of Amos, translated by John Sturdy* (New York: Shocken Books, 1970), p. 119.

prayerful intercessor for their good. This angle of Amos' prophecy was left out of Amaziah's report to the king.

"In the beginning of the shooting up of the latter growth ... after the king's mowings ..." It is not clear, exactly what custom is referred to in the second phrase here; and the scholars have no agreement about what is meant; but the meaning is clear enough: the threatened locust plague occurred at exactly the right time to have done the maximum damage.

It is agreed by all that the language here is figurative, and that the locust plague stands for some terrible threatened disaster in the past which God had averted. It is certain that the visions do not stand for something that actually happened, but for that which appeared to be impending and did not occur. Nor do they refer to the ultimate judgment which would actually befall Israel, a fate strongly predicted by other words and other visions. As Harper said, "These visions are not premonitions of coming disaster."[6] In a sense, these first two visions are the prophet's revelation that the abyss had yawned underneath Israel repeatedly during the course of the chosen people's ceaseless rebellions against God, and that again, and again God's mercy had spared the impending punishment, or rather deferred it; for it would yet occur anyway unless Israel repented. It may not be wise therefore to limit the application of the vision to some single instance of such a relenting; and yet it is doubtless true that there were historical instances of such a a thing known to all. Deane thought that, "The vision is thought to refer to the first invasion of the Assyrians, when Pul was bribed by Menahem to withdraw."[7] Certainly, such a view does no violence to the text. It was a very efficient and fruitful device to represent all such deliverances which had rescued Israel from threatened disasters in the past under the figure of a locust plague, which in Palestine, is a *recurring* phenomenon.

Verses 2,3, And it came to pass when they made an end of eating the grass of the land, then I said, O Lord Jehovah,

---

[6]W.R. Harper, *op. cit.*, p. 164.

[7]W.J. Deane, *Pulpit Commentary, Vol. 14, Amos* (Grand Rapids: Wm. B. Eerdmans Publishing Company, 1950), p. 137.

forgive, I beseech thee: how shall Jacob stand? for he is small. Jehovah repented concerning this: It shall not be, saith Jehovah.

Foremost in this is the prayer of the prophet with the resulting deliverance of the people. It would appear to be obvious that the reason for the inclusion of these visions by Amos, visions which he had actually had, in his proclamations against Bethel, is that of disarming any suspicion that the people might have entertained to the effect that Amos hoped for, or desired, any calamity to befall them. On the other hand, he was the source of prayers which had actually averted disasters from them many times in the past.

"Jehovah repented . . ." Such expressions in the scriptures do not imply any instability, fickleness, or indecision on the part of God, his repentance always meaning that some justifying change had occurred in the threatened people themselves.

"When they made an end of eating the grass of the land . . ." This indicates that the disasters which had been averted through prayer were not *totally* avoided, but that they were interrupted and averted before fatal damage was inflicted. This would fit the interpretation of such things by Deane who cited one of them thus:

> This refers to the retreat of the Assyrians under Pul, the usurping monarch who assumed the name of Tiglath-Peleser II (2 Kings 15:17ff). Some commentators consider this judgment to be literally a plague of locusts; but this is not probable.[8]

Verses 4-6, Thus the Lord Jehovah showed me: and, behold, the Lord Jehovah called to contend by fire; and it devoured the great deep, and would have eaten up the land. Then said I, O Lord Jehovah, cease, I beseech thee: how shall Jacob stand? for he is small. Jehovah repented concerning this: This shall not be, saith the Lord Jehovah.

No matter how this vision is understood, the meaning of it is exactly that of the preceding vision, namely, great

---

[8]*Ibid.*, p. 138.

disasters threatening Israel, and yet being averted through the intercession of the prophet. Since it was a *vision*, it could have been a fire so great that it burned up the sea (the "great deep"),[9] and even the earth itself was threatened, carrying with it suggestions of the great and final Judgment Day itself. "This is not for Amos a naturalistic vision. This is the supernatural fire of the Lord's judgment."[10] There is certainly nothing wrong with this interpretation. Some scholars, however perhaps overlooking the fact that this is a *vision*, have interpreted it naturalistically, making it, "A drouth so intense that the great subterranean depths which supply the springs and streams with water dried up."[11] It really makes no difference at all which view is taken; the message is the same either way. It would appear that the vision's being that of a supernatural event is preferable. Keil understood the fire as, "not an earthly fire, but the fire of the wrath of God";[12] and Barnes thought that the destruction of the sea by fire (in the vision) was a symbol of, "The fire of the Day of Judgment."[13] Schultz and others insist that it is "the summer heat."[14] Refer to the interpretation of the first vision, above, for the meaning here; for it is identical with this. Regarding some particular historical situation that may, along with others, be symbolized by this, Dean has:

> The particular calamity alluded to is the second invasion of Tiglath-Pelese II, when he conquered Gilead and the northern part of the kingdom, and carried some of the people captive to Assyria (2 Kings 15:29).[15]

The spiritual overtones of the passage describing these two visions are definite and impressive; and the introduction of what appeared to be a threat of the final judgment itself is a strong suggestion that all of the great punitive

---

[9]Erling Hammershaimb, *op. cit.*, p. 110.
[10]Henry McKeating, *op. cit.*, p. 55.
[11]W.R. Harper, *op. cit.*, p. 164.
[12]C.F. Keil, *Commentary on the Whole Bible* (Grand Rapids: Wm. B. Eerdmans Publishing Company), p. 309.
[13]Albert Barnes, *Notes on the OT, Minor Prophets, Vol. 1* (Grand Rapids: Baker Book House, 1953), p. 317.
[14]Arnold C. Schultz, *WBC* (Chicago: Moody Press, 1962), p. 835.
[15]W.J. Deane, *op. cit.*, p. 139.

judgments of God upon rebellious humanity are typical of
the ultimate and final judgment that will be executed at the
Last Day. Mankind should never forget that the entire race
of Adam's posterity are still living under the primeval sentence of death imposed in Genesis 2:17, a sentence which
was never vacated or repealed, but only deferred, and is yet
destined to be executed in its fulness upon humanity. There
are surely overtones of that in the passage before us.

**Verse 7, Thus he showed me: and, behold, the Lord stood
beside a wall made by a plumb-line, with a plumb-line in his
hand.**

The proper understanding of this vision must include the
recognition that the plumb-line was a symbol both of building and of destruction, the plumb-line symbolizing the testing required for the construction of a sound building, and
for revealing those defects that required the destruction of
a building. The figure elaborated in this vision, "represents
the Lord himself as coming to examine the conduct of
Israel, and finally deciding upon its entire ruin."[16] In this
vision, "Amos makes no prayer, and Yahweh, on his part,
confirms the meaning with an interpretative oracle."[17] It is
significant that the same plumb-line used to build Israel
was that which was used in their destruction. "By that law,
that right, those Providential leadings, and that grace
which we have received, by the same we are judged."[18]

**Verse 8, And Jehovah said unto me, Amos, what seest
thou? And I said, A plumb-line. Then said the Lord, Behold,
I will set a plumb-line in the midst of my people Israel; I
will not again pass by them any more.**

The direct conversation which Amos here mentions as
occurring between himself and the Lord was probably for
the purpose of emphasizing the truth that Amaziah later
ignored in his message to the king, namely, that the words
of denunciation uttered by the prophet were not his words
at all, but the words of the true God of Israel.

---

[16]*Ibid.*
[17]J.A. Motyer, *NBCR* (Grand Rapids: Wm. B. Eerdmans Publishing Company, 1979), p. 738.
[18]Albert Barnes, *op. cit.*, p. 318.

"A plumb-line in the midst of my people Israel . . ." This was an ominous promise:

> The plumb-line was used not only in building, but in destroying houses (2 Kings 21:13, Isaiah 28:17, 34:11, and Lamentation 2:8). It denotes that God's judgments are measured out by the most exact rules of justice.[19]

"I will not again pass by them any more . . ." Again, the clear reference to the ancient Passover is evident; only, this time, he will not do a similar thing. As Smith said:

> The word *pass by* here and in 5:17 was probably deliberately used by Amos (rather, *by the Lord*) to represent the reversal of the "passover" when God passed through Egypt in judgment, but delivered Israel (Exodus 12:23).[20]

Through the passage of time, the word *passover* had come to have somewhat the same meaning as *forgiveness*. As Motyer noted, "The phrase *pass by*, used again at 8:2, appears in Micah 7:18 in the meaning 'to forgive.' "[21]

Before leaving this passage, it should be noted that some allegations commonly made regarding this passage should be rejected. "In spite of his plans to punish Israel, for Yahweh they will always remain his beloved and chosen people."[22] As regards the secular, fleshly descendants of Abraham, nothing could be further wrong that such a view, except in its unique application to the true Israel of God, the church of Jesus Christ. That the rebellious and grossly wicked children of Abraham in the fleshly sense whose notorious rebellions against God and all righteousness are the burden of the entire OT, and who climaxed their unrighteousness by the murder of the Son of God himself— that *that* people are, in some sense, still "the chosen people of God" is a monstrous error.

---

[19]Robert Jamieson, *JFB* (Grand Rapids: Zondervan Publishing House, 1961), p. 798.

[20]Ralph L. Smith, *BBC* (Nashville: Broadman Press, 1972), p. 126.

[21]J.A. Motyer, *op. cit.*, p. 738.

[22]Erling Hammershaimb, *op. cit.*, p. 112.

Verse 9, And the high places of Isaac shall be desolate, and the sanctuaries of Israel shall be laid waste; and I will rise against the house of Jeroboam with the sword.

"The high places of Isaac . . ." "Isaac" is here a title of Israel, as the parallel in the next line shows. It is not the religious conduct of the patriarch Isaac that is under indictment here, but that of the Northern Kingdom. The amazing notion current among many scholars to the effect that there was nothing wrong with those shrines which the rebellious people had built upon the very sites of the old pagan shrines that once were there before Israel came into the land could not possibly be correct. Some of the patriarchs indeed had been associated with some of those places, through events that marked their lives; and, no doubt, the paganized priesthood of Jeroboam's Israel had, from such premises, alleged the legitimacy of their shrines; it was, nevertheless, a deception. Harper's opinion that, "Down to the days of Josiah, the nation worshipped Yahweh regularly and legitimately upon the so-called high places,"[23] cannot be allowed, the sole reason for the shrine of Bethel, for example, having been Jeroboam's repudiation of God's true religion and the institution of another, as a political device to establish his throne. "Even the priesthood which Jeroboam I appointed was absolutely illegitimate (1 Kings 12:31f)."[24] This latter fact was one of the gross sins of Israel that would be exposed by God's plumb-line, of which Thorogood gives this excellent definition:

> First, He was using the Law which he had given to the Israelites long before, as the standard of their faith and conduct. Secondly, He was using the prophets, such as Amos . . . Their preaching was a standard by which the Israelites could judge their own lives.[25]

One false idea which is almost invariably associated with these vigorous condemnations is expressed as follows, "Amos also taught that the most elaborate worship, if

---

[23]W.R. Harper, *op. cit.*, p. 168.
[24]Erling Hammershaimb, *op. cit.*, p. 112.
[25]Bernard Thorogood, *A Guide to the Book of Amos* (Valley Forge: Judson Press, 1971), p. 80.

insincere, is but an insult to God.''[26] This is true enough, except for the implication that, if the worship of the Israelites of the Northern Kingdom at the pagan shrines of Dan, Bethel and other high places had been "sincere" it would have been acceptable to God; and this is not the case at all. As Christ himself declared, "In vain do ye worship me, teaching for doctrines the commandments of men" (Matthew 15:9). This applies pointedly to the very thing that characterized the worship in the Northern Kingdom; it was founded on practically nothing that God commanded, but was built altogether upon traditional, pagan and opportunistic practices.

"The sanctuaries of Israel shall be laid waste . . ." This refers to the, "idol-temples at Dan and Bethel (1 Kings 12:29), at Gilgal (ch. 4:4), and perhaps in other places."[26] It was not merely the social indifference and oppression of the poor, and not merely a matter of their insincerity, but their whole rotten system of gross paganism, garnished and embellished with a few trappings from God's true religion, that was marked for destruction here. Furthermore, not merely the overthrow of false religion would occur, but also the overthrow of the evil dynasty that had initiated it, and the whole people of that evil generation which had received and revelled in the false religion.

"And I will rise against the house of Jeroboam with the sword . . ." As Keil pointed out, this is a reference to the dynasty of Jeroboam I, "but not to be restricted to the overthrow of his dynasty, but an announcement of the destruction of the Israelitish monarchy."[27] Three things should be noted, no special king is mentioned here, but *a dynasty,* such being the meaning of "the house of Jeroboam"; secondly, this is something which God promised to do, not Amos; and in the third place, the name, or identity of any ruler to be killed by the sword was definitely not mentioned.

Verses 10,11, Then Amaziah, the priest of Bethel sent to Jeroboam king of Israel, saying, Amos hath conspired

---

[26]George L. Robinson, *The Twelve Minor Prophets, a 1979 reprint of a 1926 copyright* (Grand Rapids: Baker Book House), p. 56.

[27]C.F. Keil, *op. cit.,* p. 311.

against thee in the midst of the house of Israel: the land is
not able to bear his words. For thus Amos saith, Jeroboam
shall die by the sword, and Israel shall surely be led away
captive out of his land.

"Amaziah . . ." Nothing has been seen any more astounding than the argument from this pagan priests' name that
he was a true priest of God! "His name (*Yahweh* is strong) is
compounded with Yahweh and would indicate that the sanctuaries of Israel maintained the worship of Yahweh."[28] The
same kind of argument would prove that the great NT
preacher Apollos was a worshipper of Apollo. One can
hardly understand the tenderness of so many commentators with regard to that utterly pagan and depraved worship of the Israelites.

These two verses (10-11) are the first of a three-fold division of this last section of the chapter, and relates to Amaziah's report to the king. The other two are: Amaziah's
taking matters into his own hands (vv. 12-13), and Amos'
answer to Amaziah (vv. 14-17). The whole passage is one of
remarkable strength and effectiveness. Smith's quotation
from George Adam Smith is appropriate:

> It "is one of the great scenes of history." It reports
> the conflict between a priest who spoke for and with
> the authority of a king, and a prophet who delivered
> the word of God.[29]

"Jeroboam shall die by the sword . . ." Incredibly, some
have defended this slander upon the basis that, "it is basically correct."[30] Indeed no! On the contrary, it is a base and
unprincipled lie. As the Catholic Bible puts it:

> The prophet did not say this, but "that the Lord
> would rise up against the house of Jeroboam with the
> sword," as was verified when Zacharias, son and suc-
> cessor of Jeroboam, was slain with the sword.[31]

[28]J. Keir Howard, *NLBC* (Grand Rapids: Zondervan Publishing House,
1979), p. 968.
[29]Ralph L. Smith, *op. cit.*, p. 127.
[30]Erling Hammershaimb, *op. cit.*, p. 115.
[31]*Catholic Edition of the Holy Bible* (New York: Catholic Book Publishing
Company, 1949), footnote on page 990.

Amaziah's report was false for these reasons:

1. It falsely reported who was to be killed.
2. It falsely attributed the prediction to Amos, instead of the Lord.
3. It is false in that it omitted any mention of the sins of Israel which were the reason for this prophecy.
4. It is false in that it made no mention of any call to repentance, or to the hope extended if they did repent.

If this report is "basically correct," it would be interesting to see one that was "basically in error!"

Note particularly the point in Amos' preaching at which this rude interrruption by the pagan priest occurred. Neither of the first two visions occasioned any objection from Amaziah, for they were accounts of deliverances which God had extended to Israel; but this third vision, which was a bold and thundering prophecy of the immediate and impending doom of the whole nation, to be effected by the overthrow of the monarchy, the destruction of the sanctuaries, and the captivity of the whole nation, aroused the "highpriest" of Bethel to action, which issued in his sending a hasty message to the king, and then, apparently not waiting for any authority, nevertheless took what action he could against Amos without any authority. It would appear that Amaziah had been listening to all that Amos said.

Some have found it amazing that Jeroboam II is not represented here as taking any action whatever against Amos; and we believe that this is evidence enough that he took none, a conclusion that might seem incredible. However, this man, Jeroboam II, had evidently known personally the prophet Jonah, upon whose prophecies he had relied when he came to the throne, and in accordance with which he had won the great military triumphs which had led so disastrously to the sin and overconfidence of Israel. Jeroboam's respect for the prophetic office must, therefore, have been very considerable. In this light, Jamieson's conclusion is reasonable, "The king, however, did not give ear to Amaziah, probably from religious awe of the prophet of

Jehovah."[32] Barnes was also of this opinion, pointing out that Jeroboam would also have had knowledge "of the true prophecies of Elisha with reference to the successes of his father, Jeroboam I."[23] The action of Amaziah in himself, taking the authority to forbid Amos to speak and ordering him to leave the country, does not nullify this; because it is exactly the kind of conduct one might have anticipated in a time-serving self-seeking pagan priest like Amaziah. The next subsection of this episode presents Amaziah's action against Amos.

Verses 12,13, Also Amaziah said unto Amos, O thou seer, go flee thou away into the land of Judah, and there eat bread, and prophecy there: but prophecy not again any more at Bethel; for it is the king's sanctuary, and it is a royal house.

"O seer, go flee thou away. . ." It is puzzling why so many find nothing contemptuous or patronizing in such a statement as this, for there would appear to be plenty of both. It is true, of course, that some have made "seer" in every way a synonym of prophet; but there were "seers" by the hundreds in antiquity who were of the devil. The word also carries the thought captured by McFadden's paraphrase of it as, "Thou visionary,"[34] which, in the light of the visions Amaziah had just been hearing from Amos, would seem to be accurate. Dummelow was doubtless correct in his equating the words of Amaziah here with, "the proverbial saying, 'eat your pudding slave, and hold your tongue.' "[35]

"Eat bread, and prophecy there . . ." the implications of this are a gross reflection upon Amaziah himself, as many have pointed out. He did not recognize any such thing as a truly prophetic office; to him *all prophets* were concerned merely with what they could get out of it, this being a perfect reflection of his own character. The argument he makes, to the extent that there is any, is that Judah would

---

[32]Robert Jamieson, *op. cit.*, p. 799.
[33]Albert Barnes, *op. cit.*, p. 320.
[34]John Edgar McFadden, *op. cit.*, p. 100.
[35]J.R. Dummelow, *Commentary on the Holy Bible* (New York: The Macmillan Company, 1937), p. 570.

pay more for prophecies against Israel than could be received for such prophecies being delivered in Israel itself! The expression "eat bread" means "make your living," "peddle your wares," or "do your thing" in Judah, and not at Bethel.

"It is the king's sanctuary..." "It was founded by the king (1 Kings 12:28), and not by God; so, in truth, it had only an earthly sanction,"[36] although it may be doubted that Amaziah noticed the self-convicting admission of these words. There is a world of difference in God's sanctuary and the king's sanctuary. Barnes said that in three places only in the OT is the alleged sanctuary of God called the sanctuary of Israel, here, and in Lamentations 1:10, and Leviticus 26:31.[37] Christ likewise designated the Jewish temple in Jerusalem (Matthew 24:38), "Behold, your house is left unto you desolate."

The balance of this chapter is comprised of Amos' undaunted response to Amaziah's peevish and blasphemous efforts to thwart the prophet's holy mission, namely, that of turning Israel to repentance before it would be everlastingly too late. It appeas that Amos was in no way intimidated or silenced by Amaziah's ill-advised interruption.

Verse 14, Then answered Amos, and said to Amaziah, I was no prophet, neither was I a prophet's son; but I was a herdsman, and a dresser of sycamore trees.

This was levelled squarely at Amaziah's unjust charge, by implication, that Amos was a cheap "seer" picking up a little money where he might for prophesying against Israel, there being also some implications in Amos' reply, namely, that the regular line of prophets, especially those identified as "the sons of the prophets," i.e., those attending the prophetic schools and following the traditions that many of them followed, were indeed the same type of "seer" with whom Amaziah sneeringly sought to identify Amos.

"I was no prophet ..." The past tense is vital to this verse, for in no sense whatever was it Amos' purpose here to deny his divine commission and calling as a true prophet

---

[36]W.J. Deane, *op. cit.*, p. 139.
[37]Albert Barnes, *op. cit.*, p. 321.

of the Almighty God. We may only deplore the fact that both the RSV and the NEB, by rendering the verb here in the present, "I am no prophet, etc.," put in Amos' mouth a denial of the very thing he so emphatically affirmed in verse 15 (next). To be sure, the passage could be rendered in either fashion. "The doubt about the tense arises because in Hebrew the verb is not expressed, but left to be understood."[38] Smith included this further explanation:

> The Hebrew language often used nominal sentences without verbs. In such a case, the tense of the verb was usually supplied by adopting that of the previous verb. If that principle were followed in this case, the past tense would be required, "I was no prophet."[39]

Our own choice of the ASV for these studies is due to the fact of there being in it strong evidence of a much greater respect for considerations of this kind than is evident in other versions.

Rowley's paraphrase of these verses was given thus by Hammershaimb:

> It is not money I prophecy for; I am a prophet by divine constraint. I had not chosen the calling of a prophet, or trained to be a prophet. God laid his hand upon me, and charged me with his word, and I have delivered it where he constrained me to deliver it.[40]

"Dresser of sycamore trees . . ." "The phrase *boles shiqmim* may mean either one who plucks mulberry-figs for his own sustenance, or one who cultivates them for others."[41] Dean thought it was the latter in the case of Amos, and Keil believed it was the other. We do not know. In any event, it was a humble calling.

Verse 15, And Jehovah took me from following the flock, and Jehovah said unto me, Go prophesy unto my people Israel.

---

[38]Henry McKeating, *op. cit.*, p. 58.
[39]Ralph L. Smith, *op. cit.*, p. 128.
[40]Erling Hammershaimb, *op. cit.*, p. 117, footnote.
[41]W.J. Deane, *op. cit.*, p. 139.

The acceptance of such a commission meant that Amos was no longer his own master, and that not even the words he was to deliver were to be his own, but the true word of God. Thus it has ever been with the true prophet or apostle. See Number 22:38, Jeremiah 20:9, and Acts 4:19-20. Therefore, "Whoever sought to oppose the message of Amos opposed the Most High God."[42] Thus, Amaziah, in his opposition to Amos, had rebelled against God's word; and therefore, God, through Amos, spoke a prophecy of doom against Amaziah. We may not, therefore, interpret Amos' rejoinder here as the mere "venting of his spite" against the priest of Bethel.

Verse 16, Now therefore hear thou the word of Jehovah: Thou sayest, Prophesy not against Israel, and drop not thy word against the house of Isaac.

"Drop not thy word . . ." Dummelow seems to have captured the thought behind this second clause thus: "Don't let it drip, drip, drip, in imbecile and wearisome fashion (Micah 2:6,11, and Ezekiel 21:2,7)."[43] Harper, and others, rejected this view: "The word does not carry with it any contemptuous idea";[44] but the idea, especially in English, is certainly there; furthermore, it fits the context perfectly.

Before leaving this verse, the rendition of this in the Catholic Bible seems pertinent and is included. It has, "Thou shalt not drop thy word upon the house of the idol (instead of "the house of Isaac.")."[45] Their authority for this rendition is not cited, and it certainly could be wrong; but, regardless of that, it properly identifies that "house" at Bethel!

Verse 17, Therefore thus saith Jehovah: Thy wife will be a harlot in the city, and thy sons and thy daughters shall fall by the sword, and thy land shall be divided by line; and thou thyself shalt die in a land that is unclean, and Israel shall surely be led away captive out of his land.

[42]Paul T. Butler, *op. cit.*, p. 350.
[43]J.R. Dummelow, *op. cit.*, p. 570.
[44]W.R. Harper, *op. cit.*, p. 173.
[45]Catholic Bible, *op. cit.*, p. 990.

This terrible prophecy against Amaziah was doubltess fulfilled exactly, as were all the other prophecies, the evident truth and divine origin of them being the primary reason that the prophecy of Amos has survived some 27 centuries of human history. It is a perpetual memorial to the grand truth that what God prophesies through his prophets will surely come to pass.

"Thy wife will be a harlot . . ." Such a result as this would have been an inevitable consequence of the great military disaster that loomed upon the horizon of the doomed people:

> Rape of women, slaying of youth, partition of property among the victors, and exile of the leaders were all part of the ordinary treatment of a conquered people by the victorious invaders.[46]

It is not necessary to assume that Amaziah's wife willingly became a harlot of the city, although some have assumed that she did. What seems more likely is that, violated by the soldiers of Assyria, and left behind with the residue of the people after the deportation, she could have had no other means of sustenance.

"Thy sons and thy daughters . . ." That these were not mentioned as among those to be "carried away," is likely because they were too young to have any value as slaves, or as objects of gratification; and they were therefore brutally slain by the heartless invaders.

"Thy land shall be divided by line . . ." that is, parcelled out as "booty" among those, including some of the soldiery, with whom the Assyrians repopulated the land.

"Thou thyself shall die in a land that is unclean . . ." This referred to any land where God was not worshipped, and where paganism was established, here, meaning the land of the Assyrians; and here is powerful evidence that the "repentance" of Ninevah under the preaching of Jonah produced no lasting changes in the character of the fierce, sadistic, and bloodthirsty Assyrians.

---

[46]Hughell E.W. Fosbroke, *IB, Vol. VI* (New York: Abingdon Press, 1957), p. 837.

Behold in this terrible fate of Amaziah the utter worth-
lessness of a false religion. The trouble in Israel was not
merely their "insincerity" in their worship, and not even
their "oppression of the poor," which is made out by most
modern commentators to be the sum and substance of all
that was wrong; but it was their total departure from the
word of God in (1) setting up shrines without divine authority, (2) commissioning priests who according to the Law of
Moses were not legitimate, (3) installing idols, such as the
golden calves of Jereboam, (4) polluting their worship
through the burning of "leavened bread" to produce an
aromatic smell, (5) omitting all sin-offerings, as if they were
not sinners, (6) introducing the unauthorized instruments
of music "like David," (7) committing fornication after the
ancient pagan rites observed by the followers of Baal, and
doing it in the very shrines and lying down by every altar (!)
in Israel "upon the clothing" extorted from the poor, (8)
drinking wine out of sacred vessels dedicated to God's
service, etc. The very suggestion that a tender regard for
the poor and a deep sincerity on the part of the people could
have sanctified and legitimatized such a bastard religion as
that is an affront to all that is written in the holy scriptures.
The religion by which men hope to receive and retain the
favor of Almighty God must be something far more than a
sensitive humanism with reference to the common needs
and sufferings of mankind, and something far more than a
"sincere" following of and participation in some traditional
system of worship. Just as ancient Israel had a plumb-line,
by which they could have measured, corrected, and con-
structed a proper and obedient faith, our own generation
has the same privilege, that plumb-line, of course, being the
teaching of the Word of God. Despite this, many, it would
appear, are still making the same fatal mistake as that of
the ancient Israelites.

As Smith said:

Amaziah undoubtedly felt secure behind the defenses of Samaria and the religious observances at
Bethel. He erred in considering the word of God to be
just the word of a man and in failing to examine himself and his society (and may we add: *and his religion*)

in light of the covenant privileges and responsibilities.[47]

The word of the Lord endureth for ever; and it is our humble prayer that the Lord's followers may never forsake that holy word.

[47]Ralph L. Smith, *op. cit.*, p. 129.

CHAPTER 8

Amos, having effectively disposed of the interruption by Amaziah, proceeded to deliver his sermon. The first four visions actually occur in pairs, the two first being of disasters averted through prayer, and the nest two announcing the summary and forthcoming end of Israel, the first of these (the third) having already been delivered. This fourth one, therefore (1-3) is not a recapitulation of the third, nor the introduction of any startling new element. Amos' denunciation continued as if nothing had occurred. "Notwithstanding the interference of Amaziah, the prophet finishes the recital of his visions."[1] Deane outlined the chapter thus: (1) the vision of the basket of the summer fruit (1-3), (2) The denunciation of the dealers (4-10), and (3) the warning of a famine of hearing God's word and a wandering all over the earth by Israel (11-14).[2]

This fourth vision cannot be, therefore, a mere "reassertion of the thought contained in the third vision, which had been interrupted."[3] We may safely reject such allegations as, "these verses were inserted by a later editor of the book,"[4] based upon the bizarre and unfounded proposition that, "Amos had been imprisoned and executed,"[5] etc. As Smith has noted:

> If Amos did not flee from Amaziah; and there is almost no reason to conclude that he did, it is conceivable that he stayed at Bethel to deliver the last two vision reports and the oracles that went with them.[6]

---

[1]J.R. Dummelow, *Commentary on the Holy Bible* (New York: The Macmillan Company, 1937), p. 570.

[2]W.J. Deane, *Pulpit Commentary, Vol. 14, Amos* (Grand Rapids: Wm. B. Eerdmans Publishing Company, 1950), p. 157.

[3]W.R. Harper, *Amos & Hosea* (New York: Charles Scribner's Sons, 1910), p. 175.

[4]Bernard Thorogood, *A Guide to the Book of Amos* (Valley Forge: Judson Press, 1971), p. 85.

[5]Rolland Emerson Wolfe, *Meet Amos & Hosea* (New York: Harper & Bros., 1945), p. 60.

[6]Ralph L. Smith, *BBC* (Nashville: Broadman Press, 1972), p. 130.

Not only is such a thing "conceivable"; but it is clearly and logically an almost mandatory conclusion. We would amend Smith's admission that there is "almost no reason" to conclude otherwise with an affirmation that there is "no reason whatever" against this.

Verses 1-3, And thus the Lord Jehovah showed me: and, behold, a basket of summer fruit. And he said, Amos, what seest thou? And I said, A basket of summer fruit. Then said Jehovah unto me, The end is come upon my people Israel; I will not again pass by them any more. And the songs of the temple shall be wailings in that day, saith the Lord Jehovah: the dead bodies shall be many; in every place shall they cast them forth with silence.

This is the vision of the basket of summer fruit, the fourth vision in Amos' sequence.

"A basket of summer fruit ..." Despite this translation being widely received, there is, nevertheless, some question about it. Most commentators and translators are greatly impressed with what they see as a kind of pun in the similarities between the Hebrew word for "basket" and their word for "end."[7] But the Hebrew word from which this is translated actually means "a receiver"[8] and might just as well be translated "hook" for plucking, or receiving the fruit from the tree. The Catholic Bible gives it that meaning: "And behold a hook to draw down fruit."[9] In either case, the meaning is essentially the same, namely that the ripeness of the fruit signals the end of its cycle. Motyer commented that, "The harvest metaphor is well suited to the passage. The crop comes to harvest as the climax of its own inner development."[10]

"The end is come upon my people Israel ..." "The harvest is past and the summer is ended; and we are not saved" (Jeremiah 8:20), was the plaintive cry of Jeremiah; and the same sad extremity is in view here.

[7]Bernard Thorogood, *op. cit.*, p. 85.

[8]C.F. Keil, *Commentary on the Whole Bible* (Grand Rapids: Wm. B. Eerdmans Publishing Company), p. 314.

[9]*The Catholic Edition of the Holy Bible* (New York: Catholic Book Publishing Company, 1949), p. 990.

[10]J.A. Motyer, *NBCR* (Grand Rapids: Wm. B. Eerdmans Publishing Company, 1979), p. 738.

"I will not again pass by them any more . . ." As repeatedly in Amos, there is an indirect allusion to the passover experience of the children of Israel in Egypt when God "passed over" them and spared them from disaster; but this can no longer be expected. The people are ripe for judgment and destruction. See under 7:8, above.

"The songs of the temple shall be wailings . . ." Here again the translation should be corrected, as in the NEB,[11] to "the palace," instead of "the temple." The Jerusalem edifice is not in view here at all, as it is particularly the sins of the Northern Kingdom that are under consideration. The mistranslation is quite understandable, since the Hebrew text actually has a "Great House," which might mean either the temple, or the palace of the king. "The word came to the Hebrews from Babylonia, and literally signifies 'Great House.' "[12]

"The dead bodies . . . many, etc . . . silence . . ." This verse is rendered differently in several versions; and Fosbroke complained that, "The phrasing is abrupt, disjointed, and with no discernible grammatical construction," but, in spite of this, went on to state that even as the text stands, "it presents effectively the horrors of the aftermath of war, or possibly of pestilence."[13] We appreciate what McKeating said; "Amos seems to specialize in these fragmentary pictures, whose very lack of clarity makes them the more menacing."[14] Hammershaimb rendered the Hebrew text literally as, "The dead bodies are many! in every place one throws out, silence!"[15]

The most pertinent of all comment upon these verses is that of the word of God itself, thus:

But if thy heart turn away, and thou wilt not hear, but shall be drawn away, and worship other gods, and serve them; I denounce unto you this day, that ye shall

[11]Henry McKeating, *CBC, Amos, Hosea & Micah* (Cambridge: At the University Press, 1971), p. 59.
[12]J.R. Dummelow, *op. cit.*, p. 570.
[13]Hughell E.W. Fosbroke, *IB, Vol. VI* (New York: Abingdon Press, 1957), p. 838.
[14]Henry McKeating, *op. cit.*, p. 60.
[15]Erling Hammershaimb, *The Book of Amos, translated by John Sturdy* (New York: Shocken Books, 1970), p. 121.

surely perish: ye shall not prolong your days in the land, whither thou passest over the Jordan to go in to possess it. I call heaven and earth to witness against you this day, that I have set before thee life and death, the blessing and the curse: therefore choose life, that thou mayest live, and thy seed; to love Jehovah thy God, to obey his voice, and to cleave unto him; for he is thy life, and the length of thy days; that thou mayest dwell in the land which Jehovah sware unto thy fathers, to Abraham, to Issac, and to Jacob, to give them (Deuteronomy 30:17-20).

Prominent in that warning was the prohibition against worshipping other gods; and this was preeminently the sin which Israel had committed.

Verse 4, Hear this, O ye that would swallow up the needy, and cause the poor of the land to fail.

Well, what has this to do with worshipping other gods? It was a condition brought about by the rejection on the part of Israel of the allocation of the land on the basis of inheritance, in order to prevent the very type of landed aristocracy with a heartless disregard of the poor, which had replaced the theocratic arrangement given by the Lord when Israel entered Canaan. Their rebellion against God by their rejection of the theocracy and the elevation of a monarch, "like the nations surrounding them," was the beginning of their sorrows. What is in view in this verse is the end result and ripened fruit of that original departure from the word of God.

Verse 5, Saying, When will the new moon be gone, that we may sell grain? and the sabbath, that we may set forth wheat, making the ephah small, and the shekel great, and dealing falsely with balances of deceit?

The heartless traders grudged even the sabbaths and feast days as interruptions in their business, which was simply that of cheating in every way possible. There had already come to its fruition in the Northern Kingdom, the diabolical sin that eventually culminated in the Jerusalem

temple, designated by Jesus as "a den of thieves and robbers."

"The new moon . . ." The feast of the new moon was
allegedly derived from the commandment of God to offer
sacrifices upon the first of each month (Numbers 28:11); but
that is a far different thing from "worshipping the host of
heaven" in any such thing as a feast of the new moon. That
this feast (evidently of pagan origin) did creep into Jewish
worship is clear enough, evidently having been introduced
and established by King David (1 Chronicles 23:31), which
in the light of other things that David did still leaves the
practice questionable. We believe this is a clear instance in
which it came to pass as declared by the martyr Stephen,
"That God turned, and gave them up to serve the host of
heaven" (Acts 7:42).

While the sabbath day was indeed a legitimate religious
day, the same was not true of the "new moons"; and thus
we have another example of the gross departure of Israel
from their duty.

The Hebrews had *twelve months*; and thus there is no
question of the first of each month falling upon the feast of
the new moon as would (or might) have occurred had the
Israelites been following a lunar month.

"Making the ephah small . . ." Amazingly, of the dozen or
so commentaries consulted on this, no two of them give the
same size to the *ephah!* Harper noted that: "The size is not
definitely known, being estimated at from 21.26 quarts to
40.62 quarts (Josephus)."[16]

"And the shekel great . . ." Coinage was unknown till a
later period; and weights were used for weighing the
amount of silver, or other substance, used as the medium of
exchange. Of course, if a dishonest tradesman used one set
of weights for buying, and another set of weights for selling
(neither of them being *true*), he would be able easily to
defraud his customers. A similar deceit was used with regard to the ephah, a fact demonstrated by the truth that,
until this day, nobody knows for sure what an ephah was!
They were indeed a vicious class of robbers, exactly like
those that Jesus ran out of the temple during his ministry.

---

[16]W.R. Harper, *op. cit.*, p. 178.

"And dealing falsely with the balances of deceit . . ."
These were dishonest scales, indicating that current laws in
every civilized state regarding weights and measurements,
and the necessity of inspecting the scales in stores and
markets continually, is anchored in the long experience of
the human race with the very practices condemned here by
the prophet Amos.

Before leaving this verse, the question at the beginning of
it should be noted, for it was that question which Amos
answered in verse 9: *"When will the new moon be gone . . .
and the sabbath . . .?"*

**Verse 6, That we may buy the poor for silver, and the
needy for a pair of shoes, and sell the refuse of the wheat?**

This reference to buying the poor for silver, etc., is probably a reference to forcing the poor into slavery, through
their unjust laws, due to their having defaulted upon some
minor and trifling debt.

"Sell the refuse of the wheat . . ." This is a third device
pointed out in this passage, used for swindling and defraud-
ing the customer. They were: (1) false measurements, (2)
false scales, and (3) delivery of inferior merchandise. The
refuse of the wheat was hardly fit for animals, as it was
derived from the sweepings of the threshing floors; but
these unscrupulous rascals were delivering it to the poor
instead of the good merchandise which they were paying
for. The corruption of the judicial system left them no
recourse, and no respite, from such crooked dealers.

**Verse 7, Jehovah hath sworn by the excellency of Jacob,
Surely, I will never forget any of their works.**

Barnes understood this as the equivalent of "God's
swearing by himself, since God was, in fact, the true excellency, or glory of Jacob (1 Samuel 15:29)."[17] In all likelihood,
this is the true meaning of the passage; but there is another
view which also has much to commend it. McKeating wrote
that Amos' intention here is "ironic. One swears by what is
fixed and unalterable, hence 'by Jacob's monumental

[17]Albert Barnes, *Notes on the OT, Minor Prophets, Vol. 1* (Grand Rapids:
Baker Book House, 1953), p. 325.

pride.' "[18] The Catholic Bible renders the place: "The Lord hath sworn against the pride of Jacob," etc.[19] Harper supported the second view, thus:

> Although Yahweh himself is Israel's glory (1 Samuel 15:29), the author of 6:8 could hardly have described Yahweh as "the glory of Jacob": it is rather the vainglorious boasting of Israel, by which, as an unchangeable fact, Yahweh swears scornfully.[20]

However the passage may be understood, or interpreted, the fact of God's utmost displeasure with the Northern Kingdom stands sharply in focus.

Verse 8, Shall not the land tremble for this, and every one mourn that dwelleth therein? yea, it shall rise up wholly like the River; and it shall be troubled and sink again, like the River of Egypt.

It seems rather strange to compare the trembling of the earth with the rising and falling of the Nile River (as most interpret this), "because the rise and fall of the Nile River are quite gradual."[21] However, since the devastation caused by the Nile at flood ("rising some 20')[22] was tremendous, it is an apt figure of the overwhelming destruction in store for Israel. Thus, it would appear better to understand "tremble" as a metaphor for such a disaster, instead of "literally" as an earthquake, which does not seem to be indicated at all. There may be something else here. Dummelow pointed out the fact followed by most interpreters that the word for "River" used in this place is regularly employed for the Nile";[23] but Barnes noted that, "It is the Egyptian name for river which Israel brought with them out of Egypt, and is used either for the Nile, or for one of the artificial trenches derived from it,"[24] hence, by extension (through time) as the name of *any* river.

---

[18]Henry McKeating, *op. cit.*, p. 61.
[19]Catholic Bible, *op. cit.*, p. 990.
[20]W.R. Harper, *op. cit.*, p. 179.
[21]Ralph L. Smith, *op. cit.*, p. 132.
[22]Robert Jamieson, *JFB* (Grand Rapids: Zondervan Publishing House, 1961), p. 800.
[23]J.R. Dummelow, *op. cit.*, p. 570.
[24]Albert Barnes, *op. cit.*, p. 325.

In this light, we interpret the verse as a reference to two rivers, not merely one, the application above pertaining to the second river, which was surely the Nile; but the other river is the one mentioned by Isaiah:

> Now, behold, therefore the Lord bringeth upon them the waters of the River, strong and mighty, even the king of Assyria and all his glory: and it shall come up over all its channels, and go over all its banks, and it shall sweep onward and pass into Judah; it shall overflow and pass through (Isaiah 8:5-8).

It will be noted that "River" in the first part of this verse is definitely not referred to as the "River of Egypt." Also, the fact that Assyria is clearly in the mind of Amos throughout this prophecy adds to the probability of their being two rivers in view. In that case, it would mean that the River (Assyria) would overflow against Israel in a manner ("as") like the well-known innundations of the Nile, "of Egypt" in that case being the identification of the river to which comparison was made, and not an identification of the first river.

Verse 9, And it shall come to pass in that day, saith the Lord Jehovah, that I will cause the sun to go down at noon, and I will darken the earth in a clear day.

This is Amos' answer to the question propounded by the dishonest traders in verse 5, "When will the new moon . . . and the sabbath . . . be gone?" Very well, the answer was: "At that time when the sun goes down at noon, and the earth is darkened in a clear day," an undeniable reference to the crucifixion of the Son of God, that being the only occasion in the history of the world when the sun set at noon, and the earth (not just a portion of it, but all of it) was darkened in a clear day! We may only marvel at the blindness of biblical interpreters who fail to see this.

Some have tried to refer this to an eclipse, even attempting to discover which eclipse was meant; but, even as McKeating admitted, "It is pointless to decide that verse 9 refers to an eclipse and then try to identify the eclipse!"[25]

---

[25]Henry McKeating, *op. cit.*, p. 63.

No eclipse ever recorded could be an example of the sun's "going down"; and, besides that, no eclipse ever involved more than the tiniest fraction of "the earth." "The language as Amos used it referred to more than just an eclipse of the sun,"[26] and it should be added, "something far different from any such natural phenomenon." It is also impossible to restrict the meaning of this passage to something that was to come to pass in the near future. As Mays pointed out:

> In general usage, the temporal phrase "in that day" would point to a time identified in the context (as in 1 Samuel 3:2). Here the context offers only the coming deeds of Yahweh as a specification of the time in question.[27]

It is clearly a supernatural event at some undetermined future time that Amos here prophesied; and, as already noted, the only event ever known that answers to it is that of the supernatural darkening of the sun for three hours, involving the entire earth, when our Lord Jesus Christ was crucified. Such an ordinary event as an eclipse could not possibly be intended; and, there is the additional fact that, "Nowhere in the OT is there direct mention of an eclipse."[28] Hammershaimb referred this prophecy to "the day of Judgment";[29] and Barnes spiritualized it and denied the reality of it: "Not that the sun was hidden, or the day disappeared, but that the mourners could see no light even at midday, for the darkness of their grief!"[30] All such interpretations appear to be blind to the circumstantial and specific fulfilment at the crucifixion. Perhaps part of the trouble (or, indeed, all of it) derives from the fact that men are unwilling to allow that we are dealing here with *the word of God.* Dummelow said, "The eclipse of June 15, 763 B.C. may have impressed his imagination powerfully."[31] This writer

---

[26]Ralph L. Smith, *op. cit.*, p. 133.
[27]James Luther Mays, *Amos, A Commentary* (Philadelphia: The Westminster Press, 1969), p. 146.
[28]W.R. Harper, *op. cit.*, p. 181.
[29]Erling Hammershaimb, *op. cit.*, p. 126.
[30]Albert Barnes, *op. cit.*, p. 126.
[31]J.R. Dummelow, *op. cit.*, p. 570.

would not spend five minutes on the prophecy of Amos, if he saw nothing in it except the imagination of an ancient shepherd. This verse is an outstanding example of that heavenly phenomenon mentioned by Peter, to the effect that the ancient prophets uttered words which they themselves did not understand, and which they diligently studied in order to try to ascertain the meaning of what they had spoken (1 Peter 1:10-12). We believe that Amos, in this prophecy, is not likely to have had the slightest idea regarding *how* such a thing as he had prophesied could ever happen, and indeed might have thought such a thing to be absolutely impossible; but he was delivering the words of God! His own interpretation of them was probably to the effect that "there never would be a time when the sabbath would be gone"; but, of course, it was summarily abolished in the cross of Christ, a fact clearly stated by Paul in Colossians 2:14-17, a passage which entails some of the exact language of this very passage in Amos.

There are some things which must be discerned as literal in the sacred scriptures, and this prophecy is surely one of them. The ancients unanimously understood this passage as we have interpreted it: Irenaeus (i:510), Tertullian (iii:167), Cyprian (v:525) and Lactantius (vii:122) all unhesitatingly reading Amos' prophecy as a foretelling of our Lord's Passion.[32] See more under v. 10. below.

Verse 10, And I will turn your feasts into mourning, and all your songs into lamentation; and I will bring sackcloth upon all loins, and baldness upon every head; and I will make it as the mourning for an only son, and the end thereof as a bitter day.

There is not a figurative or symbolical word in this verse, strongly suggesting that the previous verse (9) is also to be understood literally. We may therefore reject the interpretation that explains it thus:

> To any man, the sun sets at noon, when he is suddenly snatched away by death in the very midst of life.

---

[32]*Ante-Nicene Fathers* (Grand Rapids: Wm. B. Eerdmans Publishing Company), the small Roman numerals and Arabic numerals are for volumes and page numbers.

And this also applies to a nation when it is suddenly destroyed in the midst of its earthly prosperity.[33]

Of course, this figurative application of the passage is indeed true; but we cannot receive this as the primary meaning of it. Israel was not being destroyed at the "high noon" of their prosperity, but at its sunset, when their sin had about finished its course and at a time when they were fully ripe for destruction.

"Baldness upon every head . . ." This is not the prophecy of some kind of scalp disease; the reference is to the Jewish custom of shaving the head as a sign of mourning; and the universality of it indicated that there would be mourning everywhere.

Verse 11, Behold the days come, saith Jehovah, that I will send a famine in the land, not a famine of bread, nor a thirst for water, but of hearing the words of Jehovah.

Many great and wonderful prophets were yet to speak the message of threatened doom and the call to repentance upon Israel's part; but Amos here definitely prophesied an end to the prophetic missions. This was most remarkably fulfilled during the inter-testamental period between the OT and the NT, when no prophet spoke anything at all to the wayward and rebellious people of Israel. This literally came to pass. This verse is labelled as "a comment later inserted into the text by mistake";[34] but if that is so, how do the critics account for the truth that it was fulfilled exactly over a period of three or four centuries? That fulfilment was noticed and incorporated into the Psalms:

> We see not our signs:
> There is no more any prophet;
> Neither is there among us any that knoweth how
>   long
> —Psalms 74:9.

Only the inspiration of God could have so accurately foretold the true course of events in the future of Israel.

---

[33]Paul T. Butler, *op. cit.*, p. 357.
[34]Erling Hammershaimb, *op. cit.*, p. 127.

Verse 12, And they shall wander from sea to sea, and from the north even to the east; they shall run to and fro to seek the word of Jehovah, and shall not find it.

Although this was fulfilled by the cessation of the prophetic missions to Israel in the long centuries preceding Christ:

> The wide scope taken by the prophecy, which is not exhausted by one fulfilment, reveals here the fate of the Jews to the present time hopelessly seeking Messiah and the word of God, never finding that which they once recklessly rejected.[35]

"Shall wander from sea to sea ..." Some have tried to read this as a reference to the Dead Sea and the Mediterranean, thus confining its application to Palestine; but in Zechariah 9:10 it is a clear reference meaning, "from one end of the earth to the other." Harper, after citing the other view, admitted that, "Perhaps, the term is a more general one, meaning the ends of the earth."[36] The ancient quotation from Jerome, cited by Butler, gives the true sense:

> They roam restlessly about the world and seek the word of God; but they find it not, because they have killed the incarnate Word revealed in the written Word.[37]

Verse 13, In that day shall the fair virgins and the young men faint for thirst.

This indicates that the flower and glory of Israel shall not be spared from the disaster achieved by their leaders who were the architects of their long and stubborn rebellion against God. But it must not be thought that the terrible results of such a famine were restricted to Israel. No, indeed! Every people which forgets God and rejects the Christ shall suffer the same fate; and there is much in our own culture today to suggest that the same fate may be in store for our own nation:

[35]W.J. Deane, *op. cit.*, p. 159.
[36]W.R. Harper, *op. cit.*, p. 183.
[37]Paul T. Butler, *op. cit.*, p. 359.

Thousands and thousands of young people across our land, disillusioned and starved to death on the garbage of the contemporary "intellectualism," are "running to and fro" seeking a voice of authority, a life which consists of more than "things."[38]

Many of the very same mistakes that deceived and eventually destroyed ancient Israel are the "accepted assumptions" of our current society. See more on this under the next verse.

Verse 14, They that swear by the sin of Samaria, and say, As thy god, O Dan, liveth; and, As the way of Beersheba liveth; they shall fall, and never rise again.

"They that swear by the sin of Samaria . . ." This expression means, "The calves at Dan and Bethel, and to 'swear by,' means 'to worship.' "[39] McKeating, following the NEB, translated this, "All who take their oath by Ashimah, goddess of Samaria";[40] but this cannot possibly be correct. The NEB and other translations following this alleged "reading" represent a colossal "goof" as far as biblical translation goes. In the first place, the Hebrew text, which alone we receive as inspired, clearly has, "The guilt of Samaria, which is a refernece to the idolatrous worship carried on there."[41] Furthermore, the change to "Ashimah" in this verse involves "a change" in the Hebrew text,[42] a change for which there is no authority. By changing it a little more, they could make it read, "Diana of the Ephesians!" But that is not all of it, the intrusion of "Ashima" into this passage makes the verse applicable to a period long after the time when Amos lived; and, of course, the perverted meaning is promptly made the basis for an assault upon the integrity of the passage and the discarding of the whole verse as the work of a later author! It is merely the old device of misinterpreting, or mistranslating, a passage, and then making that error the basis of an attack upon the Bible!

[38]*Ibid.*, p. 360.
[39]Robert Jamieson, *op. cit.*, p. 800.
[40]Henry McKeating, *op. cit.*, p. 63.
[41]Arnold C. Schultz, *WBC* (Chicago: Moody Press, 1962), p. 836.
[42]Hughell E.W. Fosbroke, *op. cit.*, p. 844.

"The sin of Samaria . . ." which is under indictment here was that of worshipping the golden calves, one at Dan, the other at Bethel; and they are attributed to "Samaria," because Samaria was the capital of the country in which this monstrous departure from God's word had taken place. Deane concurred in this view, thus:

> The sin of Samaria (means) the golden calf at Bethel. The expression, "Thy god, O Dan, liveth" refers to the other calf erected at Dan, near the source of the Jordan, in the extreme north.[43]

Smith also concurred in the judgment that the best reading of the Hebrew text in this place is "the guilt of Samaria,"[44] and not "Ashimah."

"As the way of Beersheba liveth . . ." This is another instance of swearing by, or worshipping a false god, a fact deduced from the terminology employed here. Smith observed that, "The word *he* (lives) is used in both lines, always used in Hebrew to swear by false gods and nonsacral objects, *Ha* was used when oaths were taken in the name of the true God."[45] In this light, it must be true that both the god of Dan, and the way of Beersheba are references to false deities.

What a remarkable thing it is, therefore, to encounter the stout denials of commentators that there was anything wrong in that worship in Israel, except their insincerity and their oppressiveness!

> Those who, in Amos' time, swore "by the life of your god, O Dan, would not think of themselves as apostates. Neither does swearing "By the sacred way to Beersheba" in itself imply apostasy!"[46]

Although no particular false god is mentioned in connection with "the way of Beersheba," there was, in all probably such an idol there. The notion has been advanced that the Israelitish pilgrims to the place adored "the sacred way" that led to it; but, as Harper admitted, "It is possible to

[43]W.J. Deane, *op. cit.*, p. 159.
[44]Ralph L. Smith, *op. cit.*, p. 134.
[45]*Ibid.*
[46]Henry McKeating, *op. cit.*, p. 64.

understand 'way' of the method of worship at Bethel."[47]

Hammershaimb beautifully summarized this verse thus: "The god that they worship and swear by is therefore not the true Yahweh, but a god which they have fashioned to their own desires."[48] Idolatry in the Northern Kingdom had come of age. The people no longer either recognized or honored the true and Almighty God, but instead, worshipped and swore by their golden idols. Added to that was the licentious and abominable worship they practiced there; and if that was not apostasy, there never was such a thing.

"They shall fall, and never rise again ..." When God's judgment was decreed against his ungrateful and apostate people, it was determined that the pagan gods they worshipped, together with the shrines that honored them, would be utterly, completely, and finally destroyed.

It should be remembered in contemplating the fulfilment of this death sentence against the Northern Kingdom that it was *terminal*. The ten tribes which comprised it never returned to Canaan; their course through subsequent history, as regards any of their survivors, is totally unknown, buried by the dust of more than twenty-six centuries. The southern kingdom was granted some additional respite, due to God's purpose of bringing in the Messiah through their posterity; but when that was accomplished; and, after a due season in which God further extended his mercy and offered them the gospel, and after their complete rejection of that, they were perpetually hardened "until the times of the Gentiles be come in" (Romans 11:25); their vaunted temple was reduced to rubble, their capital city ravished and destroyed, over a million of them being put to death by the sword; and their state perished from the earth for the space of almost two millenniums of time!

[47]W.R. Harper, *op. cit.*, p. 184.
[48]Erling Hammershaimb, *op. cit.*, p. 130.

CHAPTER 9

This chapter comprises the fifth vision of Amos as recorded in this section of the prophecy. It is a vision diverse from all of the others and deals with a great deal more than the temporal fortunes of the kingdom of Israel (either one of the two kingdoms, Judah, or Israel). It entails the final and total destruction of both Jewish *kingdoms*, as such, including even the overthrow of the Jerusalem temple, accounted as sacred by all Israel (vv.1-4). The certainty of this was emphasized by means of Amos' third doxology (vv. 5,6). The vaunted position of the Jews as God's chosen people, a fact the Jews had mistakenly interpreted as a perpetual heavenly endorsement of their earthly, secular monarchy, is announced as being solemnly withdrawn by the Lord in the announcement that the Jews were nothing more to him than the Ethiopians and the Philistines! a fact which is sadly absent from the thoughts of most of the commentators on this passage. In this very discerning passage, the "seed of Abraham," called the "house of Jacob" (v. 8), is severed, terminally and completely from any identification whatever with a Jewish state, whether ancient Judah, or Israel, or any subsequent state (or kingdom) that might appear later in history, professing to be any kind of successor to it. (vv. 7-10). Finally, the chapter presents a prophecy of the Messiah, Jesus Christ the Lord, and the "rebuilding of the fallen tabernacle of David," which is as beautiful and circumstantial a prophecy of the church of Christ as may be found anywhere in the Bible (vv. 11-14). Without any doubt, this is one of the most important and instructive chapters to be found in the OT.

Regarding the doubts of critical scholars and their fulminations against passages in this chapter, such things are due, categorically, to their blindness to the prophetic appearance of the Lord Jesus Christ and his church in these passages, and also to their failure to understand that neither the Jewish temple (at Jerusalem) nor the secular kingdom of Solomon were in any sense harmonious with the will of God, and also to their failure to understand that *no*

kingdom, state or nation, in the sense of its corporate existence, either ever was or ever will be "the chosen people of
God," a fact made crystal clear in this chapter.

**Verse 1, I saw the Lord standing beside the altar: and he
said, Smite the capitals that the threshold may shake; and
break them in pieces on the head of all of them; and I will
slay the last of them with the sword: there shall not one of
them flee away, and there shall not one of them escape.**

"The Lord standing beside the altar . . ." The notion that
this is a reference to the pagan altars (plural) in the temple
at Bethel is false. It is utterly inconceivable that the Lord
would have taken a place beside the golden calf in the so-
called "temple," at Bethel, which, in the first place, is not
called "a temple." There was a pagan shrine there, of
course, but no temple. There were many altars there and at
other places in Israel; and no one of them could possibly
have been designated as *"the altar"* associated with the
history of the Jews. Many arguments are suggested in
order to justify the application of this verse to Bethel, such
as: "it is the only holy place at which tradition locates
Amos during his ministry;"[1] "the chief temple of Northern
Israel was located at Bethel;"[2] "Jacob saw the Lord at
Bethel;"[3] "there is a close connection with the preceding
chapter 8, which mentions Bethel in the last verse,"[4] etc.;
but none of these alleged arguments has any weight whatever. As C. G. Keil noted:

> There is no ground whatever for the assertion that
> this chapter contains simply an explanation of 8:14 . . .
> There was not any one altar in the northern kingdom
> that could be called "the altar" . . . In chapter 3:14
> Amos foretold the destruction of "the altars" (plural)
> at Bethel . . . So there was not any one altar in the

[1]James Luther Mays, *Amos, A Commentary* (Philadelphia: The Westminster
Press, 1969), p. 152.
    [2]W.R. Harper, *Amos & Hosea* (New York: Charles Scribner's Sons, 1910), p.
188.
    [3]Ralph L. Smith, *BBC, Vol. 7* (Nashville: Broadman Press, 1972), p. 135.
    [4]Hofmann, as quoted by C. F. Keil, *Commentary on the Whole Bible* (Grand
Rapids: Wm. B. Eerdmans Publishing Company), p. 320.

kingdom of the ten tribes, that could be called "the altar."[5]

Another allegation designed to support this passage as a reference to Bethel relies upon the assumption that this prophecy is not at all concerned with the southern kingdom, an assumption denied by the frequent and pertinent references to the southern kingdom, and to "the whole house of Israel, and to Judah," etc., occurring frequently enough. Some of these are: 2:5, 6:1, 5:4,5, 8:11,12, etc. It is true enough that the northern kingdom is the principal focus of the prophecy, but not for one instant is the southern kingdom left very far out of sight, as, for example, when the apostasy of David was mentioned in 6:5. One simply cannot read verse 1 as any kind of reference to Bethel.

This verse is therefore a prophecy of the destruction of the temple in Jerusalem, with the implied end of the kingdom and of the dynasty of David at the same time. Most biblical exegetes seem to be unaware of what the OT says of that Solomonic temple. To begin with, it was never God's idea at all, but David's (2 Samuel 7). It stood in exactly the same relationship to the tabernacle (which God indeed *had* given the people) as that in which the secular monarchy stood to the theocracy, namely, a *rejection* of it, neither the monarchy nor the temple ever being, in any sense whatever the true will of God. The Christian martyr Stephen made this abundantly clear in Acts 7:44-50. The summary and final end of the northern kingdom had just been announced in preceding verses; and, in this passage, preparatory to the prophecy of the eternal kingdom of the Messiah, Amos made it clear that *neither* the northern *nor* the southern kingdom, in their corporate existence, would in any manner enter into the eternal purpose of God regarding the "true Israel," which was *never* identified with either one of them.

The reason that the temple was widely viewed in Israel as "God's house" is that God indeed did accommodate to it, as also he did in the case of the monarchy; and so long as the Lord continued to send prophets to the northern kingdom, so long did they, despite all their sin, still pass as belonging

---

[5]*Ibid.*

to the "people of God." This points up the relevance of this reference to the temple at Jerusalem, which Keil defined as, "the divinely appointed sanctuary and the throne of Jehovah."[6] Thus, what happened to the temple and the kingdom of Judah was of the most vital relevance to Israel also, hence the inclusion of this fifth vision of Amos' prophecy. God appeared at the altar in Jerusalem, because *there* at the *true* sacrificial place of the nation (both of Judah and of Israel), their sins were heaped up; and from that perspective the Lord will judge and punish them.

Considerable attention has been devoted to the meaning of "altar" in this first verse; because, when this is understood as a reference to the pagan altars in Bethel, a correct interpretation of the entire passage becomes impossible.

Verses 2-4, Though they dig into Sheol, thence shall my hand take them; and though they climb up to heaven, thence will I bring them down. And though they hide themselves in the top of Carmel, I will search and take them out thence; and though they be hid from my sight in the bottom of the sea, thence will I command the serpent, and it shall bite them. And though they go into captivity before their enemies, thence will I command the sword, and it shall slay them: and I will set mine eyes upon them for evil, and not for good.

This passage is a further elaboration of what was said in the conclusion of verse 1, that, "not one of them shall escape." There is no teaching here to the effect that anyone could hide from God, or that it would be necessary for God to "search" for any who might be attempting to do so. This is highly accommodative language used to emphasize the inevitability of their destruction and the utter impossibility of any person being able to escape it.

"Hide in the top of Carmel . . ." Harper tells us that Carmel was noted for, "its limestone caves, said to exceed 2,000 in number, and to be so close together and so serpentine as to make the discovery of a fugitive entirely impossible."[7]

---

[6]*Ibid.*
[7]W.R. Harper, *op. cit.*, p. 189.

The whole passage simply wishes to say that there is no place in the whole universe where they can feel themselves secure against Yahweh.[8]

"Though they go into captivity. . . ." Amos had pointedly prophesied this fate for Israel; and this is a terrifying amplification of it, showing that the captivity in store for them will not be a benign and favorable one (as it had been in Egypt, at first); but it will be *terminal*. The historical disappearance of the ten tribes after the Assyrian captivity is proof enough of what happened. W. R. Harper, and other later commentators following his views, have supposed that this clause is addressed to an Israelitish conception (borrowed from paganism, into which the whole nation had slipped) to the effect that, "In a strange and foreign land, they would be under the power of the god or gods of that land,"[9] and not any longer under Jehovah! We do not believe there is anything like this in view, either in this place or in Jonah 1:1.

The Doxology

Verses 5,6, For the Lord Jehovah of hosts, is he that toucheth the land and it melteth, and all that dwell therein shall mourn; and it shall rise up wholly like the River, and shall sink again, like the river of Egypt; it is he that buildeth his chambers in the heavens, and hath founded his vault upon the earth; he that calleth for the waters of the sea, and poureth them out upon the face of the earth; Jehovah is his name.

This is the third of Amos' doxologies, the other two being in 4:13 and 5:8,9, the purpose of all three being quite clearly that of a reminder that the Lord, whose word to Israel Amos was faithfully delivering, was indeed all-sufficient and powerful to bring to pass exactly that which he promised. As Keil accurately discerned the intent of these verses: "To strengthen his threat, Amos proceeds (in vv. 5,6) to describe Jehovah as the Lord of heaven and earth,

---

[8]Erling Hammershaimb, *The Book of Amos, translated by John Sturdy* (New York: The Shocken Books, 1970), p. 133.

[9]W.R. Harper, *op. cit.*, p. 190.

who sends judgments upon the earth with omnipotent power."[10]

"Like the River, etc. . . ." This is almost identical with 8:8. See under that verse for the interpretation, which is identical with what is meant here.

Smith detected an interesting progression in the three doxologies of Amos, thus:

> The first doxology praises God as the creator of the universe (4:13). The second begins with creation (5:8) and goes on to refer to God's *control*. In this third doxology Yahweh's creative power is turned into destructive might.[11]

"Calling for the waters of the sea . . ." As noted in the interpretation of 8:8, which see, this appears to be a reminder of the great flood which God sent upon rebellious mankind as a punishment of their malignant wickedness.

Verse 7, Are ye not as the children of the Ethiopians unto me, O children of Israel? saith Jehovah. Have not I brought up Israel out of the land of Egypt, and the Philistines from Caphtor, and the Syrians from Kir?

Due to their gross and repeated rebellions against God, Israel had forfeited their status as "God's chosen people"; and here is revealed that God's providences for them had in no sense been heaped upon them without any concern for other nations. Israel seems to have been perpetually blind to the truth that even God's great promise to Abraham, upon which all Jewish and Christian hopes must ultimately rest, had never been given with a view to benefitting his secular posterity *alone*, but that, in Abraham, "All the families of the earth might be blessed" (Genesis 12:3). Even from the first, as demonstrated by the rejection of a great portion of Abraham's literal descendants, such as Esau, Ishmael, and the sons of Keturrah, Abraham's *fleshly* posterity was never the true possessor of the promise, which pertained to his "spiritual seed" alone, i.e., those of a like faith and disposition of their great progenitor.

---

[10]C.F. Keil, *op. cit.*, p. 325.
[11]Ralph L. Smith, *op. cit.*, p. 136.

The Jewish race, all of them, northern and southern kingdoms, had further perverted and misconstrued the promise by applying it, without reservation, to their *secular kingdoms*. This prophecy put an end to that error, for all who will read and understand Amos.

"Are ye not as the children of the Ethiopians . . .?" In a word, this means that, "Jews, in the fleshly sense, are of no more concern to Almighty God than the Ethiopians, the Philistines and the Syrians. This is still the truth. God has no more any special program for dealing with racial Jews than he does for the Japanese, the Germans, the French, or the Iranians. As Paul put it: "For *there is no distinction* between Jew and Greek: for the same Lord is Lord of all" (Romans 10:12). It must be accounted as absolutely incredible that a vast number of "Christian scholars" do not in any sense believe this!

"The Philistines from Caphtor, and the Syrians from Kir . . ." God's providence had also been showered upon these nations. Paul, in his great missionary solicitation of the Gentiles did not fail to point out that:

> God, in the generations gone by suffered all the nations to walk in their own ways; and yet he left not himself without witness, in that he did good and gave you from heaven rains and fruitful seasons, filling your hearts with food and gladness (Acts 14:16,17).

Verse 8a, Behold the eyes of the Lord Jehovah are upon the sinful kingdom, and I will destroy it from off the face of the earth.

This verse is not a promise that God will destroy "the house of Jacob," nor a promise that God will annihilate the total posterity of Abraham; but it is a promise to wipe "the sinful *kingdom*" off the face of the planet. Which *sinful kingdom*? *Every* sinful kingdom, especially the northern kingdom and the southern kingdom of Israel. The ultimate application of this to the whole world of wicked and unbelieving humanity is dramatically detailed in the prophecy of Revelation (19:11-21). In the case of the kingdoms of the Jews, the very initiation of their kingdom under Saul was a rejection of God (1 Samuel 8:7); reciprocally, this was also their rejection of their own status as "God's chosen people," a term that henceforth would apply to the "righteous remnant" and not to Israel as a whole.

McKeating interpreted this and the preceding verse 7 as "a formal contradiction of Amos 3:2, 'For you alone have I cared among all the nations of the world.' "[12] However, these verses are not speaking of the same thing. God's solicitious care for "you," means his special and unique care for those who love and obey him, a promise valid *now*, and eternally, and which in no sense nullifies or contradicts what is said here of the destruction of the *sinful kingdom*. Furthermore, in God's selection and choice of Abraham's posterity as containing "his chosen people," there were countless instances in which Israel had indeed been "cared for" by the Father in a manner absolutely unique in human history, a blesing absolutely not founded in any divine partiality for Jews, but necessary for the ultimate blessing of "all the families of the earth." At the time of God's choice of Israel, idolatry was so widespread and nearly universal on earth, that the very knowledge of God might have perished from the planet had it not been for the choice of Abraham.

McKeating's allegation of a contradiction here, as is usually the case with such allegations, is founded upon a fundamental ignorance of what this prophecy is saying. Hammershaimb correctly observed what is denoted by these verses thus:

> The point was that Israel had no entitlement to sin more than others, because Yahweh had chosen it; on the contrary, this carried with it all the greater obligations on the side of the people, and Yahweh would not spare them for that reason.[13]

There is nothing in these verses which may be interpreted as a denial that, "God is the God of all history, not of Hebrew history alone; he is behind all the great world move-

---

[12]Henry McKeating, *CBC, Amos* (Cambridge: At the University Press, 1971), p. 67.
[13]Erling Hammershaimb, *The Book of Amos, translated by John Sturdy* (New York: Shocken Books, 1970), p. 135.

ments, the migrations of people . . . are ultimately determined and effected by him."[14] Paul's great sermon in Athens emphasizes this truth (Acts 17).

Smith also observed that:

> God seems to be announcing the end of God's special relationship to Israel as *a nation* (i.e., *a kingdom*). It means that God will treat Israel like any other nation; the nation will have no special privileges; and when they sin they will be punished.[15]

This of course, is true; but it needs to be pointed out that their secular *state* had never been the object of any special favor from God (for it was contrary to his will), except in the necessity that time and again, there was no way to aid the "righteous remnant" without aiding and favoring the wicked state of which that remnant was an integral part. This mingling of the *two Israels* in the OT is one of the primary factors usually overlooked by commentators. Paul elaborated the distinction between these two Israels in Romans (chs. 9-11), and no full understanding either of the NT or the ancient prophecies is possible without keeping this distinction constantly in view. The true Israel was, and ever will be, the people who love and obey God; the other Israel, as this passage dogmatically affirms has the same status with God as the Ethiopians, the Philistines and the Syrians!

"The sinful kingdom . . ." in this verse refers to both Judah and Israel; but "the house of Jacob" in the last half of this verse is a reference to the "righteous remnant," which is the true Israel.

Verse 8b, Save that I will not utterly destroy the house of Jacob, saith Jehovah.

Having failed, completely, to understand what Amos is saying, some commentators assault the integrity of this passage:

---

[14]John Edgar McFadden, *A Cry for Justice* (New York: Charles Scribner's Sons, 1912), p. 132.
[15]Ralph L. Smith, *op. cit.*, p. 138.

> This flatly contradicts the point of the whole (verse).
> It is a later addition to the text ... The opinion ex-
> pressed in 8b is doubtless that of a Judean redactor[16]
> ... These verses are manifestly later additions,[17] etc.

Such denials of the word of God may be rejected with
impunity; they are founded upon no sufficient evidence and
are but the futile denials of some scholars whose fallacious
interpretations of previous passages are contradicted here.
It should be kept in mind, however, that it is not the previous words of the prophet Amos which this half-verse
contradicts, but the false opinions advanced in the inaccurate interpretation of preceding verses.

Smith, after taking note of the assault upon the integrity
of this verse, freely admitted that, "It must also be said
that these verses could have come from Amos."[18] The obvious truth is that any one understanding the full significance of this section finds them fully harmonious with the
whole verse and the whole prophecy and will have no hesi-
tancy whatever in receiving them as the true words of God
spoken through Amos.

Essentially, it is the good news of this passage which is so
repulsive to many interpreters, who have already decided
that there can be no good news at all in a book with so many
warnings and denunciations. As Smith said, "Many earlier
scholars did not believe that a prophet could predict judgment and hope (woe and weal) at the same time."[19] Fortu-
nately, most present-day scholars have outgrown such a
naive and foolish notion. "Present scholars recognize that
messages of weal and woe often came from the same
prophet."[20] It is surely evident that scholarly bias entered
into the rejection of this part of Amos, as did also their
failure to discern its true import.

"The house of Jacob ..." is not a mere distinction between the northern and southern kingdoms, for the term
stands for "the righteous remnant" of both kingdoms; the

[16]James Luther Mays, *Amos, A Commentary* (Westminster Press, 1969), p.
160.
[17]Henry McKeating, *op. cit.*, p. 69.
[18]Ralph L. Smith, *op. cit.*, p. 139.
[19]*Ibid.*, p. 137.
[20]*Ibid.*

true antithesis is between the "sinful kingdom" (8a) and "house of Jacob" as a "divine kernel in the nation, by virtue of its divine election, out of which the Lord will form a new and holy people."[21] This "kernel" is the "righteous remnant," the true Israel of God, who were never, in fact, identifiable as "the kingdom." Elijah and the 7,000 who had not bowed to Baal represented the totality of that remnant during the reign of the wicked Ahab (1 Kings 19:10, Romans 11:4). This righteous remnant was the remnant formed by the true believers in both the secular kingdoms of Israel and Judah, in the same sense that "the sinful kingdom" refers to the same two secular kingdoms.

Thus, here in verse 8b is introduced the subject of the concluding verses of Amos' great prophecy which foretells how God will, from that righteous remnant, develop the universal kingdom of the church of Christ and endow it with the most extravagant blessings, that new "kingdom," being not a kingdom of this world at all, but the true followers of Christ, his church being called the "rebuilt tabernacle of David" (v. 11).

Verse 9, For lo, I will command, and I will sift the house of Israel among all the nations, like as grain is sifted in a sieve, yet shall not the least kernel fall upon the earth.

The "house of Israel" here has exactly the same meaning as "the house of Jacob," having no reference at all to any secular kingdom, but to that "kernel," the righteous remnant who truly love and obey the Lord, not a single one of whom shall be lost or suffer destruction from the Lord. The simile here is that of a sieve used for screening out the trash, small stones, and chaff from the true wheat which passes through the sieve.

The historical fulfilment of this took place very shortly after the times of Amos' prophecy when the northern kingdom was carried away by the Assyrians, never more to appear any more as any kind of an entity; but, as the future of the southern kingdom comes particularly into focus here, since it was with that kingdom that "the righteous remnant" would be principally identified in the future (after the

---

[21]C.F. Keil, *op. cit.*, p. 32.

destruction of the northern kingdom), this verse is especially a reference to the southern kingdom. This "sifting" was fulfilled in the fall of their city, the destruction of their temple, and the deporting of the whole nation to Babylon; but there are overtones in the passage reaching far beyond that historical event.

It should ever be remembered that the old Israel is a type of the new; and that sifting of the house of Jacob among the nations in the OT is still going on. "The shaking of Israel in the sieve is still being fulfilled upon the Jews who are dispersed among all nations."[22] Who but God could have prophesied such a remarkable thing concerning Israel, at a time in history when it would have appeared utterly incredible? No, these verses were not added by any later editor, or redactor!

"Not the least kernel shall fall to earth ..." This means that no Israelite, or any other person on earth, who truly loves and seeks to do the will of God will be cut off, regardless of the evil nature of any kingdom, or group of people, with whom he may be environmentally associated. God knows what he is doing.

Verse 10, All the sinners of my people shall die by the sword, who say, the evil shall not overtake nor meet us.

Here again is reaffirmed the constant thesis of Amos that the two secular kingdoms, which were evil, shall surely fall, and the *kingdoms* shall be wiped off the face of the earth. The "not *utterly* destroy" of the previous verse 8b is not a denial of this, but an indication of a different fate for the "righteous remnant," in keeping with God's eternal purpose. There are two things in these verses that must be differentiated, i.e., the "kernel" and the "sinful kingdom," the great burden of the prophecy being directed against the latter.

Prophecy of the Church of Christ

Verse 11, In that day will I raise up the tabernacle of David that is fallen, and close up the breaches thereof; and

---

[22]*Ibid.*, p. 329.

I will raise up its ruins, and I will build it as in the days of old.

This verse foretells how salvation for all men "shall be effected in the house of David, in whose line Christ was to come."[23] Note that the Jerusalem temple is by-passed, absolutely, here. All of the great victories of Israel were won during the period when they had the "tabernacle," not the temple; and, as Barnes pointed out, "He speaks of the house of David, not in any terms of royal greatness; he tells not of its palaces."[24] This powerful and suggestive mention of the tabernacle speaks of the days of the humility of Israel, indicating that when God's salvation comes, it will be associated with the humble, and the simple, rather than with the royal palaces and Solomonic glory of the house of David. Some of the scholars have translated "tabernacle" here as "hut,"[25] applying it to the postexilic ruin of David's dynasty; but there is unequivocally a reference here to the ancient "tabernacle" of the Jewish wanderings in the wilderness, as proved by the sacred author James' reference to this passage in Acts 15:

> After these things, I will return,
> And I will build again the tabernacle of David, which
>   is fallen;
> And I will build again the ruins thereof,
> And I will set it up:
> That the residue of men may seek after the Lord,
> And all the Gentiles upon whom my name is called,
> Saith the Lord, who maketh these things known
>   from of old.
> (Acts 15:16-18.)

It should be remembered that James here was not quoting Amos alone, attributing his quotations to "the prophets." (Acts 15:15). However, the words of Amos in this verse are definitely among the passages referred to, making it certain that this is a reference to the building up of the Church, the

---

[23] Albert Barnes, *Notes on the OT, Minor Prophets, Vol. 1* (Grand Rapids: Baker Book House, 1953), p. 336.
[24] *Ibid.*
[25] W.R. Harper, *op. cit.*, p. 198.

238 Commentary on the Minor Prophets

antitype of the tabernacle. Note that there is no reference whatever here to the Jewish temple, itself an apostasy from the tabernacle; and, it is in the sense of that semi-pagan temple having supplanted and taken the place of the tabernacle that the "tabernacle" is here represented as "fallen," meaning that the Jews had simply discarded it and gone into the temple business.

The type of blunder into which many scholars fall in the interpretation of this place is exemplified by this: "The tabernacle of David is the Davidic dynasty, and these words presuppose that it had come to an end; they must therefore have been written later than the fall of Jerusalem in 586 B.C."[26] Such a view would, of course, remove the passage far from the days of Amos. It should be perfectly obvious to any discerning student that there is no possible reference here to "David's dynasty." *That* had not fallen when Amos wrote, but the "tabernacle" had fallen!

"In that day . . ." is a "reference to the times of the Messiah,"[27] and, in no sense was fulfilled by anything that occurred before that. After the Babylonian captivity, Israel did indeed return to their land (not the northern kingdom, but the Davidic branch of it, the southern kingdom), but they did not restore the "fallen tabernacle" at all, but merely built another temple, a far different thing, the difference being that God had given the plans and specifications of the tabernacle to Moses; but the temple was planned and built by men (Acts 7:44-47). The great error of the temple was that it was patterned after the great pagan temples of the period, and was the result of the same desire of the Israelites that led to the formation of the monarchy, namely, that they could be "like the nations around them." Thus, when Christ established his church, it was not a "rebuilding of the fallen temple," but a rebuilding of the "fallen tabernacle."

"And close up the breaches of it . . ." This does not refer to holes made in the palaces of Jewish kings, but it refers to healing the breach among God's people. Jeroboam had divided the "chosen people"; and the righteous remnant from

[26]Henry McKeating, *op. cit.*, p. 70.
[27]Robert Jamieson, *JFB* (Grand Rapids: Zondervan Publishing House, 1961), p. 801.

both divisions were thus separated; but when Messiah would come, then all of God's true Israel would be under one theocratic hand, namely, Christ.

David's kingdom is a type of Christ's; and the restoration of the fallen tabernacle is the same thing as the raising up of one of David's posterity (Christ) to sit upon David's throne forever, a prophecy of the resurrection of Christ and his enthronement in heaven, as Peter pointed out (Acts 2:30,31). No one could possibly be expected to raise up again the kingdom of David, except one of his descendants, this being the significance of the genealogies of Jesus which show him to be of "the flesh of David." Thus, in this extended meaning of the "fallen tabernacle" being restored, there is also hidden this prophecy of the restoration of David's throne "in the spiritual sense."

All kinds of errors result from a misunderstanding of the last clause of this verse:

"I will raise up its ruins, and I will build it as in the days of old . . ." This is alleged to mean that God will reproduce in the history of Israel another period reflecting the same kind of pride and glory that characterized the old Davidic and Solomonic empire; but this is definitely not the thing to be rebuilt. "The tabernacle" stands for the time when God's communion with his people had been established upon an intimate and continual communication, in short, for "their fellowship with God." It was that fellowship which had been destroyed by the sins and wickedness of the people; and it was preeminently the "broken fellowship with God," which would be restored in the church of the Lord Jesus Christ, which, alone, is foretold in this promise to "rebuild," as "in the days of old." It was the great error of Israel, during our Lord's ministry, that led them to identify the blessed Messiah himself as one who would recreate their old Solomonic empire, which, in reality, was the scandal of forty generations, and the vey last thing on earth that God would have promised to "rebuild." Christian interpreters today ought not to fall into the same error that was fatal to Israel.

Premillenial Views

Of course, those espousing a premillenial view of the Bible suppose that this passage supports their contention:

"Amos' view of the Messianic kingdom under the throne of David, represents it as universal, and as including the Gentiles."[28] The church of course is "under the throne of David" only in the spiritual sense of David's throne having been an OT type of universal reign of Christ upon his throne in heaven. No temporal restoration of David's monarchy is prophesied here.

Another unfounded theory based upon this passage is that of the projected return of the fleshly Jews to their land in Palestine and the exercise of some very wide and successful dominion from Jerusalem during the historical period of the church of Jesus Christ himself. Clarke referred to this, defining it thus:

> It must therefore refer to their restoration under the gospel, when they shall receive the Lord Jesus as their Messiah, and be by him restored to their own land. Those victories (in the return of the southern kingdom to Palestine after the captivity) could not warrant the terms of the prediction in this verse.[29]

Such interpretations overlook the fact that, long ago, God put "no distinction" between Jews and anyone else on earth (Romans 10:12); their status as "God's chosen people" was by themselves repudiated and rejected. After extended mercies and extensive opportunities repeatedly offered them, the fleshly Israel adamantly refused to have any of it, even crucifying the Son of God when he appeared upon earth; and the notion that God will, for some incredible reason, again restore secular, fleshly and rebellious Israel to "their land" in Palestine is one of the most preposterous notions ever conceived by the students of God's word. God's Israel *today* knows nothing of *race*, or any secular kingdom; it is a spiritual Israel, the only "sons of Abraham" on earth today, being, in the light of the scriptures, those who have been "baptized into Christ." And should the Jews ever receive Christ as their Messiah, they

---

[28]Arnold C. Schultz, *WBC* (Chicago: Moody Press, 1962), p. 837.
[29]Adam Clarke, *Commentary on the Whole Bible, Vol. V* (New York: T. Mason & G. Lane, 1837), p. 693.

would of necessity also be "baptized into him"; and therefore, such a proposition as that advanced by Clarke would
mean that the holy church itself, in its entirety, and not
merely some racial fraction of it, would be reestablished in
Palestine! What a fantastic misunderstanding!

James D. Bales' summary of the teaching of this place is:

> The rebuilding of the tabernacle of David, was evi-
> dently not a rebuilding of the Mosaic system, but the
> restoration of a king on David's throne; and that
> Christ is now on David's throne we have shown in
> another chapter. The Mosaical system will not be re-
> built; its mediator has now been replaced by Christ
> (Deuteronomy 18:15-17, Acts 3:22-26). The old Cove-
> nant was to pass away, and it has passed away (Jere-
> miah 31:31-34, Hebrews 8:5-10,16). Its sacrifices have
> ceased for the Lamb of God has been offered once for
> all to bear the sins of the world.[30]

**Verse 12, That they may possess the remnant of Edom,
and all the nations that are called by thy name, saith Jehovah that doeth this.**

Without any doubt, "The possession of the heathen nations by Israel is spiritual."[31] Israel's possession of the
remnant of Edom, and all other heathen nations was also
foretold by Isaiah thus:

> And the sons of them that afflicted thee shall come
> bending unto thee; and all they that despised thee
> shall bow themselves down at the soles of thy feet; and
> they shall call thee The city of Jehovah, the Zion of the
> Holy One of Israel (Isaiah 60:14).

Both passages (here, and in Isaiah) are fulfilled in this
manner: Christ is the true Israel, of which ancient Jacob
was only a feeble type; and all who are Christ's and worship
him, are therefore worshipping *Israel*! Indirect reference to
this is found in Revelation 3:9, where, in the present dispensation, the false Jews who opposed Christianity, received

---

[30]James D. Bales, *NT Interpretation of OT Prophecies* (Searcy, Ark.: College
Press), p.153.
[31]Robert Jamieson, *op. cit.*, p. 802.

242 Commentary on the Minor Prophets

the word from Jesus that they would "come and worship
before the feet" of the church at Philadelphia, fulfilled when
Jews were converted and bowed before Christ with whom,
for ages during the present order, Gentiles have been identified. "Thus, 'the taking possession' referred to here will be
of a very different character from the subjugation of Edom
and other nations to David."[32] "The relationship between
Israel and the nations will not be that of a conqueror to the
conquered because it will be the Lord 'who will do this.' "[33]
Still another excellent commentary concerning the proper
interpretation of these verses is that of J. A. Motyer:

> The warlike metaphor in many of these passages is,
> of course, to be understood in terms of the kingship of
> the Lord Jesus Christ and the missionary expansion of
> his Church. This is the interpretation authorized by
> the NT (Acts 15:12-19).[34]

"All the nations that are called by thy name . . ." A very
interesting fact regarding this passage concerns the varia-
tion of it that appears to be in Acts in the passage cited
above:

> Through slight changes, almost infinitesimal in the
> Hebrew, the Septuagint translators (c. 250 B.C.) ren-
> dered this passage: "That the residue of men may seek
> after the Lord," these last two words being supplied as
> a necessary object to the transitive verb "seek"; and
> so it is quoted by James at the Council in Jerusalem
> (Acts 15:17). This passage is especially interesting as
> an outstanding example in textual criticism.[35]

In the manner thus indicated, the scholars, some of them,
have made this example (as they call it) their *carte blanche*
permission to *change* the Hebrew text in any manner that
pleases them; but we reject this. In the first place, we have
already noted that there is no certainty that James quoted
this verse, having categorically stated that what he quoted

---

[32]C.F. Keil, *op. cit.*, p. 332.
[33]Ralph L. Smith, *op. cit.*, p. 141.
[34]J.A. Motyer, *NBCR* (Grand Rapids: Wm. B. Eerdmans Publishing Company, 1979), p. 741.
[35]Albert Barnes, *op. cit.*, p. 338.

came from more than one prophet (Acts 15:15); and the words might well have been James' own inspired words derived from interpretation of the general message of many OT prophets. But even if it could be proved that he actually quoted this *changed* translation from the LXX, the explanation would then be that offered by Barnes:

> St. James quoted the words as they were familiar to his hearers (the Gentiles accompanying Paul), not correcting those that did not impair the meaning. This showed, incidentally, that even imperfection of translation does not empty God's word.[36]

Authority for recklessly changing the Hebrew text every time some scholar thinks he could improve it is certainly not resident in this so-called "example."

Verse 13, Behold the days come, saith Jehovah, that the plowman shall overtake the reaper, and the treader of grapes him that soweth seed: and the mountains shall drop sweet wine, and all the hills shall melt.

This language, couched in materialistic metaphor is nevertheless descriptive of the "spiritual blessings" to be realized upon the earth through the ultimate coming of the Messiah and the prosperity of his kingdom, the church, upon earth. Hyperbole is also employed, the very idea of the mountain springs running sweet wine instead of water being a certain indication of this. But, despite what seems to be over-extravagant language in this description, nothing weaker than this passage could properly convey the blessings that have come to mankind through the knowledge of the Lord and Saviour Jesus Christ. In comparison to the dark heathen lands where the Lord has never been received, those portions of earth which are even in the most nominal sense "Christian" are excellent examples, even of those material blessings which carry the weight of the metaphor in this glorious promise; and this still leaves untouched the far greater and more wonderful spiritual blessings of the grace, mercy, and peace that are the inheritance of all who know the Lord.

---

[36]George L. Robinson, *The Twelve Minor Prophets* (Grand Rapids: Baker Book House, 1979), p. 58.

Jamieson interpreted the metaphor of the "plowman and the reaper" as meaning that, "Such shall be the abundance that the harvest and vintage can hardly be gathered before time for preparing for the next crop."[37] The footnote in the Catholic Bible is also excellent: "By this is meant the great abundance of spiritual blessings, which by a constant succession, will enrich the Church of Christ."[38]

It was the great misfortune of the Hebrew people to interpret such passages as this *literally*; therefore, they looked forward to the coming of their Messiah who would enlarge their secular kingdom to include all surrounding nations and miraculously bring about the supernatural wonders like mountain springs running wine! The *unspiritual* in all generations find the word of God an enigma.

Verse 14, And I will bring back the captivity of my people Israel, and they shall build the waste cities, and inhabit them; and they shall plant vineyards and drink the wine thereof; they shall also make gardens, and eat the fruit of them. And I will plant them upon their land, and they shall no more be plucked up out of their land which I have given them, saith Jehovah thy God.

Just as the materialistic metaphor of verse 13 did not indicate any of those things *literally*, the same is true here. The turning again of the captivity of Israel is a reference to the captivity of men "in trespasses and sins," and the consequent joy of salvation upon receiving the fountain of life in Christ Jesus. "Israel" is a type of the holy Church, and the peace and prosperity in evidence here are symbols of the spiritual blessings "in Christ." "The truth expressed through this imagery tells of the total reversal of the effects of sin."[39] Sin is at the root of all man's problems; it was sin that resulted in insecurity, in wretchedness, unhappiness, and want. Solving the sin problem solves them all.

Some, of course, have found here a prophecy of the return of the Jews from Babylonian captivity, a captivity that occurred over a century later; but, as Keil noted, "This was

[37]Robert Jamieson, *op. cit.*, p. 802.
[38]*Catholic Version of the Holy Bible* (New York: Catholic Book Publishing Company, 1949), p. 991.
[39]J.A. Motyer, *op. cit.*, p. 741.

no planting of Israel to dwell for ever in their land, nor was it a setting up of the fallen tabernacle."[40] It is absolutely mandatory to read this prophecy of something that applies *after* the "fallen tabernacle" was restored in the Church of Jesus Christ.

Furthermore, it is just as wrong to seek the fulfilment of this is some far-off future event (altogether mythical), "When the Jews, who have been converted to their God and Saviour Jesus Christ, will one day be led back to Palestine."[41] In this light, it is a fact that, "The land which will flow with streams of divine blessing is not Palestine, but the domain of the Christian church.[42] This divine project will be completed when, one day, the fullness of the Gentiles shall have entered into the kingdom of Christ.

"They shall build the waste cities, and shall inhabit them . . ." Barnes gave an excellent interpretation of this, thus:

> Throughout the world, amid the desert of Heathendom, which was formerly deserted by God, Churches of Christ have arisen, which, for the firmness of faith, may be called cities, and for the gladness of hope which needeth not to be ashamed.[43]

By way of summary: The raising up of the fallen tabernacle of David began with the coming of Christ and the establishment of his church, or kingdom, upon earth. The possession of the remnant of Edom and all the other Gentile nations upon whom the Lord's name is called began to take place with the missionary thrust of the apostolical church; the return of God's people from captivity, is the return of uncounted millions of men from the service and pursuit of sin, with the resultant joy that issues in such great blessings that the most extravagant metaphor is necessary to describe them. The continued sifting of "the righteous remnant" of whatever origin will continue throughout time until the full company of God's redeemed from earth shall have been completed. Blessed be the name of the Lord. Amen.

---

[40]C.F. Keil, *op. cit.*, p. 336.
[41]*Ibid.*
[42]*Ibid.*
[43]Albert Barnes, *op. cit.*, p. 339.

BIBLIOGRAPHY

The following authors and sources were quoted in this commentary on Amos:

Ante-Nicene Fathers (Grand Rapids: Wm. B. Eerdmans Publishing Company) The writings of Irenaeus, Tertullian, Cyprian and Lactantius are quoted.

Bales, James D., *NT Interpretations of OT Prophecies* (Searcy, Ark.: College Press).

Barker, William P., *Everyone in the Bible* (Old Tappan, N.J.: Fleming H. Revell Company, 1966).

Barnes, Albert, *Notes on the OT, Minor Prophets, Vol. 1* (Grand Rapids: Baker Book House, 1953).

Butler, Paul T., *Minor Prophets* (Joplin: College Press, 1968).

Catholic Edition of the Holy Bible (New York: Catholic Book Publishing House, 1949).

Clarke, Adam, *Commentary on the Whole Bible, Vols. III, V* (New York: T. Mason & G. Lane, 1837).

Deane, W. J., *The Pulpit Commentary, Vol. 14, Amos* (Grand Rapids: Wm. B. Eerdmans Publishing Company, 1950).

Encyclopaedia Britannica (Chicago: William Benton, Publisher, 1961).

Ferm, Vergilius, *Encyclopedia of Religion* (New York: Philosophical Society, 1945).

Fosbroke, Hughell E. W., *Interpreter's Bible, Vol. VI* (New York: Abingdon Press, 1957).

Good News Bible (New York: American Bible Society, 1976).

Hammershaimb, Erling, *The Book of Amos, translated by John Sturdy* (New York: Shocken Books, 1970).

Harper, William Rainey, *Amos & Hosea* (New York: Charles Scribner's Sons, 1910).

Henry, Matthew, *Matthew Henry's Commentary, Vol. IV* (Old Tappan, N.J.: Fleming H. Revell Company).

Howard, J. Keir, *New Layman's Bible Commentary* (Grand Rapids: Zondervan Publishing House, 1979).

Jamieson, Robert, *Commentary on the Whole Bible* by Jamieson, Faussett and Brown (Grand Rapids: Zondervan Publishing Company, 1961).
Josephus, Flavius, *Antiquities and Wars of the Jews, translated by William Whiston* (New York: Holt, Rinehart, and Winston).

Keil, C. F., *Commentary on the Whole Bible* by Keil and Delitzsch (Grand Rapids: Wm. B. Eerdmans Publishing Company).

Lockyer, Herbert, *All the Men of the Bible* (Grand Rapids: Zondervan Publishing House, 1958).

Mays, James Luther, *Amos, A Commentary* (Philadelphia: The Westminster Press, 1969).
McFadden, John Edgar, *A Cry for Justice* (New York: Charles Scribner's Sons, 1912).
McKeating, Henry, *The Cambridge Bible Commentary, Amos, Hosea and Micah* (Cambridge: At the University Press, 1971).
Morgan, G. Campbell, *The Minor Prophets* (Old Tappan, N.J.: Fleming H. Revell Company, 1960).
Motyer, J. A., *New Bible Commentary Revised* (Grand Rapids: Wm. B. Eerdmans Publishing Company, 1979).

Robertson, James, *International Standard Bible Encyclopaedia* (Chicago: The Howard-Severance Company, 1915).
Robinson, George L., *The Twelve Minor Prophets* (Grand Rapids: Baker Book House, 1926).
Robinson, H. Wheeler, *The Abingdon Bible Commentary* (New York: Abingdon Press, 1929).

Schultz, Arnold C., *The Wycliffe Bible Commentary* (Chicago: Moody Press, 1962).
Smart, James D., *Interpreter's Bible Dictionary* (New York: Abingdon Press, 1962).
Smith, Ralph L., *The Broadman Bible Commentary, Vol. 7* (Nashville: Broadman Press, 1970).

Thorogood, Bernard, *A Guide to the Book of Amos* (Valley Forge: Judson Press, 1971).

Unger, Merrill F., *Archeology and the OT* (Grand Rapids: Zondervan Publishing House, 1954).

Unger, Merrill F., *Unger's Bible Dictionary* (Chicago: Moody Press, 1957).

Wolfe, Rolland Emerson, *Meet Amos and Hosea* (New York: Harper and Brothers, Publisher, 1945).

Wycliffe Bible Encyclopaedia (Chicago: Moody Press, 1961).

Jonah

INTRODUCTION

The prophet Jonah is the only OT character singled out by the Lord Jesus Christ as the great type of himself; and, concerning the event of Jonah's miraculous survival (or resurrection) after three days and three nights in the belly of a sea-monster, our Lord unhesitatingly referred to it as "a sign," using exactly the same word used in John 2:11 where the apostle John speaks of the miracle at Cana as the beginning of Jesus' "signs." The NT usage of this word in Matthew 12:38,39, in which passage Jesus made the miraculous experience of Jonah a specific type of his own death, burial, and resurrection from the dead, is such as to make it absolutely certain that Jesus affirmed that the biblical account of Jonah is factual and historical. The NT word for "sign" in these passages has the technical meaning of, "a miraculous act, as a token of divine authority and power."[1]

The objections which enemies of the word of God have alleged against the book of Jonah are so weak, illogical, unscientific and ignorant as to appear absolutely worthless in the eyes of any careful scholar. As Keil stated it, "The objections . . . are extremely trivial, and destitute of any conclusive force."[2] Somewhat later in this introduction, these will be particularly examined.

Jonah stands in the OT as the most overwhelmingly complete type of the Son of God to be found anywhere in the Bible.

Jonah and Jesus

Both were asleep on board a ship at sea in a storm.
Both were awakened; Jonah by the captain, Jesus by the apostles.
Both were involved with the ship's security, Jonah for danger, and Jesus for safety.

---

[1]W.E. Vine, *An Expository Dictionary of NT Words, Vol. IV* (Old Tappan, N.J.: Fleming H. Revell Company, 1940), p. 29.

[2]C.F. Keil, *Commentary on the OT, Vol. X* (Grand Rapids: Wm. B. Eerdmans Publishing Company, 1978), p. 380.

> Both gave themselves to save others, Jonah for the sailors, Jesus for all men.
> Both produced a great calm, Jonah by being cast overboard, Jesus by fiat.
> Both were "alive" after that three days and three nights experience.
> Both converted the Gentiles, Jonah at Nineveh, and Jesus throughout the earth.
> Both were from Galilee, Jonah from Gath-hepher (2 Kings 14:25), and Jesus from Nazareth.
> Etc. (See more on this at end of commentary on Jonah)

There were also many contrasts between Jonah and Jesus, as is always the case between type and anti-type; and many of these will be noted in the discussion of the text.

The above are a few of the principal reasons why we have chosen to do a commentary on the book of Jonah.

The Historicity of Jonah

One who believes in the Lord Jesus Christ has no hesitation whatever in receiving the book of Jonah as a factual account of what really occurred; for, it is absolutely inconceivable that Jesus Christ would have made a folk tale, a fable, or a myth to be the singular type of his own death, burial and resurrection from the dead. The evidence that Jonah is indeed history is extensive and convincing.

> The symbolical and typical significance of the mission of the prophet Jonah precludes the assumption that the account in his book is a myth, a parabolical fiction, or simply the description of a symbolical transaction which the prophet experienced in spirit only. The contents of the book are at variance with all such assumptions.[3]

The Jew, the Moslem and the Christian all venerate Jonah as a prophet of God and have continuously done so throughout a time period of over 2,700 years! Jonah is read every year by the Jews on the Day of Atonement. "This

---

[3]*Ibid.*, p. 387.

speaks forcibly for the veracity of the account."[4]

The language used and the manner of relating this narrative are such as to demand their acceptance as an account of actual events.

> The style and language used give every evidence of an historical narrative. . . . The historicity of Jonah's three days and nights in the fish and the repentance of Nineveh were accepted facts, not only by Jesus who referred to them as such, but also by the Scribes and Pharisees to whom he commended the event as a sign.[5]

As Blair commented, "There is nothing in Jonah to suggest that its contents are not historic."[6] The profound scholars of the early church, the great leaders of the Reformation, and the giant exegetes of the Restoration have all viewed Jonah as a record of historical fact.

Despite Jonah's being "one of a kind" and very different from other OT books, the Jews gave it an honored place in their canon of the holy scriptures, an act that must be considered providential. "There can be only one reason why the Jews accepted this book as such, and this is the inspiration of the Holy Spirit."[7] Jonah, of course, in addition to being a type of Christ, is a type of Israel as well; and his being cast overboard prefigured the "casting away" of Israel upon their rejection of Christ. Ellul further commented:

> The Jews did not recognize this book as prophecy for the reason that it had the same characteristics as other prophetic books (for it did not have such characteristics) but for mysterious reasons which they did not fully grasp themselves and which we today can decipher. At this point they were led to bear witness precisely against themselves; though in the last resort, this was good news for them too.[8]

[4]Don W. Hillis, *Jonah Speaks Again* (Grand Rapids: Baker Book House, 1967), p. 16.

[5]*Wycliffe Bible Encyclopedia, Vol. I* (Chicago: Moody Press, 1975), p. 944.

[6]J.A. Allen Blair, *Living Obediently* (Neptune, N.J.: Loizeaux Brothers, 1963), p. 9.

[7]Jacques Ellul, *The Judgment of Jonah* (Grand Rapids: Wm. B. Eerdmans Publishing Company, 1961), p. 14.

[8]*Ibid.*, p. 15.

Josephus commented upon the facts of Jonah's experience, equating it with the activities of other prophets and of the various kings of Israel and Judah, even giving a few historical facts not mentioned in the book itself, including the place where the fish discharged Jonah.[9]

The appeal to the main facts of this historical narrative by Jesus Christ himself, affirming that a miracle indeed occurred, that Jonah indeed was vomited up alive, that he actually preached to Nineveh, and that the Ninevites repented (Matthew 12:38-41) is far more than sufficient authority for establishing the historicity of Jonah. "This testimony puts an end to all mythological, allegorical and hypothetical interpretations of those great facts."[10] And again, in the words of the matchless Adam Clarke, "In its literal sense alone, I undertake the interpretation of this book."[11]

Authorship

The facts related in the book of Jonah are such that no one except Jonah could have written them, for example, the prayer that he prayed while inside the fish. Furthermore, the fact of Jonah's being, in all probability, a great and popular hero to the entire Jewish nation as a result of his having accurately prophesied the recapture of Israel's lost cities by Jeroboam II (2 Kings 14:25), that fact means that no other person except Jonah would have written a book which casts the prophet himself in such unfavorable light as that which shines upon him in this remarkable narrative. His disobedience, his petulance, and his anger over the repentance of the Ninevites, etc., exhibit characteristics and attitudes which no later Jew could conceivably have attributed to a national hero.

The only possible reason for Jonah's being in the Jewish canon of scripture lies in their certainty that the prophet Jonah was actually the author of this book. If it had been a myth, it would have been rejected, as nothing mythological was ever accepted by them.

---

[9]Josephus, *Antiquities of the Jews, IX, 10.1.*
[10]Adam Clarke, *Commentary on the Whole Bible, Vol. IV*(New York: T. Mason & G. Lane, 1837), p. 700.
[11]*Ibid.*

No Israelite could ever have invented a story representing God as showing mercy to the Gentiles.

Various objections alleged against Jonah's authorship of this narrative will be noted under the heading, Criticism Refuted, below.

Date

The book of Jonah dates a little before or during the long reign of Jeroboam II, because his prophecies of the prosperity of that monarch occurred either at the beginning or prior to the beginning of Jereboam's long reign of 41 years. The actual dates of this reign are disputed. Butler dated that king's rule from 783 to 743 B.C.;[12] and, following this dating, the events described in Jonah probably occurred "before 745 B.C. when Assyria rebounded to dominance in the Near East under Tiglath-Peleser III."[13] Unger placed Jonah's preaching "in the reign of Assurdan III (771-754 B.C.)."[14] Michael C. Griffiths dated Jereboam's reign in 793 to 753 B.C., stating that the events of Jonah "should be assigned to the middle of the eighth century B.C."[15] W. J. Deane placed Jereboam's reign earlier, stating that, "The date of Jereboam's reign as now corrected by Assyrian chronology is 799 to 759 B.C.,"[16] going on to date Jonah a little earlier, "in 800 B.C., or a little earlier, among the first of the minor prophets, and somewhat senior to Amos and Hosea."[17] Paul Butler also agreed. "Perhaps the date of Jonah would best be put at approximately 800 B.C."[18] Because it certainly could have been a bit later than this, we shall opt for the round figure and call it within the period 800-750 B.C.

---

[12]Paul T. Butler, *Minor Prophets* (Joplin, Missouri: College Press, 1968), p. 213.

[13]*Wycliffe Bible Encyclopedia, op. cit.*, p. 945.

[14]Merrill F. Unger, *Unger's Bible Dictionary* (Chicago: Moody Press, 1957), p. 602.

[15]Michael C. Griffiths, *The New Layman's Bible Commentary* (Grand Rapids: Zondervan Publishing House, 1979), p. 975.

[16]W.J. Deane, *Pulpit Commentary, Vol. 14 ii* (Grand Rapids: Wm. B. Eerdmans Publishing Company, 1950), p. vii.

[17]*Ibid.*

[18]Paul T. Butler, *op. cit.*, p. 214.

Purpose

A number of divine purposes are clearly seen in the book of Jonah, the first of these clearly being that of demonstrating that God is the God of Gentiles and all men, as well as the God of the Jews. There is also a warning in it for Israel to show them God's displeasure at their exclusiveness and disregard of other races, Jonah himself serving as a type of Israel; and just as Jonah was thrown overboard in his disobedience, Israel too, in time, would be "cast away" because of their rejection of God's word and their refusal to receive the Messiah. Keil also pointed out God's purpose "to overthrow pharisaical reliance upon lineal descent from Abraham"[19] as being alone-sufficient for salvation. The mercy of God as extended first to Jonah, and later to Nineveh, has the purpose of showing God's willingness to forgive and redeem those who will truly turn to him, no matter what their former condition might have been. Not merely the Gentiles, as in the case of Nineveh, but also the carnal Hebrew nation also, if they should repent, will find the merciful God ready to receive and restore.

The central purpose of Jonah, however, is that of prophesying the death, burial and resurrection of Jesus Christ. It is not a mere oral prophecy but an event of historical fact designed by the God of heaven himself as the type and prefiguration of Jesus' death, burial and resurrection. The fact of Christ himself having made exactly that application and usage of the event (Matthew 12:38-42) makes this absolutely certain. It should also be noted that in that passage Jesus placed Jonah alongside the queen of the South and king Solomon, making it clear that Jesus understood all three to be historical persons. We find full agreement with DeHaan:

> In no other book do we have as clear a prophecy of the gospel of the death and resurrection of Christ as in the book of Jonah. Since the devil hates the gospel, and Jonah is the clearest picture of the gospel in

---

[19]C.F. Keil, *op. cit.*, p. 384.

prophecy, it is, therefore, no wonder that he has so desperately attacked this book.[20]

It is significant that when Jesus singled out Jonah as *the sign* by which he would refute and confound his enemies, there were a number of other OT types which he might have chosen; but he passed over them and selected Jonah. For example: (1) The dry land rose out of the deadness of the primeval seas and burst forth with abundant vegetation and fruit. "And the evening and the morning were *the third day*" (Genesis 1:13). (2) The passage of the Red Sea by the children of Israel is a historical type of Christian baptism, which, in turn, is a likeness of the death, burial, and resurrection of Christ (1st Corinthians 10:2f). (3) Another specific prophecy (by event) of the death, burial and resurrection of Christ is to be seen in the sacrifice of Isaac by his father Abraham upon Mount Moriah. "For three days Isaac was potentially dead in the mind of Abraham, but after three days of agony, he was restored to him again on Mount Moriah."[21] Abraham had already reckoned Isaac to be dead, but "accounted that God was able to raise him up, even from the dead, from whence also he received him in a figure" (Hebrew 11:19). (4) Following the death of the old world in the waters of the flood, from which Noah and his family were saved in the ark, the Genesis account recorded the exact day of the resting of the ark on Ararat, "the seventeenth day of the seventh month" (Genesis 8:4); and "Why?" it may be asked is that exact day specified? God later instituted the Passover to be observed on the "fourteenth day" of the same month. In a sense, therefore, death marked the fourteenth day, and new life marked the seventeenth day of the same month. However, it was to none of these that Jesus turned for "the sign," but to Jonah. Jesus' choice of Jonah becomes, therefore, a matter of tremendous importance and significance. Who can doubt that the events centered in Jonah were purposefully designed by God himself as a witness of the far greater wonder that

---

[20]Dr. M.R. DeHaan, M.D., *Jonah, Fact or Fiction?* (Grand Rapids: Zondervan Publishing House, 1957), p. 12.

[21]*Ibid.*, p. 10.

would eventually occur in the resurrection of the Son of God?

Another discernible purpose in the book of Jonah is that of teaching the ultimate resurrection of all men from the dead. Since the resurrection of Christ itself is a prophecy of this same thing; and, since Christ made Jonah's experience a type of his own, the events in Jonah become in a genuine, although secondary, sense a prophecy of the resurrection of all men from the dead. There are echoes of this truth in some of the writings of the third century. Methodius wrote as follows:

> As Jonah spent three days and as many nights in the whale's belly, and was delivered up sound again, so shall we all, who have passed through the three stages of this present life (the beginning, the middle, and the end), rise again.[22]

Still another purpose of this magnificent book is to demonstrate that there is always an element of contingency in the promises of God, whether of judgment and destruction on the one hand, or grace and salvation on the other. Jonah is a vivid example of the truth revealed by Jeremiah:

> At what instant I shall speak concerning a nation, and concerning a kingdom, to pluck up, and to pull down, and to destroy it; if that nation, against whom I have pronounced, turn from their evil, I will repent of the evil that I thought to do to them. And at what instant I shall speak concerning a nation, and concerning a kingdom, to build and to plant it; if it do evil in my sight, that it obey not my voice, then I will repent of the good, wherewith I said I would benefit them (Jeremiah 18:7-10).

Of course, this is exactly the truth of which Jonah was ignorant; but the experiences related in the book that bears his name abundantly illustrate it. People who cavil at the fact that after God, through Jonah, promised to destroy Nineveh "in forty days," he did not do so, are exactly as

---

[22]Methodius *in Ante-Nicene Fathers, Vol. VI* (Grand Rapids: Wm. B. Eerdmans Publishing Company, 1951), p. 378.

ignorant as was Jonah of this matchless truth. The whole religious world of our day which receives a "once saved, always saved" doctrine of salvation is dwelling in the same darkness. If a wicked man turns from his wickedness and obeys the Lord, he shall be saved; and, if a righteous man turns from his righteousness and disobeys the Lord, he shall be lost.

> It is precisely because God is immutable, that his relation to men, and his treatment of them vary with the changes in their character and conduct. In a word, *he changes because he is unchangeable.*[23]

As Henderson expressed it, "Neither God's promises nor his threatenings are unconditional."[24] This applies to God's promise to the chosen people, no less than it applies to all who ever lived, as spelled out so dramatically in Deuteronomy 28th chapter.

Criticisms Refuted

Here, we shall give some attention to the objections which evil men have made regarding the book of Jonah. The great reason underlying all objections and criticisms directed against Jonah is the unbelief of sinful men who reject out of hand the doctrine of the supernatural, not believing, really, in God at all, hooting at any such thing as a miracle, categorically denying any such things as the inspiration of the Bible, predictive prophecy, or any such thing as divine concern with the affairs of men. It is this reason, whether stated or not, and usually disguised or concealed, that actually underlies the vast majority of the multitude of criticisms and objections against this holy book in the name of alleged "scholarship," but which to an amazing extent are anchored in the "lack of information" on the part of objectors. Before moving to a consideration of the great issue, which is that of the supernatural, we shall try to swat a few of the gnats!

1. "We can be certain that Jonah is not the author of the book that bears his name . . . from the fact that the book is

---

[23]John W. Haley, *Discrepancies of the Bible* (Nashville: B.C. Goodpasture, 1951), p. 65.

[24]Henderson, as quoted by John W. Haley, *op. cit.*, p. 148.

262 Commentary on the Minor Prophets

composed almost entirely in the third person."[25] This objection results from an astonishing ignorance upon the part of the objector. The use of the third person "is not uncharacteristic of historical narrative."[26] Moses always referred to himself in the third person throughout Exodus and Deuteronomy. Other OT authors who used the third person extensively in their writings are: Exra, Nehemiah, Solomon, Amos, Jeremiah, Haggai, and Daniel.[27] The same style is extensively followed in the NT. Matthew told the story of his own conversion in the third person; John almost always referred to himself in the third person as "the disciple that leaned upon Jesus' breast." Paul used the third person frequently, especially in recounting the record of his being caught up to the third heaven, etc., etc. In fact, Barnes went so far as to say, "It is the exception when any sacred writer refers to himself in the first person."[28] Barnes also said, "It is strange that, beyond the babyhood of criticism, any argument should be drawn from the fact that the Prophet writes of himself in the third person!"[29]

But it is not merely the sacred writers who have employed the third person in their writings.

> There is nothing unusual about historians using the third person. *The Anabasis of Xenophon, The Commentaries of Julius Caesar,* and the works of Josephus, Thucydides, and Frederick the Great are among examples that might be cited.[30]

The genuineness of none of these works has ever been questioned on the basis of their being written in the third person. What, then, must be thought of the arrogant certainty with which some "scholars" use a false argument like this? It would appear that only two logical explanations may be offered, (1) on the basis of the objector's lack of information, or (2) on the basis of his lack of integrity.

---

[25]Jacob M. Myers, *The Book of Jonah in the Layman's Bible Commentary* (Atlanta: The John Knox Press, 1979), p. 160.

[26]*Wycliffe Bible Encyclopedia, Vol. I. op. cit.,* p. 945.

[27]Albert Barnes, *Barnes Notes on the OT, Minor Prophets, Vol. ii* (Grand Rapids: Baker Book House, 1953), p. 373.

[28]*Ibid.*

[29]*Ibid.*

[30]W.J. Deane, *op. cit.,* p. v.

Perhaps it is more charitable to take the former.

2. Basing the argument principally upon the existence of "a number of Aramaisms in Jonah," James D. Smart wrote, "It seems clear, therefore, that the book was written in the period after the exile."[31] Of course, the meaning of this argument is that Jonah is not the author, and that it may be considered either as some kind of an allegory or even fiction. But what about the argument? It is true, to be sure, that there are a few Aramaisms in Jonah. "We need only say that the so-called late Aramaisms cannot be proved to be unknown to the earlier Hebrew."[32] The *only* non-Hebraic word in the whole book is *taam*, a Syriac expression meaning "decree," which Jonah doubtless heard in Nineveh in connection with the kings published edict. Keil pointed out that the "so-called Aramaisms belong either to the speech of Galilee or to the language of ordinary intercourse";[33] and of course Jonah was a Galillean! As a matter of plain fact, the presence of Aramaisms in Jonah are in no sense whatever an indication of a late date.

> Aramaisms cannot be made a criterion for determining the date or the authorship since Aramaisms occur in OT books from both early and late periods. Furthermore, the recently discovered texts from Ras Shamra contain Aramaic elements, and they date as early as 1500-1400 B.C.![34]

Such information as this should be known to any competent scholar, but the argument we are refuting takes no account whatever of the archaelogical discoveries that deny and contradict it. The Ras Shamra discoveries (1929-1937) are from the north Syrian coast just opposite the pointed peninsula of Cyprus. C. F. A. Schaeffer led the French expedition which uncovered this extremely important corpus of Canaanite religious epic poetry dating back beyond 1400 B.C.,[35] and in which there were many of the very

---

[31]James D. Smart, *Interpreter's Bible, Vol. VI* (New York: Abingdon Press, 1956), p. 873.

[32]W.J. Deane, *op. cit.*, p. viii.

[33]C.F. Keil, *op. cit.*, p. 381.

[34]Paul T. Butler, *op. cit.*, p. 213.

[35]Merrill F. Unger, *op. cit.*, p. 912.

same kind of Aramaisms, a few of which are in Jonah, and upon which the "scholars" are quick to conclude that the book (Jonah) could not possibly have been written before the 2nd, 3rd, of 4th century B.C.! It is precisely this kind of critical attack upon the Bible that has absolutely discredited the so-called "higher criticism" in the last quarter of the 20th century. The Canaanite discoveries demonstrate that the Aramaisms in Jonah had been in common usage in Jonah's area of residence for at least six centuries prior to the date we have assigned his book.

3. The extension of God's blessings beyond the narrow borders of Israel, as dramatically presented in Jonah, is declared to be due to "the influence of Isaiah 40-60 upon Jonah, inspiring him with his vision of a world upon which God might yet have compassion";[36] leading to the conclusion that the book was written in the period after the exile, and not earlier than 400 B.C. Such a view is not at all logical. Isaiah lived long after Jonah's time; and Jonah's vision of the world-wide view of salvation for all the world by no means originated with Isaiah, but dates from the days of Abraham himself in whom God made very clear his intention of blessing "all the families of the earth" (Genesis 12:3).

4. Hillis speaks of those who charge that Jonah is a fraudulent book, based upon their argument that he "quoted from some of the Psalms that were written in a period later than Jonah."[37] As Dean pointed out, however:

> The phrases in the prayer (ch. 2), which are also found in the Psalms, are either taken from those written by David and his comtemporaries, which of course were well known long before Jonah's day, or (in the case of two in v. 2 and v. 7), may have been borrowed by the authors of Psalm 120:1, and 142:3 from Jonah.[38]
>
> To be sure, it is absolutely impossible to prove that a similar phrase to one found in Jonah is also found in a Psalm written long afterwards is any kind of proof that the later writer was copied by the earlier one! An

[36]James D. Smart, *op. cit.*, p. 873.
[37]Don W. Hillis, *op. cit.*, p. 15.
[38]W.J. Deane, *op. cit.*, p. viii.

argument based upon such an allegation is worthless. As Hillis put it, "Did Jonah quote from the Psalms, or did the psalmist quote Jonah?"[39]

5. This objection is complex. It alleges that:

> Jonah could not have spoken their language in preaching, that it is not reasonable that such a great city should have repented so easily, and that there is no secular record of such.[40]

The totality of Jonah's message, as delivered to Nineveh, according to the book itself, consisted of only eight words! Any ordinary person could have learned such a sentence in twenty minutes; and the desperate nature of the critic's cause is surely evident in the presentation of such a so-called argument as this. Besides that, Jonah, in all probability, was a friend of King Jeroboam II and might easily have had a passing knowledge of his friend's powerful enemies, including Assyrians, and including an elementary knowledge of their language. The two countries were adjacent; and such an objection as this is equivalent to saying that a prominent Texas politician could not have had a sufficient knowledge of Spanish to speak a single sentence of it in Mexico.

The notion that it is not reasonable that a great city like Nineveh repented so easily springs out of a double ignorance (1) of the times in which the repentance occurred, and (2) of the import of certain passages in Jonah itself.

(1) As Deane wrote, "It is possible that Jonah's mission was executed . . . at a time when the Assyrian monarch was weakened by revolt, and the country was suffering from plague and famine."[41] It is also possible that Jonah's mission was synchronized with the famous eclipse of the sun which occurred on June 15, 763 B.C.[42] Certainly God would have aided the prophet's mission. Such things as these would surely have pre-conditioned the people to repentance.

(2) However, it was the action of the king himself, in

---

[39]*Ibid.*
[40]*Wycliffe Encyclopedia, Vol. I*, p. 947.
[41]W.J. Deane, *op. cit.*, p. viii.
[42]*Ibid.*

conjuction with his nobles, that led to the general repentance. In a sense, of course, it is amazing that the king would
have led the way in repentance, this being quite atypical of
ancient monarchs; but it is more than accounted for by a
short sentence in Jonah 3:6, "And the word came unto the
king of Nineveh." This is doubtless a reference to the king's
hearing from some source (perhaps even from the sailors
who threw Jonah overboard) that Jonah was indeed a man
of Almighty God, his being alive after being cast into the
sea being all the proof anyone ever needed that he was
indeed God's man. It was this knowledge on the part of the
king that triggered his favorable response to Jonah's message and issued in his leading the whole people into repentance.

Such considerations as these far more than justify our
outright rejection of the picayune objection that the repentance of Nineveh is "unreasonable." Given all the facts and
circumstances, which admittedly we do not have, but may
only surmise, the repentance that issued from Jonah's
preaching would appear most reasonable indeed.

The *fact* of there being no "historical record" of the repentance of Ninevah is not really a fact, but a half-truth.
There is indeed no secular history of Nineveh's repentance,
but Jonah has a record of it, given in vivid detail. The
silence of pagan history regarding this repentance is merely
what should have been expected. The repentance probably
wore off quickly and may have been only superficial to
begin with; and it would be a genuine surprise indeed if
pagan historians had paid any attention whatever to it.
Christ himself affirmed that the Ninevites "repented at the
preaching of Jonah," this testimony of the Christ being
recorded in Matthew. Thus there are two documentary histories of that repentance, Jonah and Matthew.

There is absolutely nothing in such quibbles as these
upon which to challenge the historicity of the book of Jonah.

6. It is popular among critics to make such an allegation
as this: "It is significant that in 3:3 Nineveh is spoken of as
a city of the distant past."[43] The verse in question reads:

---

[43]James D. Smart, *op. cit.*, p. 873.

"Now Nineveh was an exceeding great city of three days' journey." This emphatically does not say anything resembling the critic's allegation. Unger pointed out that:

> "Ninevah was a great city" does not imply a date after 600 B.C., but merely points to the dimensions of the city as Jonah found them. Luke 24:13 constitutes a parallel. This verse says that Emmaus "was from Jerusalem about three-score furlongs."[44]

Grammarians have pointed out that the past tense with reference to the size of Nineveh is synchronous; that is, it harmonizes with the past tense used in this part of the narrative. Critics are supposed to know this, but apparently many of them do not.

Far from being an argument for a late date, this verse (3:3) is actually a very good argument for an early date, as pointed out by Jamieson:

> The mention of the greatness proves rather that the book was written at an early date, *before* the Israelites had that intimate knowledge of it which they must have had soon afterwards through frequent Assyrian inroads.[45]

7. It is objected that no writer living when Jonah is thought to have lived would have referred to the ruler of Assyria as "the king of Nineveh." As Dummelow put it:

> No writer at a time when Assyria was the greatest of the world-powers would have described its ruler as the "king of Nineveh," any more than Napoleon at the height of his power would have been called "the King of Paris."[46]

In this instance, it is clear that Jonah followed the usages of his own nation, rather than that of the hated Assyrians. As Unger observed, "The Israelites normally spoke of the

---

[44]Merrill F. Unger, *op. cit.*, p. 602.

[45]Jamieson, Fausset, and Brown, *Commentary on the Whole Bible* (Grand Rapids: Zondervan Publishing House, 1961), p. 805.

[46]J.R. Dummelow, *Commentary on the Holy Bible* (New York: The Macmillan Company, 1937), p. 575.

ruler of Assyria as 'king.'[47] Furthermore, there are a number of OT examples of the Israelites associating the title 'king' with the ruler's capitol city, rather than with his entire domain. An example of this is in I Kings 20:43 and 21:1, where the King of Israel (the whole northern kingdom) is called "the king of Samaria." It is, therefore, mere cavil to suppose that Jonah would not have followed the same usage when speaking of the King of Assyria. Incidentally, if Jonah did not come till after Isaiah, who is alleged to have had so much influence upon him, there is no way that Jonah would not have followed the lead of Isaiah who did refer to the "king of Nineveh" as "the King of Assyria." (Isaiah 8:7). Thus Jonah's particular usage of "king of Ninevah" (3:6) shows positively that he wrote long before Isaiah, when a more primitive method of addressing their kings was the order of the day.

8. Jonah's prophecy of the destruction of Ninevah did not come true. One of the purposes of the book of Jonah is that of demonstrating that all of God's promises, whether of blessing or judgment, are conditional, always and without exception. This objection was refuted more fully under the title Purpose, above.

9. Another type of objection is that which denies the book is history on the grounds that many details are left out. As Hitzig declaimed:

> The author leaps over the long and wearisome journey to Nineveh, says nothing about Jonah's subsequent fate, or his place of abode, or the spot where he was cast upon the land, or the name of the Assyrian king . . . all the more minute details which are necessarily connected with true history.[48]

As Keil pointed out, if such an impractical test as this should ever be imposed upon any of the historical writings that have come down to us through history, "The whole would be exposed to criticism, but their truth could not be shaken."[49]

[47]Merrill F. Unger, *op. cit.*, p. 602.
[48]C.F. Keil, *op. cit.*, p. 380.
[49]*Ibid.*

Such "minute details" demanded by such critics could do nothing, even if they were available, except gratify the curiosity of men, rather than aid them in understanding the divine message. Many details are omitted from all histories; and it is an unreasonable quibble that intrudes such an objection into the examination of the holy scriptures.

10. Some infidels classify the book of Jonah in the same category as a number of ancient fables which are alleged to resemble it. (1) There is the heathen fable of Andromeda's deliverance from a sea-monster by Perseus, (2) or the tale from Herodotus of Arion the musician thrown into the sea by sailors, and carried safely to shore by a dolphin, (3) or, again, that of Hercules who sprang into the jaws of a sea-monster and was three days in his belly when he undertook to rescue Hesione! Apart from the fact that there is no pagan myth or fable that is worthy to be compared with Jonah, questions of sin and righteousness, repentance and forgiveness, accountability to Almighty God, etc. are foreign to all such heathen tales. There has never been one of them that exhibited the slightest moral or ethical value; and any alleged resemblance is so slight as to deny any connection whatever with the sacred narrative. Besides all that, if there is some slight connection, it would have to be derived from the fact of pagans having corrupted and perverted the Jonah account in order to adapt it to their own purposes. As Jamieson said, "If there is a connection, the heathen fables are probably corruptions of the sacred narrative."[50] Satan has always imitated the divine miracles, as in the case of the magicians of Pharaoh casting down their staffs and changing them into serpents in order to imitate the greater miracle of Moses' rod-serpent; but Moses' rod-serpent swallowed them all up. Enemies of the book of Jonah will have to come up with something better than heathen fables.

11. Jonah is the only OT book that does not mention Israel, and the only prophecy in it concerns a heathen city, Nineveh. This objection was raised by the Jews themselves, although it was not considered any sufficient reason for keeping the book out of their canon. It seems that Israel

---

[50]Jamieson, *op. cit.*, p. 805.

was omitted from any reference in Jonah by design. The entire experience of Jonah was intended as a rebuke to Israel; and the silence of the prophetic word for them indicated a time future when, because of their rebellions and rejection of the Messiah, God's face would be turned away from them forever until such a time as they might repent.

12. The whole story is a parable! This objection is embalmed as a title for a subdivision of the Interpreter's Bible, and would appear to be the most popular of the current style of objections; but it is absolutely impossible for the book of Jonah, logically, to be understood as a parable.

> If the three days' confinement of Jonah in the belly of the fish really had the typical significance which Christ attributes to it in Mathew 12:38-41, and Luke 11:29, it can neither be a myth, a dream, nor a parable, nor a merely visionary occurrence experienced by the prophet; but it must have had as much objective reality as the facts of the death, burial, and resurrection of Christ.[51]

Of course, the only reason for denominating Jonah as a parable is to get rid of the miracle; but the prime beauty of all parables is that they "could have occurred." Therefore, if a miracle will not do in history, it will not do in a parable either.

We have little patience with the school of interpreters who allege that Jonah is some kind of fable, parable, allegory, myth or legend. If they do not believe in the Saviour of the world, then let them say so; but to profess Christianity and deny the Saviour's accuracy in designating this book as history is antithetical to everything in the Bible. As Unger brilliantly stated it:

> The book is correctly evaluated as history. There is not the slightest reason to stumble over the miraculous and to brand it as legend or myth. The miracles of the book of Jonah are a piece with those that honeycomb all scripture, particularly the Pentateuch.[52]

---

[51]C.F. Keil, *op. cit.*, p. 388.
[52]Merrill F. Unger, *op. cit.*, p. 601.

The miracles of Jonah are no more incredible than the miracles performed by Moses, the crossing of the Red Sea, the pillar of cloud by day, the pillar of fire by night, the manna, the water from the rock, and numerous other miracles of the OT. It is not any more wonderful than the changing of the water into wine, the raising of Lazarus from the dead, Christ walking on the sea, feeding a multitude from a lad's lunch basket; and it is, in fact, a far lesser wonder than the death, burial and resurrection of Christ which it typifies.

It is simple infidelity which can assert, "The large number of miracles recorded (in Jonah) precludes a historical basis."[53]

There are, of course, just as many objections to the book of Jonah as the cunning and ingenuity of biblical enemies can invent; and this examination of a few of them is by no means exhaustive; but these are more than sufficent to show the character of *all objections*, which are clearly seen to be illogical, unscholarly, unscientific, grounded in misinformation, or a lack of information, and generally exhibiting qualities which are very unflattering to the objectors.

The Problem of the Supernatural

If there is any genuine objection to the book of Jonah, it has to be grounded in the unwillingness of men to believe in the supernatural, or miracle, or divine concern and intrusion into the affairs of humanity. This is really the *only* issue. As Dr. Robert Flynt of the University of Scotland once said, "In the last analysis, all issues resolve into the existence, or not, of the supernatural; all else fades into the cosmic background." In any generation, the rejection of the faith in the supernatural entails consequences of the most hurtful and devastating nature. In essence, it means that there is nothing in the entire universe any higher than a man; creation was an accident; life was developed fortuitously; and man himself is but a disease of the agglutinated dust! Every man who rejects supernaturalism claims for himself the same cosmic value as a dog or a rat. He will-

---

[53]G. Herbert Livingston, *Wycliffe Bible Commentary* (Chicago: Moody Press, 1962), p. 843.

ingly assents to a destiny that leaves him in the rottenness of a grave forever, and spurns all of the wonderful promises which have been certified to mankind through the holy mission of Jesus Christ our Lord. No wonder that,"Jesus marvelled because of their unbelief" (Mark 6:6).

It is precisely the supernatural element of it that constitutes the glory of the book of Jonah. Its miracles, far from being superfluous, unnecessary or capricious are carefully synchronized and fitted together with marvelous intricacy to fit perfectly the greater miracle they were designed to typify. This fact is so completely lost from the thinking of all the students of this book whose works this writer has had opportunity to examine, that a little time will be devoted to the elaboration of this truth, the most amazing fact, actually, in the entire book of Jonah.

The Complex of Seven Miracles

The miracles in Jonah are not one but seven. Don W. Hillis listed them as follows:[54]

1. The tempest (1:4).
2. The sudden calm (1:15).
3. The prepared sea-monster (1:17).
4. Jonah's deliverance from the sea-monster (2:10).
5. The God-prepared gourd (4:6).
6. The God-prepared worm (4:7).
7. The scorching east wind (4:8).

A few writers have included an eighth miracle in the matter of the casting of the lots, leading to the identification of Jonah as the one to be blamed for the storm; but there are many providences of God which may not be accurately classed as miracles, and this we believe to be one of them. Certainly, it could have fallen upon Jonah by chance; and that is a difference which cannot pertain to any of the other wonders in the above list of seven.

This seven-fold complex of miracles is in the exact nature of its complexity an eloquent witness of its divine origin. A similar complex of the miraculous is found in the event of Jesus walking on the sea to go to the disciples struggling

---

[54]Don W. Hillis, *op. cit.*, p. 12.

with the contrary wind, as recorded in Matthew 14:45ff, and parallels. There were seven wonders exhibited in that event also:

1. The contrary wind was evidently due to the design of the Saviour himself.
2. Christ could see the struggling apostles in the midst of the sea, at a distance of several miles in the fourth watch of the night.
3. He walked on the sea to go to their rescue.
4. He commanded Peter to walk on the waves, which for awhile he actually did.
5. He rescued Peter from drowning.
6. There was immediately a great calm.
7. The boat was immediately at the landing (John 6:21).

This characteristic of God's wonders occurring in families is one of the hallmarks of divine truth. As the scriptures affirm, "God setteth the solitary in families!" (Psalm 68:6). Of course, evil and unbelieving men stubbornly reject and scorn such demonstrations of the divine power; but even more distressing than that is the fact of allegedly "Christian" scholars rejecting any acceptance of miracle. Infidelity is sore pressed when it would resort to the type of rationalizations that would explain biblical wonders as ordinary events. As Bickersteth said of such rationalization, "They are a laughable insult on logic, hermeneutics, good sense, and honesty."[55]

Take another instance, the greatest of all, in which God has set the "solitary" in a family of miracle. The solitary, of course, is the resurrection of the Son of God, attested and supported by six lesser miracles, themselves exceedingly great wonders, but completely overshadowed, obscured, and eclipsed by the far greater miracle which they support and surround, the resurrection of Christ himself. These are:

1. The darkening of the sun for three hours.
2. The rending of the veil of the temple.
3. The earthquake.

[55] E. Bickersteth, *Pulpit Commentary* (Grand Rapids: Wm. B. Eerdmans Publishing Company, 1950), p. 249.

4. THE RESURRECTION OF CHRIST.
5. The opening of the graves of the righteous.
6. The undisturbed grave clothes.
7. The resurrection of the saints who came out of their graves after Jesus' resurrection.

We refer the student to our Commentary on Matthew, pp. 483-497 for an extended discussion of these Calvary Miracles. It is a matter of astonishment to any who may never before have discerned it, that those wonders surrounding the resurrection of Christ fall into a definite pattern, two of them being from above the earth, two from the ground level, and two from beneath the surface of the earth. This most amazing truth was first revealed to this writer in a small booklet, entitled, "The Calvary Miracles," authored by Bishop Nicholson of the American Anglican Church.[56] A look at the designed pattern of these Calvary Miracles shows that:

> The darkened sky
> The rent veil
> > —were wonders "from above"
>
> The earthquake
> The opened graves
> > —were from the dead level
>
> The undisturbed grave clothes
> The resurrection of the saints
> > —were from beneath the earth's surface.

It was not until twelve years afterwards (after publishing the Commentary on Matthew) that we suddenly saw exactly that same pattern of design in the wonders of the book of Jonah. There also:

> The great tempest
> The scorching east wind
> > —were from above the earth
>
> The gourd vine
> The great calm
> > —were from the dead level

---

[56]William R. Nicholson, *The Calvary Miracles* (Chicago: Moody Press, 1928), p. 6.

The prepared fish
The prepared worm
      —were from beneath the earth's surface.

There is another amazing correspondence in the third wonders listed in each group above. The earthquake and the gourd vine have this in common, that each of them extends above the earth as well as below it. The epicenter of the earthquake is quite high, but still beneath the surface, whereas the rocks were cast up considerably above the earth's surface, as any traveller in Jerusalem can still see. Likewise, the gourd vine's roots were beneath the surface, but it came up above Jonah's head. This justifies the classification of both of them as dead-level phenomena!

It seems to this writer that only a boundless gullibility can enable one to suppose that the author of some fairy tale, legend, parable, allegory, or fable could have "accidentally" produced such an accurate prefiguration of that entire family of seven great wonders bound together in the resurrection of the Son of God. No! The hand of Almighty God has to be in the book of Jonah!

With the deepest reverence and appreciation, we shall now turn to a consideration of the text itself in this marvelous book.

CHAPTER 1

This chapter recounts the divine commission which came to Jonah, instructing him to prophesy against the city of Nineveh because of their great wickedness, the prophet's rebellious disobedience in trying to avoid the assignment by fleeing in the opposite direction, the judgment of God against him in the great storm that threatened the wreck of his ship, the prophet's guilt exposed, his being cast overboard by the mariners, the great calm that ensued immediately, the worship of the true God on the part of the sailors, and the swallowing of the prophet by a great sea monster, in the belly of which Jonah remained for three days and three nights (1-17).

As noted in the introduction, the denials of the historical and factual nature of this narrative raise far more questions than are answered; and absolutely nothing is gained by the attempts to make Jonah any kind of fictional character. We agree with Banks, then, "To approach the study of this book, believing it as an historical acount."[1]

Verse 1, Now the word of Jehovah came unto Jonah the son of Amittai, saying.

Now . . ." Enemies of this book do not hesitate to take the ax to the very first word in it, affirming that, "Jonah is a fragment, the continuation of a larger work";[2] but, of course, such criticisms are apparently founded in ignorance of the truth that, "This is a common formulary linking together revelations and histories, and is continually used in the OT at the beginning of independent works."[3] Joshua 1:1, Judges 1:1, 1 Samuel 1:1, Esther 1:1, and Ezekiel 1:1 all have this same beginning. "This by no means warrants the assumption that Jonah is the fragment of a larger work."[4]

---

[1]William L. Banks, *Jonah the Reluctanct Prophet* (Chicago: Moody Press, 1966), p. 8.

[2]W.J. Deane, *Pulpit Commentary, Vol. 14, Jonah* (Grand Rapids: Wm. B. Eerdmans Publishing Company, 1950), p. 1.

[3]*Ibid.*

[4]C.F. Keil, *Commentary on the OT, Vol. X* (Grand Rapids: Wm. B. Eerdmans Publishing Company, 1978), p. 389.

Barnes pointed out that the sacred writers used this word to join their writings to other portions of the word of God, thus affirming their reliability and inspiration.[5]

"The word of Jehovah came unto Jonah the son of Amittai . . ."

There is no sacred record of just how God spoke to Jonah, the great fact revealed being that God indeed spoke to him and that Jonah recognized the validity of God's message. "God having of old time spoken unto the fathers in the prophets by divers portions and in divers manners, etc." (Hebrews 1:1) gives the only clue we have as to *how* God spoke to the prophets. Nevertheless, "The basis of the prophet's life is the confidence that God is able to communicate with man, making known to him his will. Without a revelation of God there can be no prophet."[6] Strangely enough, this is the primary evidence of the supernatural in the whole book, but it seems to be curiously inoffensive even to some who vehemently reject the miracles of the same book. Granted that the infinite God is the one who spoke to Jonah and dealt with him as revealed in this history, there can actually be no problem whatever with the miraculous element in the record.

This passage unquestionably identifies Jonah with the prophet mentioned in this OT passage:

> Jeroboam the son of Joash (Jeroboam II) restored the border of Israel from the entrance of Hamath unto the sea of the Arabah, according to the word of Jehovah the God of Israel, which he spake by his servant Jonah the son of Amittai, the prophet who was of Gath-hepher (2 Kings 14:25).

Such a prophecy was doubtless made before the beginning of Jeroboam's reign, or at least very early in it; and one sure result of such a favorable prophecy's being remarkably fulfilled would have been the establishment of Jonah as a national hero among the Israelites of the northern kingdom. It cannot be imagined that any Israelite at some later

---

[5]Albert Barnes, *Notes on the OT, Minor Prophets*, Vol. I. (Grand Rapids: Baker Book House, 1953), p. 395.

[6]James D. Smart, *Interpreter's Bible*, Vol. VI (New York: Abingdon Press, 1956), p. 875.

time would have forged or invented a story such as this which portrays the prophet in such an unfavorable light.

The word *Jonah* means "dove," the same "being a symbol of Israel,'"[7] and thus a most appropriate name for one whose life in this record must be seen as a typical prophecy of the future fate of Israel. The word "Amittai" means *truth*. This word comes from the root of the Hebrew term which gives us "Amen"; thus, "Jonah son of Amittai means 'mourning dove, son of truth.' "[8]

All that is definitely known concerning the prophet Jonah is found in the little book that bears his name and in the single reference cited here from 2 Kings 14:25.

Verse 2, Arise, go to Nineveh that great city, and cry against it, for their wickedness is come up before me.

As Myers noted, "This command points to the prophetic conception of the Lord as the Ruler and Controller of all history, who had power over Nineveh just as he had over Jerusalem."[9]

This verse also shows that God is angry with wickedness. The present day conception of God as a mild, indulgent father-image of one who loves everybody no matter what they do, and as one who will never actually *punish* anyone, is a gross perversion of the truth. Every sin is an affront to God, who is "angry with the wicked every day" and who will by no means accommodate himself finally to human sin and unrighteousness. Abel's blood still cries to God from the ground (Genesis 4:10); Sodom and Gomorrah; Tyre and Sidon; the whole antediluvian world; and many other wicked civilizations were wiped off the face of the earth by divine judgments against their wickedness; and it is no contradiction of the love and justice of God who will surely spare the penitent, that he will also ultimately overthrow and destroy the wicked.

"Nineveh that great city. . ."

---

[7]*Ibid.*, p. 876.
[8]William L. Banks, *op. cit.*, p. 14.
[9]Jacob M. Myers, *The Layman's Bible Commentary* (Atlanta: The John Knox Press, 1979), p. 164.

Nineveh

Nineveh, the capital of the Assyrian kingdom, and the residence of the great kings of Assyria, was founded by Nimrod (Genesis 10:11), and by Ninos, the mythical founder of the Assyrian empire, according to Greek and Roman writers who repeatedly referred to it as "that great city." The size of it is given as "three day's journey" (3:3); and this agrees with the writings of the classical Greek and Roman writers who called it the "greatest city in the world at that time."[10]

Butler gives the following description of Nineveh from an ancient writer, Diodorus:

> It was the greatest city of antiquity with a population of 600,000, some 80 miles in circumference. Upon its walls 100' high, flanked with 1,500 towers, each 200' high, four chariots could drive abreast. It filled, together with the adjoining suburbs, the whole space between the rivers Tigris, Khosr, the Upper, or Great Zab, the Gasr Su, and the mountainous boundary of the Tigris Valley on the east.[11]

We need not be concerned with the speculations of writers who are intent upon discrediting the biblical record, affirming that, "Its area was at most not more than three square miles!"[12] The ancient writings are much more dependable in matters of this kind than the speculative guesses of those who have already compromised their objectivity by denying Jonah as historical truth. The smaller dimensions of the city are actually founded upon excavations dating back to Sennacherib who fortified the city more than a hundred years after the times of Jonah; and the lesser dimensions of those fortifications should be applied to the inner citadel *alone*, and not to the whole city. As Livingston noted:

> Nineveh comprised its occupied area and the surrounding territory, including the neighboring villages

---

[10]C.F. Keil, *op. cit.*, p. 390.
[11]Paul T. Butler, *Minor Prophets* (Joplin, Mo.: College Press, 1968), p. 218.
[12]William C. Graham, *Abingdon Bible Commentary* (New York: Abingdon Press,1929), p. 787.

under its control. In Genesis 10:11,12, Rehoboth, Ca-
lah, and Resen are mentioned with Nineveh as "that
great city."[13]

The Encyclopaedia Britannica gives the reason why so
many cities were grouped together, "The country is fertile
and prosperous wheat land, which no doubt accounts for so
many ancient cities so close to one another."[14]

The wickedness of Nineveh was a scandal in the whole
ancient world. "The city was widely known as a center of
fertility cult worship, and for its cruelty to the victims of
warfare."[15] For twenty years, New York City's Metropolitan
Museum of Art exhibited friezes from the palaces of Ashur-
nasapal and Ashur-banipal, (later than Jonah) in which the
numerous human figures were depicted with all of the muscles and tendons of the body articulating separately and
exposed with almost surgical accuracy, indicating that the
Assyrian artists were more familiar with the human body
without its skin than they were with its normal appearance.
The Assyrians normally flayed all their victims, and frequently while they were still *alive.*

Nineveh did not long survive after Jonah, only about 200
years passing till it was utterly and completely destroyed,
showing that their repentance was partial and incomplete.
Yet, significantly, God's purpose in using Nineveh as his
razor to punish Israel was made possible by the greater
power and glory that came to the great Assyrian city after
their brief period of repentance and seeking the blessing of
God. The city fell in 612 B.C.

About 612 B.C., the city was destroyed by a coali-
tion of armies from Babylon and Medo-Persia. It happened exactly as the prophet Nahum predicted it. Its
destruction was so complete that its size was forgotten. When Xenophon and his 10,000 passed by 200
years later, he thought the mounds were the ruins of
some Parthian city; and when Alexander the Great

---

[13]G. Herbert Livingston, *Wycliffe Bible Commentary* (Chicago: Moody
Press, 1962), p. 845.
[14]*Ibid.*
[15]*Encyclopaedia Britannica, Vol. 16* (Chicago: William Benton, Publisher,
1961).

fought the famous battle of Arbela near the site of
Nineveh in 331 B.C., he did not know there had ever
been a city there.[16]

Thus it was no empty warning that the prophet uttered
against this great center famed for its terrible sins. Sure,
God spared them for awhile when they repented; but when
they turned again to their evil ways, the judgment fell upon
them forever.

**Verse 3, But Jonah rose up to flee unto Tarshish from the
presence of Jehovah; and he went down to Joppa, and found
a ship going to Tarshish: so he paid the fare thereof, and
went down into it, to go with them unto Tarshish from the
presence of Jehovah.**

"But Jonah rose up to flee . . ." It is a mistake to suppose
that Jonah did not know that God was in Tarshish as well
as in Jerusalem; for it is impossible to associate such an
ignorance as that with a true prophet of God. His conduct
in this was exactly the same as that of Adam and Eve who,
after their sin, hid themselves from the presence of God. Today, it is the same. When men renounce their sacred duty to
the church, they flee as far away from it as possible, knowing full well that they cannot escape God's presence no
matter what they do. Fleeing from the scene of one's duty is
the reflexive action of a soul in a state of rebellion and
disobedience to the Lord. And it is called in this passage,
"fleeing from the presence of the Lord." Banks gave as
plausible an explanation of this as any we have observed:

> Jonah knew that the Lord was unlike pagan deities
> whose power was believed not to extend beyond the
> boundaries of a given area; but he thought running
> away to a distant place would make it physically im-
> possible for him to discharge his commission.[17]

Many have inquired as to why Jonah did not wish to obey
the word of Jehovah regarding the commission to cry
against Nineveh. Certainly, some of the reasons which
might have influenced him may be surmised.

[16]Paul T. Butler, *op. cit.*, p. 219.
[17]William L. Banks, *op. cit.*, p. 18.

(1) Jonah doubtless knew of the sadistic cruelty of the hated Assyrians, and he could not have failed to confront an element of physical fear of what might befall him in a place like Nineveh, especially in the act of delivering a message which he supposed would be most unwelcome to all of them. Yet, the great physical courage exhibited by the prophet in this very chapter is an effective refutation of the notion that this was what caused him to run away.

(2) National prejudice certainly entered into it, because no true Israelite could imagine such a thing as preaching to Gentiles, notwithstanding the fact that God, from the beginning, had intended for Israel to be a light to all nations, a function which they had signally failed to honor.

(3) The reason given by Jonah himself (4:3) was that he feared that Nineveh might repent and that God, after his usual gracious manner, would spare them and refrain from destroying their city. As to why such an eventuality was so distasteful to Jonah, there are two conjectures: (a) The prophet was mightily concerned with his own loss of face, including the prospect of his becoming widely known as a prophet whose words did not come to pass. (b) Keil thought that Jonah's real objection to Nineveh's conversion sprang out of the deep love he had for his own nation, "fearing lest the conversion of the Gentiles should infringe upon the privileges of Israel, and put an end to its election as the nation of God."[18] This latter observation strikes us as a genuine discernment of the truth. As a matter of fact, the conversion of Gentiles did typify the ultimate rejection of Israel as "the chosen people" and the receiving of Gentiles all over the earth in a "new Israel" which would include both Jews and Gentiles. Jonah seems to have sensed this; and out of the fierce love of his own country, he was loth to see Nineveh converted. Whatever the reasons that motivated him, he was wrong; and God would overrule his disobedience to accomplish his will despite the prophet's unwillingness to obey.

"To flee unto Tarshish . . ." Present day commentators usually identify this place with a seaport just west of Gibralter on the southern coast of Spain, which was at the

---

[18]C.F. Keil, *op. cit.*, p. 392.

opposite extremity of the Mediterranean and exactly opposite from the direction of Nineveh. It is far from certain, however, that this is the place referred to. Josephus stated that it was Tarsus in Cilicia;[19] "Tarshish apparently refers to more than one place in the OT (1 Kings 22:48)."[20] Myers thought it was, "more probably a place in Sardinia where there was a great iron smelter."[21] Many questions which excite human curiosity are left unanswered in Jonah, as is true throughout all the Bible.

"And he went down to Joppa, and found a ship going to Tarshish . . ." Joppa was about the only seaport that Israel ever had until Herod built Caesarea Philippi hundreds of years after Jonah. Jonah might have been surprised to find ready transportation available for the very place to which he had decided to flee. Satan always provides transportation for the soul running away from the Lord. And, as Spurgeon once said, "Evil also has its mysterious providences, and it is not always right to do what seems to be convenient."

"So he paid the fare thereof . . ." What an exciting text for a sermon is this! Whatever soul turns from the Lord finds always that a price is exacted. The prodigal son paid for his excursion into the far country with a sojourn in the swine pen; Judas paid for his "thirty pieces of silver" with a hangman's rope in the "field of blood" (Acts 1:19);

> Attempting to run away from God is like fleeing light and falling into darkness, relinquishing wealth and welcoming poverty, abandoning joy and receiving sorrow, or giving up peace in order to have chaos and confusion![22]

Every sinner on earth today is paying the fare!

"And went down into it to go with them unto Tarshish . . ." There is a glimpse in this verse, and in verse 5, of the kind of ship Jonah boarded. "The Hebrew word for ship (v.

[19]Flavius Josephus, *Antiquities of the Jews, translated by William Whiston* (New York: Holt, Rinehart, and Winston), p. 292.
[20]W.B. Robinson, *New Bible Commentary, Revised* (Grand Rapids: Wm. B. Eerdmans Publishing Company, 1970), p. 748.
[21]Jacob M. Myers, *op. cit.*, p. 164.
[22]William J. Banks, *op. cit.*, p. 19.

5) is *shephinah*, and is found nowhere else; and from its derivation (from *saphan = to cover*) implies that the vessel was decked."[23] Thus, Jonah's going "down into it" indicates that he went below decks into the hold of the ship.

Verse 4, But Jehovah sent out a great wind upon the sea, and there was a mighty tempest on the sea, so that the ship was like to be broken.

"Jehovah sent out a great wind . . ." The scriptures abundantly teach that all of the forces of nature are under the direct command of the God of heaven; and there are many instances in which these have been specifically deployed in the accomplishment of God's will. The miracle (yes, this is undoubtedly a miracle) here is not capricious. There is a moral and ethical reason behind it. "It was not a purposeless demonstration of the Lord's power over the elements, nor even just to smash inflexible Jonah, but to give him a sense of concern for the sailors, and thus for the Ninevites."[24]

"So that the ship was like to be broken . . ." Some of the old versions translate this, "So that the ship thought to be dashed to pieces."[25] Such expressions were sometimes used of inanimate things; and this one has the exact meaning of that given in our text. The ship was in dire straits, and was threatened every moment by complete destruction. It was not evidently the time of the year when such storms were expected, else the ship would not have been bound for Tarshish at all; and the sailors immediately attributed the violent and ususual storm to the wrath of "some god," as they supposed, having no knowledge whatever of the one true God.

Verse 5, Then the mariners were afraid and cried every man unto his god; and they cast forth the wares that were in the ship into the sea, to lighten it unto them. But Jonah was gone down into the innermost parts of the ship; and he lay, and was fast asleep.

---

[23]W.J. Deane, *op. cit.*, p. 3.
[24]Michael C. Griffiths, *New Layman's Bible Commentary* (Grand Rapids: Zondervan Publishing House, 1979), p. 981.
[25]C.F. Keil, *op. cit.*, p. 392.

See under v. 3, above, for comment concerning the word for ship as used in this verse.

The word for "mariners" here means "salts," that is sailors of the salt seas; they are usually thought to have been Phoenicians engaged in the corn trade with western Mediterranean ports, or the iron trade with Sardinia. The variety of "gods" mentioned indicates that they were not all of a single nationality, but of mixed heathen origin, some worshipping one god, some another. Their concern for the safety of the vessel, their diligent efforts to lighten its burden, and their frantic prayers "every man unto his god" contrasts vividly with the amazing indifference of the prophet Jonah fast asleep in the hold of the vessel.

We think Butler is right in rejecting the usual comments about Jonah's conscience being seared, blaming his deep sleep upon his spiritual condition.

> It is hardly justifiable to attribute his deep sleep through the storm to a perverse, stupefied, seared conscience. He was probably so exhausted from the long trip from Gath-hepher to Joppa, (60-70 miles) and from the psychological wrestling with his soul (which causes physical exhaustion) that he fell into a deep sleep.[26]

One should contrast this account of Jonah's being asleep on a ship at sea in a storm with the NT account of Jesus in a similar situation, as recorded in Mark 4:38.

Verse 6, So the shipmaster came unto him, and said unto him, O sleeper? Arise, call upon thy God, if so be that God will think upon us, that we perish not.

"Shipmaster . . ." This officer was actually "the captain," or as the literal import of the word implies, "the chief of the ropemen." The nautical terms used in this book were doubtless well known to the inhabitants of Galilee who lived in close proximity to the Phoenicians, who were a sea-faring people, and from whom the inhabitants of the northern kingdom would have adopted many words, due to their contact with the Phoenicians who carried the burden of

---

[26]Paul T. Butler, *op. cit.*, p. 225.

Israel's foreign trade. Criticism of Jonah based upon the appearance of a few such nautical terms is petty and irresponsible quibbling.

How sin degrades and reduces God's servant. Behold Jonah, who, had he been doing his duty, might have been reproving the king of Nineveh, is instead himself here upbraided by a heathen shipmaster!

"Call upon thy God ..." Jonah had evidently mentioned the God of Israel at the time he boarded the ship; and, as many ancient nations had heard of Jehovah's power, there seems here to be some hope on the part of the shipmaster that the feared God of the Israelites might be enlisted to aid them in their extremity.

"If so be that God will think upon us, that we perish not ..." These words vividly recall Psalm 40:17, "The Lord thinketh upon me," which has the meaning that God succours and defends those who call upon him.

Verse 7, And they said every one to his fellow, Come and let us cast lots that we may know for whose cause this evil is upon us. So they cast lots, and the lot fell upon Jonah.

A few commentators wish to make a miracle of this; but since it has to be true that the lot had to fall upon someone, and since it certainly could have fallen upon Jonah "by chance," we shall not construe this as any kind of miracle comparable to the others in this book. Besides that, the sailors themselves did not rely entirely upon the lot, even though it fell upon Jonah, basing their subsequent actions upon Jonah's confession, rather than upon the uncertainty of the lot. Yes, the scriptures reveal that even the apostles relied upon the casting of lots in their selection of Matthias to succeed Judas Iscariot (Acts 1:26); but in that case, the lots were cast after the apostles had earnestly prayed unto God to show by that manner who was chosen. No such prayer to the true God occurred in this instance. Of course, today, there is no need for the casting of lots on the part of them who have the word of God, after "that which is perfect has come."

This verse apparently presupposes that Jonah had indeed prayed unto "his God," but that his prayer had not been answered any more than the prayers of the heathen, hence their concern with casting lots to expose the guilty party.

There is in the verse a strong example of the almost universal conviction that sin is connected with all human disasters. The citizens of Malta thought that Paul must have been a murderer because he was bitten by a poisonous serpent (Acts 28:4); and even the apostles supposed that the man born blind had experienced such a tragedy due either to his own sin, or that of his parents (John 9:2). Although in specific instances, such conclusions may be absolutely inaccurate, the principle, nevertheless is profoundly true; and that terrible storm which threatened the destruction of Jonah's vessel is a prime example of such a thing.

"The lot fell upon Jonah . . ." Whether by providence or by chance, the lot left Jonah defenseless before his accusers; and he at once accepted the blame as indeed pertaining to himself alone.

Verse 8, Then said they unto him, Tell us, we pray thee, for whose cause this evil is upon us; what is thine occupation? and whence comest thou? what is thy country? and of what people art thou?

There would have been no need whatever to elicit any confession of guilt from Jonah, if the sailors had had any faith, absolutely, in their casting of lots. But with that, as a starting point, they plied the suspected prophet with a series of urgent questions; and Jonah did not disappoint them.

Verse 9, And he said unto them, I am a Hebrew; and I fear Jehovah the God of heaven, who hath made the sea and the dry land.

"I am a Hebrew . . ." Jonah answered their last question first. "*Hebrew* is the name by which the Israelites designated themselves in contradistinction to other nations, and by which other nations designated them (Genesis 14:13)."[27]

"I fear Jehovah the God of heaven . . ." The Interpreter's Bible calls this, "A common postexilic title for Yahweh, and in wide use in the book of Ezra, and in the Elephantine

---

[27]C.F. Keil, *op. cit.*, p. 395.

papyri of the fifth century B.C.!"[28] Such irresponsible comments as this are designed to support a postexilic dating of
Jonah, long after the times when Jonah lived; but such
allegations are completely refuted and contradicted by the
fact that Abraham himself, the ancestor of all the Hebrews,
refers to God in exactly these same words (Genesis 24:7). It
is more charitable to charge Smart (in Interpreter's Bible)
with ignorance than it is to charge him with a lack of
integrity.

"Who hath made the sea and the dry land . . ." Such a
confession on Jonah's part was calculated, whether by design or not, to arouse the most anxious fear on the part of
the sailors. It was precisely "the sea" which was the source
of all their troubles at the moment; and the knowledge that
Jonah had offended the God who created the sea would
have been the cause of the most urgent alarm.

"I fear Jehovah . . ." This should not be taken to mean
that Jonah, at the moment, was in mortal fear that God
would destroy him, or that he was here professing innocence and righteousness in his behavior toward God; but it
is a simple statement of his relationship to the God of
Israel, having this meaning:

" . . . Namely, that he adored the living God who
created the whole earth, and, as Creator, governed the
world. He admits directly afterwards that he has
sinned against this God.[29]

**Verse 10, Then were the men exceedingly afraid, What is
this which thou hast done? For the men knew that he was
fleeing from the presence of Jehovah, because he had told
them.**

"Exceedingly afraid . . ." See the above verse and comment for the reason of this increased and intensified fear.

"What is this that thou hast done . . ." "This is not a
question, but an exclamation of horror."[30]

"For the men knew that he was fleeing from Jehovah . . ."
This passage reveals that Jonah had explained to the

---

[28]James D. Smart, *op. cit.*, p. 882.
[29]C.F. Keil, *op. cit.*, p. 395.
[30]Michael C. Griffiths, *op. cit.*, p. 982.

sailors at the time of his boarding the ship that he was fleeing from God. "We shall meet later examples of the writer's economy of words in supplying necessary information omitted earlier."[31]

Verse 11, Then said they unto him, What shall we do unto thee that the sea may be calm unto us? for the sea grew more and more tempestuous.

The concern and reserve of these pagan sailors in this instance is most commendable. Instead of moving at once to rid their ship of its offending passenger, which they might have done upon the basis of the lot's having fallen upon Jonah, they nevertheless sought Jonah's own advice and consent of what they should do.

Verse 12, And he said unto them, Take me up, and cast me forth into the sea; so shall the sea be calm unto you: for I know that for my sake this great tempest is upon you.

A number of the most important considerations appear in this verse. Jonah here designated the terrible tempest as an act of God directed against himself on account of his disobedience. He unselfishly offers up his own life to save the lives of the mariners, an action of such nobility as to enroll his name forever among the children of God. In this sacrificial act, he stands as one of the noblest types of our Lord Jesus Christ, this being only one of a great number of particulars in which that relationship appears. Moreover, Jonah here discharges his prophetic office effectually by his promise that as soon as he is cast overboard the sea will be calm to the distressed sailors. Such nobility was not lost upon the anxious sailors, for they tried with all their strength to avoid executing the sentence which Jonah, through inspiration, had passed upon himself.

This is the very heart of one of the most wonderful events that ever took place. Till that hour, Jonah had hated "foreigners"; but in the agony of that great storm, they found their common humanity, and Jonah's heart went out to them; and his soul was touched because of their unfortunate plight, a situation to which he himself had so effec-

---

[31]*Ibid.*

tively contributed. Indeed, he had brought it all upon them. "All that he had fled to avoid happens before his eyes; and through his own mediation, he sees the heathen turn to the fear of the Lord."[32] Nothing any more wonderful than this ever happened to one of God's servants!

Verse 13, Nevertheless, the men rowed hard to get them back to land, but they could not; for the sea grew more and more tempestuous against them.

"Ships of ancient times hugged the coastline, keeping in sight of the shore."[33] The sails were not being used, for the wind was off shore; and the sails would have been no value at all; but they tried to beach their ship by the use of oars, struggling with all their might, due to their reluctance to execute Jonah. It was all to no avail, and their only source of hope lay in obeying the words of the prophet of God.

Verse 14, Wherefore, they cried unto Jehovah and said, O Jehovah, we beseech thee, let us not perish for this man's life, and lay not upon us innocent blood; for thou, O Jehovah, hast done as it pleased thee.

This very remarkable prayer on the part of the sailors attributes to Jonah an innocence which, at first, surprises us; but this, no doubt, was due to the divine plan. Jonah is a type both of Israel and of the Lord Jesus Christ; and when the Jews insisted upon the crucifixion of our Lord, the Gentiles in the person of Pontius Pilate proclaimed his innocence, even washing his hands and saying, "I am free from the blood of this innocent man." Jonah's experience in being cast overboard is a type of Israel's casting the Saviour "overboard" by crucifying him on Calvary; and the proclamation on the part of the sailors that Jonah was innocent and that they did not wish God to lay his blood upon them, prefigures the protest of the Gentiles in the person of Pilate when Christ suffered on Calvary. Jonah enacted the part of both types here, insisting upon his being cast overboard, just as Israel insisted upon the death of Christ, but standing also innocent in the eyes of the

[32]Michael C. Griffiths, *op. cit.*, p. 982.
[33]*Ibid.*

Gentiles. Of course, Jonah was actually guilty; and Christ was "made sin" upon our behalf.

Verse 15, So they took up Jonah and cast him into the sea; and the sea ceased from its raging.

Jonah was here the cause of a great calm, even as Christ stilled the stormy sea (Matthew 8:26). See introduction for a list of a number of correspondences between the type Jonah and the antitype Jesus Christ.

"They took up Jonah . . ."

> It does not say, "laid hold on him," or "came upon him," but lifted him; bearing him, as it were, with respect and honor, they cast him into the sea, not resisting, but yielding himself to their will.[34]

Verse 16, Then the men feared Jehovah exceedingly; and they offered a sacrifice unto Jehovah, and made vows.

"The men feared Jehovah exceedingly . . ." The old versions have, "They feared the Lord with a great fear." Why? They had seen things contrary to nature; they had confronted the knowledge of the true God; they had seen his just judgment upon one of his disobedient servants; and they were aware of their own sins and accountability before the God of heaven and earth. "Events full of wonder had thronged upon them, things beyond nature and contrary to nature, things which betokened HIS PRESENCE, who holds all things in his hands!"[35]

"A sacrifice unto Jehovah . . ." This shows that not everything on the ship had been cast overboard, some of the animals, no doubt, which were used for food, were still available for the sacrifice mentioned.

"And made vows . . ." indicates that whatever sacrifice they made was deemed by them to be insufficient, hence their intention of doing a more thorough and acceptable service of worshipping and sacrificing to the true God, as soon as circumstances would permit it.

---

[34]Albert Barnes, *op. cit.*, p. 406.
[35]*Ibid.*

Verse 17, And Jehovah prepared a great fish to swallow up Jonah; and Jonah was in the belly of the fish three days and three nights.

The word "prepared" as used here actually means "commissioned" or appointed, or "ordered."[36] It may be assumed that the great fish was ready at the instant God needed it, just as the tree had been growing by the bitter waters of Marah for a long time prior to the moment when Moses was commanded to cast it into the waters for the purpose of making the bitter waters sweet (Exodus 15:23f). The miraculous nature of the event narrated here is seen in the timing of the fish's appearance and swallowing Jonah and in the fact of the experience not being fatal to Jonah.

"Three days and three nights ..." Most commentators move quickly to protect the popular superstition regarding this being a reference to the so-called "Hebrew idiom," in which any part of three days and three nights, as for example two partial days, one whole day, and two nights may properly be called "three days and three nights!" However, we reject this, not only as it is alleged to apply here to the experience of Jonah, but in the fact of its application to the experience of Christ as well, who was in the grave "three days and three nights," rising the third day. Sunday was described in the book of Luke as "The third day since" the crucifixion (Luke 24:21); and there is no honest way to make that mean that Sunday is the third day since Friday! See dissertation on this entire subject in CMK, pp. 343-351.

The Great Fish

The King James translators made an unfortunate mistranslation of Matthew 12:38-40, in which this great fish was called "a whale"; but that word is nowhere found in the scriptures in connection with the events recorded here.

As to what kind of fish this was, there is utterly no way of knowing. Many scholars have needlessly exercised themselves in trying to help God out (!) by finding a record of some great fish that could actually swallow a man; but such

---

[36]Harold E. Monser, *Cross-Reference Bible* (New York: The Cross-Reference Bible Company, 1910), p. 1683.

"findings" have no value at all. The event here described is
clearly beyond nature and above it. The supernatural is
written on every word of this narrative. In nature, there is
no such thing as a fish that could swallow a man without
killing him; and it is a futile kind of vanity that looks for
such a thing. As a type of the death, burial, and resurrection of Christ, this event was designed to be altogether
above and beyond the ordinary occurrences in the realm of
nature.

A more pertinent question, it seems to this writer, is that
of whether Jonah remained alive for that three days and
three nights within the belly of the great fish, or if God
raised him from the dead upon the occasion of the great
fish's vomiting him out upon the dry land. The record of the
prayer which Jonah prayed after being swallowed seems to
argue that he was alive; but, since the prayer was only a
matter of a very few minutes duration, it falls short of
proving Jonah's continued life within the fish's belly for a
whole three days and three nights. Basing argument upon
the fact that Jesus Christ certainly was not alive for three
days and nights in the tomb, DeHaan did not hesitate to
affirm that, "Jonah was *dead* for three days and three
nights, and then was resurrected and sent forth to
preach."[37] The event must be accepted as "a sign from
heaven," no matter how it is understood, that is, whether
Jonah was maintained alive inside the fish for that extended period, or if he was resurrected after the fish vomited him up.

It really serves no purpose to find examples of extraordi-
narily large specimens of ocean life such as the Mediterranean white shark, and others, which are alleged to have
swallowed men, or even horses; what of it? No such event
ever heard of even approaches what is said here of Jonah.
This is intended as a sign from God, the particular sign to
which Jesus appealed in his struggle against the Pharisees,
and the one which he made, preeminently above all others,
the sign of his own death, burial and resurrection (Matthew
12:38-40).

---

[37]Dr. M.R. DeHaan, M.D., *Jonah, Fact or Fiction?* (Grand Rapids: Zondervan Publishing House, 1957), p. 7.

Then certain of the scribes and Pharisees answered him, saying, Teacher, we would see a sign from thee. But he answered and said unto them, an evil and adulterous generation seeketh after a sign; and there shall no sign be given to it but the sign of the prophet Jonah: for as Jonah was three days and three nights in the belly of the fish; so shall the Son of Man be three days and three nights in the heart of the earth (Matthew 12:38-40).

It is poor exegesis that attempts to explain Jesus' words here as anything other than an acceptance of the events in Jonah as factual. He even went on to declare in that same passage:

The men of Nineveh shall rise up in the judgment with this generation, and shall condemn it: for they repented at the preaching of Jonah; and, behold, a greater than Jonah is here (Matthew 12:41).

And in the very next line, Jesus went on to mention the queen of the south who would rise up in judgment and condemn the generation of the Pharisees, "For she came from the ends of the earth to hear the wisdom of Solomon; and, behold, a greater than Solomon is here" (Matthew 12:42). The only logical deduction that may be made from this statement is that Christ considered Jonah just as historical as the queen of the south.

Three Miracles in this Chapter

There are no less than three miracles in this first chapter: (1) the great tempest which God sent out into the sea, (2) the immediate calm which ensued when Jonah was cast overboard, and (3) the great fish appointed at the right instant to appear and swallow up Jonah. Strangely enough, one finds little objection to the first two of these wonders. Why is that? The same applies to the other miracles that appear subsequently in the narrative, such as (4) the worm, (5) the gourd vine, and (6) the scorching east wind. De-Haan explained the complacency with which the lesser wonders are received as follows:

The one incident in the book of Jonah upon which almost all the attacks are levelled is the story of Jonah's sojourn in the belly of the fish. We hear little objection to the worm, or the supernatural gourd, or the stilling of the storm. The reason for this becomes immediately evident in the fact that Jonah's experience was a picture of the gospel of the death and the resurrection of Christ! That is why the enemies of Christ can swallow the storm, and the calm, and even the worm and the gourd vine, etc; but the fish, the fish (!)—that is just too big a mouthful for them.[38]

We conclude the study of this chapter with Deane's comment regarding the wonders related in it:

The historical nature of these occurrences is substantiated by Christ's reference to them as a type of his own burial and resurrection. The antitype confirms the truth of the type. It is not credible that Christ would use a mere legendary tale, with no historical basis, to confirm his most solemn statement concerning the momentous fact of his resurrection.[39]

Before leaving this chapter, it should be noted that Jonah here appeared as a remarkable type of Israel. Christ of course is the "new Israel," Jonah being also a vivid and instructive type of the Lord Jesus Christ; but it also follows that his life in certain particulars is also typical of the old Israel.

Jonah a Type of Secular Israel

Both Jonah and Israel were satisfied in Jerusalem, or Samaria.

Both Jonah and Israel despised the Gentiles.

Both Jonah and Israel were unwilling to preach to Gentiles.

For Jonah's failure, he was "cast overboard"; and for Israel's failure, they were rejected as "the chosen people."

---

[38]Dr. M.R. DeHaan, M.D., *op. cit.*, p. 19.
[39]W.J. Deane, *op. cit.*, p. 6.

Jonah was overruled by God who required him to preach the word to Gentiles; and Israel too in the person of the apostles was required to preach the truth to the Gentiles.

Jonah's preaching converted many Gentiles; and Israel's witness to the Gentiles (by the Jewish apostles and Paul) also converted a host of Gentiles.

Jonah was sorely displeased by the Gentiles' conversion; and secular Israel also stubbornly rejected all allegations that Gentiles should be saved by the gospel.

CHAPTER 2

All ten verses of this brief chapter relate almost entirely to the prayer uttered by Jonah from inside the fish. Jonah was a close student of the holy scriptures, especially of the Psalms, as indicated by his use of much terminology found also in them. Destructive critics have exercised the most valiant and persistent efforts to make this common terminology between Jonah and the Psalms a basis of their insistence upon a postexilic date; but, as we shall more pointedly observe in the notes, below, such allegations are groundless. Many of the Psalms having words or clauses in common with Jonah were doubtless dated long before the prophet appeared; and in a very few cases where this is alleged not to be the case, the correspondence clearly indicated that the Psalmist was influenced by Jonah, and not the other way around. In addition to this, there is convincing evidence of the most positive nature found in the prayer itself which indicates a date long before that favored by OT enemies.

Verse 1, Then Jonah prayed unto Jehovah his God out of the fish's belly.

The first threat to Jonah's life was, of course, that of drowning; and, for whatever period of time he might have been conscious inside the sea-monster, he was profoundly grateful for his being saved from drowning; and that salvation led him to believe that God would preserve him alive throughout the entire experience. This situation explains the double application of some of the expressions in the prayer. Critics like to complain that the passage (chapter 2) "is not a prayer but a thanksgiving for deliverance."[1] However, in the words of Young who refuted such statements, "Is not thanksgiving of the very essence of prayer?"[2]

Such critical censure is pointless, displaying ignorance of the fact that thanksgiving is the very heart of

---

[1]Paul T. Butler, *Minor Prophets*, (Joplin, Mo.: College Press, 1968), p. 235.
[2]Edward J. Young, *Introduction to the OT*, p. 280.

prayer; but this is not a psalm of deliverance from the great fish. It is rather a psalm of deliverance from drowning.[3]

The Problem of the Psalm

The fact of a number of words, phrases, and clauses from Jonah's prayer (or psalm) resembling or corresponding rather closely to similar expressions in the book of Psalms is a big point of contention to some. It is true that a number of parallels exist:[4]

Jonah 2	Psalm
3b	18:7, 120:1
4b	18:6 30:4
5	42:8
6	31:23, 5:8
7	18:8, 69:2f.
8	18:17, 30:4, 103:4
9	142:4, 143:4, 18:7, 5:8
10	88:3, 31:7, 26:7,
	50:14,23, 42:5, 116:7

All that is actually proved by these similarities is that Jonah was steeped in a thorough knowledge of the devotional language of God's people. Keil was correct in his flat denial that Jonah's prayer was in any way "compounded from passages in the Psalms."[5] Knobel and DeWette, as quoted by Keil, affirm that:

> Jonah's prayer is the simple and natural utterance of a man versed in the holy scripture and living in the word of God, and is in perfect accordance with the prophet's circumstances and the state of his mind.[6]

There are no quotations from the Psalms in Jonah's words, but only the usage of certain words, phrases, etc., known to all faithful Hebrews.

---

[3]Merrill F. Unger, *Unger's Bible Dictionary* (Chicago: Moody Press, 1957), p. 602.

[4]Paul T. Butler, *op. cit.*, p. 236.

[5]C.F. Keil, *Commentary on the OT* (Grand Rapids: Wm. B. Eerdmans Publishing Company, 1978), p. 399.

[6]*Ibid.*

The words (in Jonah's prayer) fit none (of the Psalms) well enough to conclude that they are specific quotations. More likely, many Psalms were in mind and freely paraphrased to fit the particular situation and in a manner which expressed Jonah's appropriate emotions.[7]

Critics will have their way, however; and one of the strategies is to date all of the Psalms at a point long after Jonah lived; but we shall not play games with dating OT scriptures. If the Psalms are later than Jonah, then the Psalmist was influenced by the Prophet! And, as Deane said, "It is a matter of controversy, incapable of settlement, whether Jonah or the Psalmist is the original!"[8]

Concerning the date of the Psalms, certainly,

The most of these had then (in the times of Jonah) been written, and, as the Church Psalter, would be familiar to a prophet of God . . . and so in all times, all over the world, the saintly praise and pray "in the words of David."[9]

The nobility and spiritual import of this matchless psalm-prayer were commented upon by Blaikie:

Only tell us what a man says into the secret ear of God and you have told us all that is in his heart, have revealed what microscope could not detect, not scalpel lay bare . . . It shows Jonah at bottom, a regenerate and saintly man.[10]

Peculiarities of the Prayer

Its brevity. One of the startling things about this remarkable utterance on the part of Jonah is the brevity of it,

---

[7]*Wycliffe Bible Encyclopedia* (Chicago: Moody Press, 1975), p. 946.

[8]W.J. Deane, *Pulpit Commentary, Vol. 14, Jonah* (Grand Rapids: Wm. B. Eerdmans Publishing Company, 1950), p. 43.

[9]J.E. Henry, *Pulpit Commentary, Vol. 14, Jonah* (Grand Rapids: Wm. B. Eerdmans Publishing Company, 1950), p. 49.

[10]W.G. Blaikie, *Pulpit Commentary, Vol. 14, Jonah* (Grand Rapids: Wm. B. Eerdmans Publishing Company, 1950), p. 51.

being easily read in less than sixty seconds! Hillis thought
this suggested that Jonah "did not live long inside the
fish."[11] There is no certain way by which this question may
be dogmatically resolved; and we shall leave it open. Many,
along with Banks, have observed that, "Conservative Bible
scholars believe that he died and point out that this best
typifies what happened to Christ."[12]

The use of the past tense. According to Matthew Henry,

> This indicates that he (Jonah) afterwards recollected
> the substance of it, and left it upon record. He reflects
> upon the workings of his heart towards God when he
> was in his distress and danger, and the conflict that
> was then in his breast between faith and sense, be-
> tween hope and fear.[13]

Unity of Jonah

This psalm-prayer is alleged by some to be an ill-fitting
addition to the narrative, thus compromising the unity of
the book of Jonah, and leading to the allegation that this
chapter is not a part of the original record. This is false. As
Young pointed out, "If 2:2-9 be removed, the symmetry of
the book is most certainly destroyed."[14] Besides that, there
is not the slightest historical or textual evidence that the
2nd chapter of this book is any less original than the rest of
it. All of the objections to this prayer-psalm disappear upon
a careful examination of the text itself.

Verse 2, I called by reason of my affliction unto Jehovah,
> **And he answered me;**
> **Out of the belly of Sheol cried I,**
> **And thou heardest my voice.**

This marvelous prayer which God heard and answered
was not offered from any formal position such as kneeling,
standing, etc. "The Bible shows by example that men may

---

[11]Don W. Hillis, *Jonah Speaks Again* (Grand Rapids: Baker Book House,
1976), p. 69.

[12]William L. Banks, *Jonah the Reluctant Prophet* (Chicago: Moody Press,
1966), p. 46.

[13]Matthew Henry, *Commentary on the Bible* (Old Tappan, N.J.: Fleming H.
Revell Company), p. 1287.

[14]Edward J. Young, *Introduction to the OT*, p. 280.

pray in any posture."[15] The scriptures show that men prayed kneeling (1 Kings 8:54), standing (Nehemiah 9:5, Luke 18:13), bowing down on the earth with face between the knees (1 Kings 18:42), lying in a sickbed and turning the face to the wall (2 Kings 20:2), falling prostrate upon the ground (Matthew 26:39), and walking along or standing in public (John 11:41,42, 12:28f).

This prayer is totally unsuitable for an allegory, "And, as no one could have known its substance except Jonah, we have here an argument for his authorship of the book."[16]

"Out of the belly of Sheol . . ." "*Sheol* means netherworld, or underworld, and is equivalent to *Hades* in the NT."[17] "It is the regular word in Semitic literature for the realm of the dead."[18] De Haan made a strong argument from this that Jonah actually died, basing it upon the contrast between the belly of the fish and the belly of Sheol, in which different words were used by the Holy Spirit;[19] but it may very well be that Jonah meant, "That the Lord had snatched him from the Jaws of death, delivering him *before* the gates of Sheol closed upon him."[20] We remain uncertain whether or not Jonah actually died and was raised up from death. There was no problem at all for the Lord either way. It appears to this writer that the argument from the antitype to the effect that since Christ actually died, the type, Jonah, also, in all likelihood died, is more convincing than the argument from the use of Sheol in this passage; but as Banks pointed out "A type should never be unduly pressed; and there is no one else in the Bible who, having been brought to life again, gives a detailed account of his experience in death."[21]

Verse 3, For thou didst cast me into the depth, in the heart of the seas,

---

[15]Paul T. Butler, *op. cit.*, p. 236.
[16]W.J. Deane, *op. cit.*, p. 43.
[17]William L. Banks, *op. cit.*, p. 56.
[18]Jacob M. Myers, *Layman's Bible Commentary* (Atlanta: John Knox Press, 1979), p. 170.
[19]Dr. M.R. DeHaan, M.D., *Jonah, Fact or Fiction?* (Grand Rapids: Zondervan Publishing House, 1957), p. 81.
[20]Jacob M. Myers, *op. cit.*, p. 170.
[21]William L. Banks, *op. cit.*, p. 46.

> **And the flood was round about me;**
> **All thy waves and thy billows passed over**
> **me.**

"Thou didst cast me . . ." Jonah here attributed to God the action of the mariners who cast him overboard, because it was upon God's command as given through Jonah that they did this.

"And the flood was round about me . . ." The Hebrew word here for *flood* means literally *river*.

> This may mean "the current" as in Psalm 24:2, which in the Mediterranean sea flows west to east, and, impinging on the Syrian coast, turns north; or it may have reference to the notion familiar to us in Homer, which regarded the ocean as a river.[22]

"Thy waves and thy billows . . ." Thus Jonah acknowledged God's hand in the dreadful punishment he received.

Verse 4, And I said, I am cast out from before thine eyes;
Yet I will look again toward thy holy temple.

Apparently, Jonah, at the instant indicated by these words, had already been rescued from drowning by the great fish, encouraging him to believe that he would yet be spared alive to worship God in Jerusalem. Thus, in the last clause here, he envisions a deliverance which had not at that moment come to pass; but which the inspired prophet already considered as a reality.

"I will look again toward thy holy temple . . ." "Thus, Jerusalem was not yet destroyed, for the temple was still standing."[23] Now the Babylonian army had completed the destruction of the temple in 586 B.C., after a siege of 18 months, consequent upon Zedekiah's rebellion."[24] However, the moral and spiritual ruin of the temple had occurred much earlier under Rehoboam, Abijah, and Asa, in whose reigns the golden treasures of the temple had been robbed

---

[22]W.J. Deane, *op. cit.*, p. 44.
[23]Adam Clarke, *Commentary on the Whole Bible, Vol. V*(New York: T. Mason & G. Lane, 1837), p. 704.
[24]*International Standard Bible Encyclopaedia* (Chicago: Howard-Severance Company, 1915), p. 2934.

and all kinds of abominations introduced into its services,[25] leaving us with the certainty that such an affectionate mention of the temple as that which occurs here could not have been made by a prophet like Jonah except about the approximate time we have assigned as the date of this book. This mention of the temple as still standing completely explodes the efforts to date this in the fifth century or in postexilic times. The critics know this, of course; so they insist that Jonah was not actually referring to the temple in Jerusalem, but to God's eternal temple in heaven! However, the dual mention of God's "holy temple" both here and in verse 7, below, has its most simple and obvious meaning as a plain reference to the temple of Solomon then standing in Jerusalem. Denials of this are invariably grounded in a determination to deny the whole prophecy by late dating it.

Verse 5, The waters compassed me about, even to the soul;
The deep was round about me;
The weeds were wrapped about my head.

"Even to the soul . . ." "The meaning is that the waters so press in that life itself is threatened."[26]

"The weeds were wrapped about my head . . ." Some of the critics have really hooted at this, screaming that "weeds do not grow in a great fish's belly!"[27] Indeed, indeed, indeed! Neither did Jonah "grow in the belly of the big fish," but there he was; and, of course, both Jonah and the sea weed got there in the same swallow. It is nothing short of amazing how commentators are intimidated by blatant assertion, risking all kinds of bizarre guesses as their answer to this phantom objection. Livingston supposed that, "Jonah had become entangled with other material within the fish";[28] and thought that maybe Jonah mistook "the

---
[25]*Ibid.*
[26]J.R. Dummelow, *Commentary on the Holy Bible* (New York: The Macmillan Company, 1937), p. 577.
[27]Paul T. Butler, *op. cit.*, p. 235.
[28]G. Herbert Livingston, *Wycliffe Bible Commentary, OT* (Chicago: Moody Press, 1962), p. 847.

whale's viscera!"²⁹ and merely thought it was seaweed! Blair stated the truth:

> Doubtless the fish had swallowed not only Jonah but considerable seaweed as well. There was Jonah floundering in the entangling mass, all adding to the confusion of his distressing dilemma.³⁰

It seems hardly credible that intelligent men could find any kind of objection to this mention of the seaweed. This writer has seen accumulations of this weed so thick that one could almost be tempted to try walking on them in the open sea; and, especially off the coast of Nova Scotia, and following a storm, the accumulations of this material are very extensive. Remember that Jonah and his co-sailors were in a storm; and the presence of masses of seaweed at the place where Jonah was cast overboard would have made it absolutely impossible for a big fish to swallow him without taking on a substantial load of the seaweed at the same time, which, of course, is evidently what happened. Deane attempted an explanation of it by suggesting that, "Jonah sank to the bottom before he was swallowed by the fish."³¹ Well, maybe he did; but none of this type of explanation is necessary. If the fish swallowed Jonah in three seconds after he hit the water, he would still have swallowed a lot of seaweed also. Dummelow understood the situation perfectly when he wrote, "Floating seaweed entangles him as he sinks."³²

Verse 6, I went down to the bottoms of the mountains;
  The earth with its bars closed upon me for ever;
  Yet hast thou brought up my life from the Pit, O Jehovah my God.

"Bottoms of the mountains . . ." The roots or foundations of earth's mountains lie far beneath the sea, and this expression reveals the apparant hopelessness of Jonah's situation.

²⁹Michael C. Griffiths, *The New Layman's Bible Commentary* (Grand Rapids: Zondervan Publishing House, 1979), p. 983.
³⁰J. Allen Blair, *Living Obediently* (Neptune, N.J.: Loizeaux Brothers, 1963), p. 74.
³¹W.J. Deane, *op. cit.*, p. 44.
³²J.R. Dummelow, *op. cit.*, p. 44.

"Earth with its bars closed upon me for ever . . ."

The thought is that as he sinks he goes far from the earth, the home of the living, and its doors are closed and barred against him for ever. No return to the light and sunshine seems possible.[33]

Verse 7, When my soul fainted within me, I remembered Jehovah; and my prayer came in unto thee, into thy holy temple.

See under verse 4 for the significance of this reference to the temple in Jerusalem as still standing. There is no dependability whatever in denials that this is a reference to that temple. Griffiths asserted that, "This is probably not the literal Jerusalem temple";[34] but that is the *only* temple that any of the Jews of that era knew. As Blaikie put it:

Jonah thinks of the temple (the literal temple), the sacred ark, the mercy seat, the over-shadowing cherubim, the promise of Moses: "There will I meet with you, and I will commune with you from above the mercy seat.[35]

At first thought, it appears that Jonah was a bit late remembering God; but remember him he did and therefore received the blessing.

Verse 8, They that regard lying vanities
Forsake their own mercy.

The prophet's deep-seated hatred of idolatry appears in this. He had just observed the distressed mariners each appealing to his god; but, as yet, Jonah's attitude towards them would appear to be colored by that detestation in which all the Jews held other peoples. That this was the case appears in Jonah's displeasure when the Ninevites actually repented and were spared by the Lord.

[33]*Ibid.*
[34]Michael C. Griffiths, *op. cit.*, p. 983.
[35]W.G. Blaikie, *op. cit.*, p. 54.

"Lying vanities . . ." Dummelow pointed out that this is in every way the equivalent of "idol gods"[36] (Deuteronomy 32:21). The word "vanity" means literally "something evanescent and worthless."[37] It exemplifies a strange trait of human nature that Jonah who himself was not at that time out of danger should nevertheless have uttered these derogatory remarks about the pagan sailors (who seem to be in his thoughts), even addressing such remarks to God himself! Despite the fair and even magnanimous actions of the sailors towards himself, Jonah appears in this passage not to have entertained any generous thoughts concerning them.

Banks pointed out the relevance of the teaching against idolatry in this verse by affirming its relevance to our own times:

> We do not bow and scrape before heathen images, but we are also idolaters. Not in the crude way of Jonah's time, but in a more subtle, sophisticated, and therefore a more sinister way. We have merely made some substitutions. In the place of Ashtaroth, Baal, Chemosh, Dagon, Diana, Isis, Mammon, Molech and Nebo we have put alcohol, ambition, automobiles, greed, Hollywood, jazz, money, nicotine, pleasure, science, sports and sex. Moreover, many in "Christian" America classify themselves as Buddhists, Muslims, etc.; and hundreds of millions in other lands still worship the heathen gods.[38]

Verse 9, But I will sacrifice unto thee with the voice of thanksgiving;
I will pay that which I have vowed. Salvation is of Jehovah.

"I will sacrifice . . ." These are bold words indeed for one in the precarious situation of Jonah at the time he uttered this promise; and Deane must surely be correct in pointing out that "The Hebrew words here denote rather, 'I would

---

[36]J.R. Dummelow, *op. cit.*, p. 577.
[37]*Ibid.*
[38]William L. Banks, *op. cit.*, p. 62.

fain sacrifice,' as it depended not on him but upon God whether or not he would be able to worship again in the Holy Land."[39]

Livingston commented that, "The true act of sacrifice is an expression of gratitude to God, rather than an effort to appease his wrath."[40] However, the experience through which Jonah had so immediately lived surely indicates that penalties exacted for sin and disobedience are directly connected with the appeasement of the wrath of God, as when Jonah's being cast overboard was followed by the great calm. Thus, there is an element of propitiation, and not merely expiation alone, both in the experience of Jonah the type, and in the greater wonder of the atoning death of the Christ upon Calvary.

Verse 10, And Jehovah spake unto the fish, and it vomited out Jonah upon the dry land.

"Jonah's deliverance is the only pleasant usage of the word *vomit* in the whole Bible."[41] We do not know, of course, exactly where Jonah was deposited on dry land; but Josephus stated that it was upon the shore of the Euxine sea.[42] If that was true, the great fish passed through the Dardenelles before depositing him, thus following the strong current which is mentioned in Jonah's prayer. Some have quibbled about how Jonah got his information about being in the fish "three days and three nights"; and we cannot give a positive answer to that either; however, as an inspired prophet of God he accurately foretold the calm that would follow his being thrown overboard; and it appears that this was a far more wonderful knowledge than that of the exact time he was inside the fish. We may therefore trust the holy record implicitly.

An ancient poem attributed to Tertullian describes Jonah's deliverance thus:

[39]W.J. Deane, *op. cit.*, p. 45.
[40]G. Herbert Livingston, *op. cit.*, p. 847.
[41]William L. Banks, *op. cit.*, p. 67.
[42]Flavius Josephus, *translated by William Whiston* (New York: Holt, Rinehart and Winston), p. 293.

His sails . . . the intestines of a fish;
Himself shut in by waters, yet untouched;
In the sea's heart, and yet beyond its reach;
Mid wrecks of fleets
Half eaten, and men's carcasses dissolved
In putrid disintegrity: in life
Learning the process of his death; but still—
To be a sign hereafter of the Lord,
To witness was he in his very self,
Not of destruction, but of death's repulse![43]

---

[43]Tertullian. *Appendix, in Ante-Nicene Fathers* (Grand Rapids: Wm. B. Eerdmans Publishing Company), p. 293.

CHAPTER 3

This brief chapter of ten verses tells of the renewal of Jonah's commission, his obedient response, his preaching the word God had commanded, and the remarkable repentance of the Ninevites.

Verse 1, And the word of Jehovah came unto Jonah the second time, saying.

The narrative passes over a number of intervening incidents which arouse our curiosity. Nothing is given concerning where Jonah was deposited by the fish, what Jonah did next, or where he was when this second commission came from the Lord. As a speculation, it seems reasonable to suppose that as soon as Jonah was able to do so, he went up to Jerusalem and worshipped and paid his vows in the temple as he had indicated he would do in the psalm-prayer.

> Jonah, delivered from the great fish, doubtless went up to Jerusalem to pay his vows and thank God there; perhaps he also thought that his punishment had been sufficient, and that he would not again be commanded to go to Nineveh.[1]

At any rate, it was certain that Jonah had settled down "somewhere"; for the word of God that came the second time, said, "Arise and go (v. 2)"; and that is inconsistent with the idea that Jonah was already on the way.

Verse 2, Arise, go unto Nineveh that great city, and preach unto it the preaching that I bid thee.

No preacher of God's word has any other message than the divine revelation, his first and only duty being to proclaim the truth of God unto all alike. It is a shame that in our own times, as in many others, "All this is changed into vain show at the will of the multitude, and the breath of popular favor."[2]

---

[1]Albert Barnes, *Notes on the OT, Minor Prophets, Vol. I* (Grand Rapids, Baker Book House, 1953), p. 413.
[2]*Ibid.*

The Hebrew in this verse literally means, "Cry the cry that I bid thee";[3] and it has reference to the fervor, earnestness, and urgency which are to mark the preaching. Any message, the urgency of which is denied by the manner of its delivery, will be fruitless.

"The preaching that I bid thee . . ." As Butler said, concerning this, "Men who do not declare from the pulpit, 'Thus saith the Lord,' are not fit to stand in that sacred spot."[4]

Verse 3, So Jonah arose and went unto Nineveh, according to the word of Jehovah. Now Nineveh was an exceeding great city, of three days journey.

"So Jonah arose and went . . ." As we detected in the psalm-prayer, Jonah still entertained a deep prejudice against the pagan worshippers of idols; and Smith may be correct in his remark that, "He obeyed, but with his prejudice as strong as though it had never been humbled, nor met by Gentile nobleness."[5]

"Now Nineveh was an exceeding great city . . ." "The past tense shows that the writing belongs to a period after the destruction of Nineveh in 612 B.C."[6] We consider it a duty to warn young students of God's word against observations like this comment from Interpreter's Bible. It is a curious example of pedantic sophistry which pretends a discernment which is actually blindness, and which falsely alleges an intellectuality which is nowhere to be found in it. To begin with, "The Hebrew has no true past tense, indeed has no tenses in its verb system."[7] An argument from "tense" in this place is therefore worthless. "All that is intended here is, that, 'Nineveh existed in Jonah's day as a great city.' "[8] The greatest scholars on earth have been

---

[3]Adam Clarke, *Commentary on the OT, Vol. V* (New York: T. Mason & G. Lane, 1837), p. 705.

[4]Paul T. Butler, *Minor Prophets* (Joplin: College Press, 1968), p. 243.

[5]George Adam Smith, *Twelve Prophets, Vol. II* (New York: Jennings & Graham), p. 529.

[6]James D. Smart, *Interpreter's Bible, Vol. VI* (New York: Abingdon Press, 1956), p. 888.

[7]G. Herbert Livingston, *Wycliffe Bible Commentary, OT* (Chicago: Moody Press, 1975), p. 848.

[8]*Ibid.*

pointing this out now for a hundred years, but the so-called "liberal" scholars go right on parroting the same old worn-out arguments that have been exploded for a century! Dozens of writers have pointed out that the tense in this passage is synchronistic, that is, it corresponds with the whole narrative which is cast in the past tense. "The statement that, 'Nineveh was an exceeding great city,' need imply no more than that this is how it was when Jonah went there."[9]

If the false allegation that Jonah was written after 612 B.C. is accepted, the entire book of Jonah would be pointless; "Should not I pity Nineveh?" would then be, "not only a hypothetical consideration, but a particularly ill-chosen one."[10] A number of similar usages of the past tense (in our translations) in both OT and NT refute the critical allegations against this verse. For example:

> Now Bethany *was* nigh unto Jerusalem, about fifteen furlongs off (John 11:18). Who would stress the verb *was* to the point of denying that the town of Bethany existed in Jesus' day, or even when Luke wrote?[11]

Or take 1 Kings 18:2:

> Elijah went to show himself unto Ahab. And the famine *was* sore in Samaria.

Could this verse possibly mean that the famine, on account of which Elijah went to see Ahab, was a thing of the remote past, some two or three hundred years earlier? Indeed no!

There is no need to multiply instances of this well known and frequent use of the past tense in the Bible. As a matter of fact, such arguments as that concocted from "was" in this verse are not even believed by those using them, but they are for the purpose of deceiving people who are not supposed to know any better. Robinson wrote:

---

[9]W.B. Robinson, *The New Bible Commentary, Revised* (Grand Rapids: Wm. B. Eerdmans Publishing Company, 1970), p. 750.

[10]*Ibid.*, p. 747.

[11]William L. Banks, *Jonah the Reluctant Prophet* (Chicago: Moody Press, 1966), p. 76.

The chief reason why some scholars hold the book to be a product of postexilic times is that ... the general thought and tenor of the book ... presupposes the teaching of the great prophets, including Jeremiah (and Isaiah).[12]

It should be noted that the actual reason has nothing to do with the type of insinuation used against this verse. The chief reason, as Robinson went on to point out is "highly subjective,"[13] having nothing at all to do with any factual or substantive evidence.

Now, with regard to the "chief reason," Jeremiah and Isaiah both were doubtless influenced by Jonah, especially Isaiah who, in full harmony with the inevitable deductions that appear mandatory in the book of Jonah, prophesied again and again the rejection of Israel and the acceptance of the Gentiles into the kingdom of God. The entire 9-11th chapters of Romans are fully devoted to this.

"Great city of three day's journey ..." The unanimous voice of the ancients attests the accuracy of this statement. The subjective objections of some who would like to have it otherwise are not sustained by either fact or substance. Excavations of the ancient fortifications of Nineveh are considerably smaller than the area indicated here; but the citadel should not be confused with the whole city. All ancient, walled cities, were actually composed of a vast inhabited area outside the walls, and frequently at considerable distances beyond them, in addition to the comparatively small area encompassed by the walls proper. Keil, quoting Niebuhr (p. 277), wrote:

> The circumference of the great city of Nineveh, or the length of the boundaries of the city in the broadest sense was nearly ninety English miles, not reckoning the smaller windings of the boundary; and this would be just three day's travelling for a good walker on a long journey.[14]

---

[12]W.B. Robinson, *op. cit.*, p. 747.

[13]*Ibid.*

[14]C.F. Keil, *Commentary on the OT, Vol. X* (Grand Rapids: Wm. B. Eerdmans Publishing Company, 1978), p. 406.

Verse 4, And Jonah began to enter into the city a day's journey, and he cried, and said, Yet forty days, and Nineveh shall be overthrown.

"Began to enter into the city ..." This says nothing about Jonah's going a whole day's journey into Nineveh and then starting to preach, but points out the fact that as he "started" the day's journey into Nineveh, he began to cry the cry that God gave him. This mention of a "day's journey" in this verse "must not be understood as relating either to the diameter or the circumference of the city."[15] It merely means that after Jonah had gone some distance into Nineveh he started to preach.

"Yet forty days and Nineveh shall be overthrown ..." The word "overthrown" here, literally means, "Destroyed from the very foundation and is the same word used in speaking of the destruction of Sodom and Gomorrah."[16]

"And he cried ..." What language did Jonah use? Of course, no one can actually say; but since his message contains only five words in Hebrew, it could hardly have been inconvenient if he had learned it in three or four different languages! Besides that, Aramaic, which according to Griffiths, "was a *lingua franca* for the educated classes, understood by Jews and Assyrians alike, as the language of diplomacy."[17]

"Yet forty days ..." Why *forty*? "The number *forty* is often associated in the scripture with humiliation. It was forty days that Moses, Elijah and Christ fasted."[18] Furthermore, Israel's probation in the wilderness lasted forty years; and forty years elapsed between the end of the ministry of Jesus Christ and the final overthrow and destruction of Jerusalem. When the flood came, it rained, a rain of judgment upon the earth, for a total of forty days and forty nights. Banks added that, "The number *forty* is considered the number of probation, testing, punishment, chastise-

---

[15]*Ibid.*

[16]Paul T. Butler, *Minor Prophets* (Joplin: College Press, 1968), p. 243.

[17]M.C. Griffiths, *The New Layman's Bible Commentary* (Grand Rapids: Zondervan Publishing House, 1979), p. 984.

[18]Jamison, Faucett, and Brown *Commentary on the Whole Bible* (Grand Rapids: Zondervan Publishing House, 1961), p. 809.

ment and humiliation."[19] In NT times, those who were punished with stripes usually were given "forty lashes, save one." "The more definite form of the denunciation (in this verse) implies that Nineveh has now almost filled up the measure of her guilt."[20]

Verse 5, And the people of Nineveh believed God, and they proclaimed a fast, and put on sackcloth, from the greatest of them even to the least of them.

"The people of Nineveh believed God . . ." Actually, the Hebrew text in this would be better translated "believed in God," according to Barnes, who also made the distinction between the two expressions thus:

> To *believe God* means to believe what God says, to be the truth; to *believe in God* expresses not belief only, but that belief resting and trusting in God; it combines hope and trust with faith and love, since without love there cannot be trust.[21]

That the people of Nineveh should have done such a thing as that which is here related must be accounted one of the wonders of all time. That a lone Jewish prophet, a member of a hated and despised race, who reciprocated in every way the hostility and hatred in which their respective nations held each other — that a man like that could simply walk into the city, declare its immediately forthcoming destruction, and be greeted by the enthusiastic and wholesale repentance which greeted Jonah's denunciation — all that is such an extraordinary occurrence, that some of the commentators have hailed it as a miracle. However, this was no miracle. The people heard the word of God, believed it, and obeyed it; and that same opportunity to hear, believe, and obey the truth is still available today for every man on earth.

The people of Nineveh, however, did have a very remarkable "sign" from God that Jonah's message was the truth.

---

[19]William L. Banks, *op. cit.*, p. 79.
[20]Jamison, Faucett, and Brown, *op. cit.*, p. 809.
[21]Albert Barnes, *op. cit.*, p. 415.

To the Ninevites, Jonah himself was not merely a
prophet, but a wonder in the earth, as one who had
tasted of death, and yet had not seen corruption, but
had now returned to witness among them for God.[22]

Such an observation as this is undoubtedly true, as attested by the following scripture:

This generation is an evil generation: it seeketh after
a sign; and there shall no sign be given to it but the
sign of Jonah. For even as Jonah became a sign to the
Ninevites, so shall also the Son of Man be to this
generation (Luke 11:29,30).

"Jonah became a sign to the Ninevites . . ." This is the
only proof needed that the Ninevites were fully aware of the
supernatural wonder involved in Jonah's deliverance. Here
again, we have that great NT word used also in John 2:11,
etc., which "denotes a miraculous act, given as a token of
divine power and authority."[23] The scriptures do not tell us
"how" Nineveh learned about this, but they do clearly
inform us that they did learn of it. As to the "how"; it may
be assumed that Jonah himself related his experience with
God's anger, and with God's punishment, and following his
repentance, with God's mercy. If Jonah did not himself tell,
there were other witnesses, the mariners; at any rate there
was ample human testimony.

There is also another very important possibility, and that
regards the matter of Jonah's appearance following his
deliverance. Many writers have wondered if he carried in
his body any evidence of the terrible ordeal through which
he had passed. Was his skin for ever altered in color by the
digestive juices in the fish? Were there scars that he would
carry to the grave? We have no answers to such questions;
but our Lord Jesus Christ exhibited the pierced hands and
feet, and invited Thomas to thrust his hand into our Saviour's side *after* the resurrection! Again, the likeness between the antitype and type suggests that one of the ways

---

[22]Jamison, Faucett, and Brown, *op. cit.*, p. 808.
[23]W.E. Vine, *An Expository Dictionary of NT Words* (Old Tappan, N.J.:
Fleming H. Revell Company), vol. iv, p. 29.

in which Jonah was a sign to the Ninevites might very well have been that of the evidence exhibited in his body of what had occurred. Certainly, it was true in the case of Jesus our Lord.

To be sure, the critics of the NT have moved every part of heaven and earth they could reach in order to make "the sign" here anything except the wonder of Jonah's deliverance. As Summers asserted:

> In Luke, the "sign" was not the experience but the preaching. Jonah proclaimed God's message . . . the ancient heathen city responded in repentance.[24]

It is a mystery how any student either of the Bible or of human nature could believe that Jonah's preaching, unsupported by any substantive proof, would be hailed in scripture as a "sign." Jonah's preaching would never have been believed at all, except for the fact that Jonah's deliverance from death was such an astounding wonder that "when the word came unto the king of Nineveh," he immediately believed every word of it! Without the prior miracle of Jonah's deliverance from death, only a fool could believe that the king of Nineveh would have come down from his throne, cast off his royal robes, clothed himself in sackcloth and ashes, and led the whole nation in repentance. "Preaching" alone was never made the "sign" of anything!

Before leaving this verse, we should note that the first step in the conversion of the Ninevites was their "belief in God." As, noted above, this refers to a genuine, deep-seated, and sincere conviction that God is God and that all of our allegiance is owed to him. The NT evangelists referred to it as "believing with all of one's heart." (Acts 8:37 AV). It may be feared, as Butler thought, that:

> Preachers are guilty of expecting nominal Christians to lead lives of repentance when their belief is only nominal. Conviction must come before conversion! Persuasion precedes penitence![25]

---

[24]Ray Summers, *Commentary on Luke* (Waco: Word Books, Publisher, 1973), p. 144.
[25]Paul T. Butler, *op. cit.*, p. 247.

In this connection, it should also never be forgotten that our Lord was absolutely fair and equitable in his dealings with the Pharisees who had demanded a "sign." "No sign," said Jesus, would be given "except the sign of the prophet Jonah"; and then Jesus went on beyond that to affirm that:

> Just as Jonah was delivered from death after having been inside of the great fish for three days and three nights, SO SHALL THE SON OF MAN be in the heart of the earth (dead and buried) for three days and three nights, and then RISE FROM THE DEAD. (Paraphrase).

Of course, this was a far greater wonder for the Pharisees, and all mankind, than the wonder of Jonah's deliverance. Furthermore, the Pharisees would have a much closer view of the wonder than that which was accorded the Ninevites, whose belief, at best rested upon tenuous and uncertain testimony; but the Pharisees themselves had witnessed the crucifixion, procured the guard at the grave, and instigated the action that sealed it. Yes indeed, the Lord was more than fair with them.

Nevertheless, Jonah's deliverance was indeed a marvelous sign in its own right; and it is to the eternal credit of the Ninevites that they honored God by believing it. The action of the Ninevites in this matter proved to be an accurate prophecy of what would happen in the days of the Lord Jesus Christ. It was the deliverance of Jonah which convinced them; and it was the resurreciton of Jesus Christ which convinced the whole Gentile world of the power and godhead of the Son of God.

Verse 6, And the tidings reached the king of Nineveh, and he arose from his throne, and laid his robe from him, and covered him with sackcloth, and sat in ashes.

"The tidings came to the king ..." What tidings? A thorough and accurate account of Jonah's miraculous deliverance, of course.

> We cannot imagine the people of Nineveh (including the king himself) having been motivated to fasting and cessation of violence and wickedness on the mere cry

of impending ruin by a stranger of whom they were totally ignorant.[26]

The Saviour's words that Jonah was a "sign" unto the Ninevites (Luke 11:30) has often been cited by Bible scholars as the basis for understanding that, "Jonah's experience in the great fish was made known to the Ninevites."[27] Such knowledge would have included the fact of Jonah's rebellion against God and the subsequent mercy that came to him; and, in the matter of Jonah himself, though in rebellion against God, having received God's mercy, there also appears the slender little thread of hope upon which the Ninevites based their hopeful surmise that he might also spare them.

"The king of Nineveh . . ." Upon this phrase, we are again treated to the profound wisdom (!) of the critics:

> The reference to the "king of Nineveh" is another indication of the nonhistorical character of the book, for nowhere else is the king of Assyria so named.[28] It is another indication of the author's remoteness from an actual historical situation, that he uses this title, instead of King of Assyria, and gives the king no proper name.[29]

To begin with, Nineveh was not the capital of Assyria until a period about a hundred years after the times of Jonah; and there is not the slightest evidence anywhere that "The King of Assyria" ever lived in Nineveh until the times of Sennacherib and Ashur-banipal (704 B.C. till the total destruction of the city).[30] Thus, the expression "king of Nineveh," as used by Jonah proves that he wrote earlier at a time when the historical situation is exactly represented by the title he ascribed to the ruler of Nineveh, i.e., somewhere in the half century 800-750 B.C. Pinches also affirmed that, "It is unknown how long Nineveh was the capital of Assyria."[31]

[26]Paul T. Butler, *op. cit.*, p. 248.
[27]Michael C. Griffiths, *op. cit.*, p. 984.
[28]Jacob M. Myers, *The Layman's Bible Commentary* (Atlanta: The John Knox Press, 1979), p. 172.
[29]James D. Smart, *op. cit.*, p. 890.
[30]T.G. Pinches, *ISBE* (Chicago: Howard-Severance Company, 1915), p. 2150.
[31]*Ibid.*

Another fact which refutes the allegations of the NT enemies on this passage was given by Banks:

> The Hebrew word from which "king" comes in this phrase is a Semitic word *mlk*, in its Akkadian sense meaning "prince" or "governor."[32]

Wycliffe Bible Encyclopedia summarizes the refutation of critical objections to the title, "king of Nineveh," thus:

> "The king of Nineveh" is a metonmy with adequate precedent in the OT (1 Kings 21:1, 2 Chronicles 24:23, Genesis 14:18, and Jeremiah 8:19), in which references the chief officer, or ruler of each of the cities: Samaria, Damascus, Salem, and Zion is called "king of Samaria, etc." Furthermore, Nineveh was not yet the capital of Assyria. Also, the word *melek* may be used here as a transliteration of the Akkadian *malku* meaning "governor."[33]

It is simply monotonous how invariably and completely the objections to the divine record are frustrated, exploded, and exposed as fradulent by a little investigation.

As for the quibble that Jonah did not include the name of the king of Nineveh, it should be observed that it was not in his style of writing to include such personal designations. He did not give the name of the ship, nor of the captain with whom he sailed, nor any one of a dozen other things that would have satisfied human curiosity. This is after the manner of holy writers throughout the Bible.

"Covered him with sackcloth, and sat in ashes ..." It is quite significant that the ancient governor of Nineveh, along with his people, knew exactly the posture and attitudes of repentance, as a comparison with Job 2:8 and Ezekiel 27:30 will reveal. Surely, there is a trace of the original monotheism in this, a residual remembrance in the heart of dissolute and wicked men of the righteousness and mercy of God. This fundamental conception of God's righteousness and of human wickedness appears to be from the

---

[32]William L. Banks, *op. cit.*, p. 88.
[33]*Wycliffe Bible Encyclopedia* (Chicago: Moody Press, 1975), p. 947.

very beginning of man's creation, not instinctive, perhaps, but nearly so.

Verse 7, And he made proclamation and published through Nineveh by the decree of the king and his nobles, saying, Let neither man nor beast, herd nor flock, taste anything; let them not feed, nor drink water.

We shall not bother with noting various and sundry objections as to how Jonah might have known certain words used in this passage, such as robe, decree, etc. Jonah was an eyewitness of what he described in this passage; and the various unusual words used entered his vocabulary upon the same occasion as the events related.

What a bellowing must have gone up to God when none of the cattle were watered or fed. Anyone who ever witnessed the lowing of thirsty cattle can never forget the terrible impact of it. This action initiated by the king was evidently designed to achieve just such an impact upon the whole population.

The king's decree is continued in the next verse.

The involvement of animals in the general mourning was not due to any notion that the animals had sinned; it was merely an Oriental custom.

> Herodotus relates that the Persians, when mourning for their general, Masistios, who had fallen in the battle of Platea, shaved off the hair from their horses, and adds, "Thus did the barbarians in their way, mourn for the deceased Masistios."[34]

This ancient custom of causing the animals to participate in the occasions of public mourning is still evidenced in the world by the custom of reversing the harness or saddles of horses in some funeral cortege of a president or some other famous person.

Verse 8, But let them be covered with sackcloth, both man and beast, and let them cry mightily unto God; yea, let them turn every one from his evil way, and from the violence that is in his hands.

---

[34]Paul T. Butler, *op. cit.*, p. 249.

"Let them turn every man from his evil way . . ." No matter how terribly the conscience of man may be seared, there must always remain within him some basic knowledge of what is right or wrong. It does not appear that Jonah elaborated the sins of the Ninevites; he did not need to do so; they already knew what actions of theirs were sinful in the eyes of the one true and Almighty God.

The Ninevites also recognized the fundamental truth that the mere putting on of sackcloth and ashes would be futile and useless without the fundamental change in their lives which such outward tokens of repentance promised. In a manner that reminds us of the words of John the Baptist who commanded the people to "Bring forth fruit worthy of repentance" (Matthew 3:8), this ancient governor of Nineveh laid the same commandment upon himself and his fellow-citizens.

The fact of there being no mention of this great turning unto the Lord by the Ninevites in any of the books of the Hebrew Bible has, to be sure, been alleged as argument against the historicity of Jonah; but all such allegations ignore the very nature of secular Israel. Their hatred and prejudice against Nineveh was exactly like that manifested by Jonah, and we may be absolutely certain that they omitted, by design, any reference whatever to the conversion of any Gentiles, especially of the hated Ninevites. Furthermore, we shall dare to engage in a little speculation with reference to this very thing. Jonah himself, after having successfully turned an entire pagan city to the Lord, would for ever afterwards have been *persona non grata* in the whole nation of Israel. Jonah could not have failed to be aware of that, and it may accordingly be doubted that he ever went back, either to the northern or to the southern kingdom. There has to be some good reason why tradition places the grave of Jonah in Nineveh! Furthermore, if the animus of "the chosen people" against Jonah in any wise matched that which they directed towards the destruction of the apostle Paul, another Jew who converted many Gentiles, then, they would have held a public funeral for Jonah, buried him in effigy, and engraved his name on a grave near Gath-Hepher, which was Jonah's home; and if this supposition appears in any manner unreasonable to anyone, let him explain how, otherwise, it was possible for Jonah to have two graves, one at Gath-Hepher, and the other in Nineveh! We shall devote a little further space to the examination of this hypothesis at the end of the commentary on Jonah. We conclude it here with the comment by Deane to the effect that the records of the Jews, "never touched" such things, especially events happening so far away, and to a people whom they so thoroughly disliked.[35]

Verse 9, Who knoweth whether God will not turn and repent, and turn away from his fierce anger, that we perish not?

The marvel of this repentance of the Ninevites is nowhere more evident than in this:

> They repented with no invitation to repent.
> They repented without promise that it would do any good if they did repent.
> They repented without any wish or hope on the part of the preacher that they would repent.
> They repented even in the face of Jonah's anger at their doing so.
> They repented *en masse*, from the greatest of them to the least of them.
> They backed up their repentance by turning away from their violence and wickedness.
> Such repentance was rewarded by the blessing of God!

Some have supposed that the Ninevites had no hope when they turned to repentance, but that is inaccurate. God had given them the "sign" of the prophet Jonah (Luke 11:30); and they knew that Jonah, in the very midst of his rebellion against God, had nevertheless received mercy, and they may well have surmised that it could be even so with them. There was also the matter of the forty days promised by the Lord before the destruction; they evidently understood this accurately as an opportunity for them to amend their ways and appeal for mercy. Otherwise, God would

---

[35]W.J. Deane, *op. cit.*, p. 61.

have destroyed them instantaneously, without any time-lapse at all.

Certainly, those pagans did not believe that God was fickle. "Instead, they believed that God's greatest desire was not to destroy men, but to save them";[36] and in this they were profoundly correct.

Many have marvelled at the fact that the repentance of the Ninevites did not last; but, as far as we know, it lasted for that generation, and the blessing of God was continued for an extended time afterwards. In fact, the greatest period of Nineveh's power and prosperity came a century after the events of this chapter. The eventual falling of the whole nation into debauchery and violence again was nothing more than the normal human reaction to God's blessings, nations finding it quite easy to renounce God and all righteousness in times of prosperity, and thus making the very blessing of the Father the occasion of their turning away from him. It may also be surmised that Israel, herself increasingly hardened and sinful, offered no encouragement to Gentile converts.

Verse 10, And God saw their works, that they turned from their evil way; and God repented of the evil which he said he would do unto them; and he did it not.

"God repented . . ." For a full discussion of the questions raised by this, see in the introduction under the subtitle, Purpose, in the last three or four paragraphs, above. All of God's promises, whether to bless or to destroy, in the last analysis, are *conditional*; and one of the purposes of Jonah is to exemplify that principle. See Jeremiah 18:7-10. In fact, Griffiths said that, this passage from Jeremiah "is a general rule, demonstrated in the particular case of Jonah."[37]

"And God saw their works . . ." It is most significant that the sparing of Nineveh was altogether contingent upon their good works, and this in no sense meant that they had earned any respite from the punishment which was justly due them; and God's sparing them was an act of grace, despite the fact that if they had not repented and

[36]G. Herbert Livingston, *op. cit.*, p. 848.
[37]Michael C. Griffiths, *op. cit.*, p. 985.

turned he would never have blessed them. "It was not until the repentance of Nineveh was manifested through works that their salvation was effected by God."[38] This is a plain doctrine of both the OT and the NT, and it is opposed in every way to the popular misconception which alleges that people are saved "through faith alone."

Some have complained that there is no archeological or documentary testimony regarding this wholesale repentance in Nineveh, but no thoughtful person could really be surprised by that. "It is very unusual in monumental history to find mention of any events except wars and the execution of material works."[39] Those who allege that "There is no ancient documentary proof of the great repentance in Nineveh," are profoundly mistaken. There is documentation of it in the Gospel of Matthew; and there has nothing ever come out of antiquity that is any more historical than the sacred gospels. Jesus Christ himself said, concerning the Ninevites, that, "They repented at the preaching of Jonah" (Matthew 12:41). To be sure the critics have tried every device known to them to get rid of that testimony in Matthew; but, as Bruce said, "The verse cannot be challenged on critical grounds."[40]

Before leaving this verse which has the record of God's sparing Nineveh, it should be remembered that the punishment was merely deferred, not cancelled, and that, in time, after the people had turned again to terror and violence, God indeed executed his wrath upon them. Keil summed up that point thus:

> The punishment was therefore deferred by the long-suffering God, until this great heathen city, in its fuller development into a God-opposing imperial power, seeking to subjugate all nations, and make itself the mistress of the earth, had filled up the measure of its sins, and had become ripe for that destruction which the prophet Nahum predicted, and the Median king

---

[38]Paul T. Butler, *op. cit.*, p. 251.

[39]W.J. Deane, *op. cit.*, p. 60.

[40]Alexander Balmain Bruce, *Expositor's Greek NT, Vol. I* (Grand Rapids: Wm. B. Eerdmans Publishing Company, 1967), p. 191.

Cyaxares inflicted upon it in alliance with Nabopolas-
sar of Babylon.[41]

That final overthrow and total destruction of Nineveh is
usually dated in 612 B.C. See introduction for the record of
the utter removal of Nineveh from the face of the earth.

[41]C.H. Keil, *op. cit.*, p. 410.

CHAPTER 4

This whole chapter of eleven verses deals almost exclusively with Jonah's disappointment, anger, and resentment because of the conversion of the Ninevites, and with the gentle persuasion of the Lord, who provided motivation for Jonah, pointing him towards a more acceptable attitude.

Verse 1, But it displeased Jonah exceedingly, and he was angry.

Bible students have imagined all kinds of reasons for the anger of Jonah, and it is surely possible that there were a number of different considerations making up a complex basis for it. Certainly, this amazing anger on Jonah's part is one of the strangest things in the Bible; and yet, we must believe that it was grounded in very human and very understandable attitudes in Jonah himself. "Here is absolutely the most amazing reaction to spiritual awakening we can find anywhere. Of all people, one would think the preacher would be happy about converts!"[1]

There are different opinions about the exact point in this history that Jonah became angry. Keil was of a very positive opinion that Jonah's anger did not flair until the forty days were concluded, and it became evident that God would not destroy Nineveh. "There is nothing whatever to force us to the assumption that Jonah had left Nineveh before the fortieth day."[2] Dean, on the contrary, thought that:

> The fact that God would spare Nineveh probably was made known to Jonah before the forty days expired by Divine communication, in accordance with the saying in Amos 3:7. "Surely the Lord will do nothing, but he revealeth his secret to his servants the prophets."[3]

---

[1]James T. Draper, Jr., *Jonah Living in Rebellion* (Wheaton, Ill.: Tyndale House, Publishers, 1971), p. 87.

[2]C.F. Keil, *Commentary on the OT, Vol. X.* (Grand Rapids: Wm. B. Eerdmans Publishing Company, 1978), p. 413.

[3]W.J. Deane, *Pulpit Commentary, Vol. 14, Jonah* (Grand Rapids: Wm. B. Eerdmans Publishing Company, 1950), p. 79.

Both of these viewpoints, of course, are plausible; but we believe there is a clue in the text itself, in the very next verse (2). Jonah had observed the wholesale conversion of the people; and his knowledge of God's true nature, mentioned by Jonah in the next verse, led him to the conclusion that God would in no wise destroy a penitent and pleading people. That Jonah acted upon this deduction would explain the element of uncertainty in the clause, "to see what would become of the city" (v. 5). At any rate, the question is one of interest, but not one of importance.

A far more urgent question is the one of "why was Jonah angry"?

Reasons for Jonah's Anger

(1) There was a terrible "loss of face" on Jonah's part. His words concerning the restoration of Israel's cities (2 Kings 14:25) had been gloriously fulfilled; but now,

> His reputation as a prophet was irreparably damaged. He would be called a false prophet, a liar, a deceiver, and would be ridiculed and denounced for prophesying something which did not occur.[4]

(2) It may very well be that Jonah was also aware of the prophetic implications of Nineveh's conversion, forecasting the ultimate rejection of Israel as God's people, and the coming of the Gentiles into that sphere of God's favor, which until then was the sole prerogative of Israel. A true prophet of God (which Jonah surely was) could not have failed to read the dire implications for Israel in the astounding events he had just witnessed.

(3) Deep-seated prejudice and hatred of the Gentiles on the part of Jonah are also mentioned frequently as the cause of his anger; and there is little doubt of the truth of this. Jonah himself confessed that his flight to Tarshish in the first place had been prompted by his unwillingness to see Nineveh converted and spared.

(4) Jonah recognized that the sparing of Nineveh would ultimately result in the loss of Israel's territory, the very

---

[4]William L. Banks, *Jonah the Reluctant Prophet* (Chicago: Moody Press, 1966), p. 106.

territory which, following his prophecy, Jeroboam II had
recovered for Israel. He also projected prosperity of
Nineveh as a sign that God would ultimately use Assyria to
punish Israel for their disobedience, a fact which Isaiah
later pointed out (10:5). Thus, Jonah's patriotism and love
of his own country could have been at the root of his anger.
The Jews of Jonah's time, "could only see God's kingdom
being established by the overthrow of the kingdom of the
world,"[5] a misunderstanding that persisted and finally resulted in their rejection of the Christ himself. In fact, one of
the shameful and destructive influences on earth till this
day is the savage, malignant, and carnal patriotism which
equated love of one's own nation with the hatred of every
other nation.

(5) There may have been in Jonah a deep desire for the
destruction of Nineveh that could be used by himself as an
example of God's anger with sin, such an example being, in
Jonah's mind, the very last hope of arresting the degener-
acy and rebellion of Israel against God. With the conversion of Nineveh, his hope of converting Israel through the
use of such a terrible example was frustrated, leaving him
nothing to look forward to (in regard to Israel) except their
ultimate overthrow by the faithful God whose will they had
so consistently violated. It was this hopelessness of Jonah
on behalf of Israel that angered him, according to some. As
Jamieson said,

> When this means of awakening Israel was set aside
> by God's mercy on the repentance of Nineveh, he was
> bitterly disappointed, not from pride or mercilessness,
> but by hopelessness as to anything being possible for
> the reformation of Israel, now that his cherished hope
> is baffled.[6]

(6) Common jealousy is discerned by some as the cause of
Jonah's anger; and this could surely have entered into it.

---

[5]Michael C. Griffiths, *New Layman's Bible Commentary* (Grand Rapids:
Zondervan Publishing House, 1979), p. 979.
   [6]Jamieson, Faucett, and Brown, *Commentary on the Whole Bible* (Grand
Rapids: Zondervan Publishing House, 1961), p. 810.

> At the root of all this was jealousy. Jonah was jealous because the Ninevites, who had been hated and despised by the Jews for their extreme wickedness and cruelty, were now standing with the Jews in their worship of the one supreme God. . . . Such a thing is vividly prevalent, even in our day.[7]

Despite the plausibility of such reasons as those cited above, and without denying that traces of the attitudes mentioned must surely have existed in Jonah, there is, it seems to this writer, a far more compelling reason for his anger.

(7) The conversion of Nineveh was the doom of Jonah himself, as far as any further acceptable relationship with Israel was concerned. Jonah could not, after the conversion of the greatest pagan city on earth, return in triumph and honor to his native land. No indeed! Take a look at the case of Saul of Tarsus. The uncompromising hatred and animosity of Israel which already existed toward Nineveh, would, after the conversion of that city, have been intensified and transferred to Jonah. "He saw the utter weakening of his hands, the destruction of his usefulness among his countrymen."[8] All of Jonah's hope of bringing his own nation to do the will of God perished, in the event of Nineveh's conversion, which as it seemed to Jonah, "would eclipse the honor of God, destroy the credit of his ministry, and harden the hearts of his countrymen."[9] To ascribe Jonah's anger to such motivations as this explains his desire to die (vv. 3,8). Did not Paul also prefer to die rather than accept the lost condition of Israel? (Romans 9:2). Regarding the speculation mentioned in the previous chapter concerning the funeral for Jonah in Israel, see under *Jonah, the Great OT Type*, at the end of this chapter.

Whatever the reasons for Jonah's anger, he was wrong in it.

---

[7]J. Allen Blair, *Living Obediently* (Neptune, N.J.: Loizeaux Bros., 1963), p. 160.

[8]Hugh Martin, *The Prophet Jonah* (Grand Rapids: Baker Book House, 1979), p. 442.

[9]*Ibid.*, p. 453.

The whole of chapter 4 is an account of Jonah's displeasure. His anger was as much a repudiation of God as was his flight in chapter 1. It was an anger that could not tolerate the thought of God having compassion upon the heathen.[10]

Verse 2, And he prayed unto Jehovah, and said, I pray thee, O Jehovah, was not this my saying, when I was yet in my country? Therefore I hasted to flee unto Tarshish; for I knew that thou art a gracious God, and merciful, slow to anger, and abundant in lovingkindness, and repentest thee of the evil.

"He prayed . . ." Even when men are not in harmony with God's will they often continue to use the old forms of worship and prayer to God.

This is true to life in every age, for the most thorough-going rejection of God's will often takes place in persons who observe the forms of piety, and in their own minds count themselves believers.[11]

If, as we have mentioned, Jonah believed that the destruction of Nineveh might have resulted in Israel's conversion, he was totally wrong. God's summary intervention on behalf of the chosen people had been dramatic and spectacular on a number of occasions, and no such thing had ever had the slightest influence in arresting the sinful course of Israel. As Butler said, "Everything of this sort had already been tried with Israel, and still their hearts waxed hard and cold."[12]

"Gracious . . . merciful . . . slow to anger . . . etc." How terrible is the thought that Jonah made these very attributes of the loving God the basis of rejecting his will!

Jonah is here quoting the 'Thirteen Attributes' (Exodus 34:6,7 and Joel 2:13); he may have memorized them as a child, but he did not want to accept them.[13]

---

[10]James D. Smart, *Interpreter's Bible, Vol. VI* (New York: Abingdon Press, 1956), p. 891.

[11]*Ibid.*

[12]Paul T. Butler, *Minor Prophets* (Joplin: College Press, 1968), p. 257.

[13]Michael C. Griffiths, *op. cit.*, p. 985.

Verse 3, Therefore now, O Jehovah, take I beseech thee, my life from me; for it is better for me to die than to live.

Even in the state of rebellion which still marked Jonah's condition, there are elements of nobility in it. Desiring death, he would not take his own life, but rather pray the Lord to remove him. The entire world of spiritual reality, as Jonah had misunderstood it, had come crashing down around him; and his frustration was complete. "He saw, or thought he saw, all of his usefulness destroyed."[14]

> Why live any longer? His attitude is reminiscent of Elijah (1 Kings 19:4), both men having apparently risked their lives for nothing, and Israel's enemies remained powerful. Both men seem close to a nervous breakdown.[15]

Verse 4, And Jehovah said, Doest thou well to be angry?

Having extended mercy to a great pagan city, God extends mercy also to his servant. Anger and frustration over what God allows, or what God does, are understandable human reactions, wrong to be sure, but arising in part from an inadequate understanding of God's larger purpose. The Father was concerned for other nations besides Israel, incomprehensible as that might have seemed to Jonah.

"Doest thou well to be angry. . .?" This remonstrance is a gentle endeavor on the part of the Lord to provoke in Jonah a self-examination of his own emotions and attitudes. How unreasonable it must appear in any objective examination of the facts, that a preacher whose business it was to convert men should have been angry when his efforts met with wholesale success!

Verse 5, Then Jonah went out of the city, and sat on the east side of the city, and there made him a booth, and sat under it in the shade, till he might see what would become of the city.

See under verse 1, above for a note on the reason for the apparent uncertainty on Jonah's part as to whether the city

---

[14]Hugh Martin, *op. cit.*, p. 453.
[15]Michael C. Griffiths, *op. cit.*, p. 986.

would be destroyed or not. It appears that Jonah had already concluded that the city would be spared, a conclusion based upon his knowledge of the character of God (v. 2), and the evident and overwhelming fact of Nineveh's wholesale repentance.

"East side of the city . . ." This was the elevated portion of the terrain and provided a better vantage point for seeing the city overthrown, an event Jonah hoped for, contrary to his expectations. His preaching had probably begun on the west side of the city; and thus it may be concluded that he had completed his warning of the entire metropolis.

"Made him a booth . . ." "This was a rough structure made of poles and leaves, like those of the Feast of Tabernacle."[16] Jonah evidently expected to stay a considerable time, yet hoping for the overthrow of hated Nineveh. Although Jonah had already decided that God would spare the city, he was not yet certain of it; and as long as there was hope of its destruction, he would wait. Sure, he knew that Nineveh had repented; but there were examples in God's dealings with Israel in which severe punishment was inflicted even after repentance (2 Samuel 12:10-14); and perhaps Jonah hoped for that pattern to be followed in the case of Nineveh. In any case, there he was, as full of derogatory thoughts about Nineveh as ever, and intently hoping for its utter destruction. As a prophetic type of the old Israel, this attitude of Jonah indicated the hatred which the Jews of the times of Jesus would exhibit against any idea of salvation for the Gentiles. As Barnes stated it, "He prefigured the carnal people of Israel, for these too were sad at the salvation of the Gentiles."[17]

Still another reason why Jonah appears in this verse still expecting and hoping for the destruction of Nineveh may be in the estimate which he had of the depth and sincerity, or rather, of the lack of such depth and sincerity, in which case Jonah would have supposed that the punishment was only deferred, not cancelled altogether, and thus he would go ahead and wait for it!

---

[16]J.R. Dummelow, *Commentary on the Holy Bible* (New York: The Macmillan Company, 1837), p. 577.

[17]Albert Barnes, *Notes on the OT, Minor Prophets, Vol. I* (Grand Rapids: Baker Book House, 1953), p. 423.

One of the practical lessons that should not be overlooked in connection with Jonah's actions here was stated thus by Blair, "He overlooked the importance of following through."[18] If there was ever a time when the Ninevites needed Jonah it was immediately after their repentance. Uncounted thousands had turned to the Lord, but they were still as newborn babes without any complete knowledge of what turning to God really meant. His petulant departure from the city without addressing himself to the spiritual needs of those new believers "in God" was as reprehensible as anything that the prophet ever did.

Verse 6, And Jehovah God prepared a gourd, and made it to come up over Jonah, that it might be a shade over his head, to deliver him from his evil case. So Jonah was exceeding glad because of the gourd.

"God prepared a gourd . . ." All kinds of fanciful "explanations" of this have been attempted, one of the favorite devices being that of making this "gourd" to be a "castor bean plant," the remarkably rapid growth of which leads some scholars to accept it as the "gourd" mentioned here. These notions should be rejected.

> The attempt to find a plant which would grow high enough in a single day to provide shade for Jonah is beside the point. *This* plant grows suddenly, at God's command, just as the great fish swallowed Jonah at God's command. The author does not mean to describe natural happenings.[19]

The supernatural appearance of this "gourd" overnight is one of no less than six lesser wonders that surround, confirm, and support the far greater wonder of Jonah's deliverance from death. See full discussion of this under *Jonah, the Great OT Type,* at the end of the commentary on Jonah.

Verse 7, But God prepared a worm when the morning rose the next day, and it smote the gourd that it withered.

---

[18]J. Allen Blair, *op. cit.*, p. 164.
[19]James D. Smart, *op. cit.*, p. 893.

Here, too, the record plainly refers to a supernatural event, that of God's preparing and commissioning a worm to destroy the gourd which had enjoyed such a short period of growth. This also is one of the "six supportive miracles" mentioned under verse 6, above.

This worm struck effectively against the very source of Jonah's great gladness, which, strangely enough, was not connected in any way with the great repentance of Nineveh, but was derived from a wretched gourd vine which provided him shade! If there was ever an example of a man's being "exceedingly glad" for the wrong reasons, here it is in these two verses. There are millions of Jonahs everywhere in our society today, people who are glad, exceedingly so, for the comforts and luxuries they enjoy, rather than for the great hope of the soul's eternal redemption in Jesus Christ our Lord. They are more thankful for sports contests, outings on the beach, air-conditioning, soft drinks, plenty of beer, etc., than they are for the right to worship God without molestation. Yes, there are a lot of Jonah's who are still "exceedingly glad" for gourds!

Regarding the "worm" mentioned in this verse, Deane wrote that the term could be used here collectively, as in Deuteronomy 28:39, thus meaning "worms,"[20] that is, a sudden massive infestation of them. This appears unnecessary, however; one worm operating strategically upon the main stem of the gourd at, or near, ground level, would have destroyed it as effectively as any army of 10,000 worms, especially when aided by the scorching east wind that arrived almost simultaneously to hasten the destruction of the gourd. There is no use for the commentators to help the Lord out with little problems of this kind. The whole account clearly deals with events which the inspired author attributed to the direct intervention of God. In short, they are *miracles*.

Verse 8, And it came to pass, when the sun arose, that God prepared a sultry east wind; and the sun beat upon the head of Jonah, that he fainted, and requested for himself

---

[20]W.J. Deane, *Pulpit Commentary, Vo. 13, Jonah* (Grand Rapids: Wm. B. Eerdmans Publishing Company, 1950), p. 81.

**that he might die, and said, It is better for me to die than to
live.**

Paul also had a similar thought:

> But I am in a strait betwixt the two, having a desire
> to depart and be with Christ; for it is very far better:
> yet to abide in the flesh is more needful for your sake
> (Philippians 1:23,24).

This is the third miracle in as many verses, the gourd and
the worm having already been cited. It is a blind and un-
learned objection, however, which fails to see the connection which these lesser wonders have with the central event
of the book, i.e., Jonah's delivery from death. These lesser
wonders are not capricious, unnecessary, or useless miracles
at all. For an elaboration of the greater meaning of these
supernatural events as they stand related to God's eternal
purpose, see under, *Jonah, the Great OT Type,* at the end of
this chapter.

**Verse 9, And God said to Jonah, Doest thou well to be
angry for the gourd? And he said, I do well to be angry,
even unto death.**

The almost incredible stubbornness of Jonah is matched
historically by only one thing, and that is the obstinate
unwillingness of Israel to accept the Lord Jesus Christ,
that being exactly the very event which this conduct on the
part of Jonah was designed to foretell.

"Doest thou well ...?" How frequently in the divine
solicitations concerning sinful mankind has the Father
pressed home the truth with questions? Note these examples:

> Doest thou well to be angry? (Jonah 4:9).
> Adam, Where art thou? (Genesis 3:9).
> Where is thy brother, Abel? (Genesis 4:9).
> What doest thou here, Elijah? (1 Kings 19:13).
> Betrayest thou the Son of Man with a kiss? (Luke
>   22:48).
> Lovest thou me more than these? (John 21:24).
> Wilt thou be made whole? (John 5:6).
> Saul, Saul, Why persecutest thou me? (Acts 22:7).

Before leaving this verse, it should be noted that a different word in the Hebrew is used for God, than is used in other verses of this chapter. In fact, the following pattern is evident:

Verse 4, "Jehovah," meaning *God the Creator* is used.

Verse 6, "Jehovah-Elohim," the compound name of God found in the book of Genesis.

Verse 8, "Elohim," the personal God, sends the worm.

Verse 9, "Elohim," the Ruler of Nature sends the east wind.[21]

C. F. Keil, and other scholars, have also marvelled at this selective use of several different names for God in this book. The significant truth here is that the critical conceit of trying to determine the origin of OT books by the variations of God's name found in them is effectively refuted by this single book, which has a number of different names for God in the same passage!

Verse 10, And Jehovah said, Thou has had regard for the gourd, for which thou hast not labored, neither madest it grow; which came up in a night, and perished in a night.

"Jonah's unreasonableness stands fully unmasked."[22] Yes, Jonah can be appreciative of a gourd, but has no feeling for the vast city with its teeming populations. He did not like to see even a gourd destroyed, but he would gloat over the destruction of half a million precious souls! A gourd is an ephemeral thing, here one day, gone the next, but the soul of a human being will outlast the sun itself! Yet Jonah's delight is focused on the gourd! How unreasonable, and how reprehensible in the eyes of God must many of the preferences of men appear to be. Even if Jonah was unwilling to get the point, God gave it to him anyway, in the very next verse:

Verse 11, And should not I have regard for Nineveh, that great city, wherein are more than sixscore thousand persons

[21]W.J. Deane, *op. cit.*, p. 81.
[22]W.J. Deane, *op. cit.*, p. 81.

that cannot discern between their right hand and their left hand; and also much cattle?

Jonah's reply is not given. He could make none. The logic of the Father is unassailable, and Jonah's selfish and peevish attitude stands exposed for what it is. How strange that this remarkable book should come to such a dramatic and shocking end, with Jonah still standing on his under lip, pouting and dissatisfied with God's purpose of redeeming anybody except him and his fellow Jews! As Dummelow wrote:

> There is no finer close in literature than this ending. The Divine question, "Should not I have pity?" remains unanswered. Its echoes are heard still above every crowded haunt of men. Above the stir, and din, and wickedness the Infinite Compassion is still brooding.[23]

This book began with Jonah running away from God; "And when the book is over, Jonah is still rebelling against God."[24] He is not any longer running away, but he is far away from him in mind and spirit.

The evangelical message of the book of Jonah was thus summarized by Robinson:

> What shall we say then? Is there injustice on God's part? By no means! For he says to Moses, "I will have mercy on whom I have mercy, and I will have compassion on whom I have compassion" (Romans 9:14,15).[25]

"No man has the right to question or resent the outpouring of God's love in saving man, any man, from sin and destruction."[26]

"Sixscore thousand persons who cannot discern between their right and their left hand . . ." Efforts to apply these words to the entire population of Nineveh are fruitless,

---

[23]J.R. Dummelow, *op. cit.*, p. 577.

[24]James T. Draper, Jr., *op. cit.*, p. 89.

[25]W.G. Robinson, *new Bible Commentary, Revised* (Grand Rapids: Wm. B. Eerdmans Publishing Company, 1970), p. 751.

[26]G. Herbert Livingston, *Wycliffe Bible Commentary* (Chicago: Moody Press, 1962), p. 850.

being usually for the purpose of showing that Nineveh, after all, was not "that exceeding great city" which Jonah called it. The simple and obvious meaning of these words is that there were 120,000 infants and little children in Nineveh. As Deane said:

> This limitation would include children of three or four years old; and taking these as one fifth of the population, we should set the inhabitants at six hundred thousand in number.[27]

Commentators who try to downgrade the size of Nineveh in order to challenge the authority of scripture have been silenced and refuted by certain discoveries by archeologists.

A recently discovered inscription of Asshurnasirpal II (883-859 B.C.) (that is, about a century prior to Jonah), tells of a banquet with a total of 69,574 invited guests! Taking into account the surrounding population and the foreigners, the figures given here in Jonah do not appear as fantastic as is sometimes thought.[28]

Having now examined the text of this remarkable book, we shall take a more particular look at the astounding significance of it as revealed in the typical nature of its contents. Jonah is not merely *a type* of the Lord Jesus Christ, as revealed by Jesus himself; but he is far and away the most important type to be found in the entire OT, and not merely of Christ, but also of the first Israel.

Jonah, the Great OT Type

Many of the lists of OT types do not include Jonah at all, despite the truth that this book has the unique distinction of being the only one singled out by the Christ himself as having material in it which he designated as typical of himself. An exploration of this truth reveals some very extraordinary scriptural information. Since the Lord Jesus

[27]W.J. Deane, *op. cit.*, p. 81.
[28]Jacob M. Myers, *Layman's Bible Commentary* (Atlanta: The John Knox Press, 1979), p. 176.

himself was typified by the first Israel, there being many particulars in which the old Israel was a type of Christ the true Israel, Jonah is therefore a type of the Old Israel also. This typical resemblance and correspondence between the old Israel in their wilderness wanderings, for example, and the experiences of the church of our Lord (the body or Christ) during this present period of their probation and suffering, is usually thought of as pertaining merely to Christ's spiritual body, but it also includes Christ. Israel as a type of Christ may be seen in other comparisons. Matthew, for example, quoted Hosea, "Out of Egypt have I called my son," applying it first to the coming up out of slavery in Egypt by the Israelites, and in the second instance to Christ's coming up out of Egypt, following the flight of Joseph, Mary and Jesus into that country, during the period of Jesus' infancy (Matthew 2:15). The apostolical church pointed out many of such similarities. As Richardson noted:

> The apostolic church saw in the action of Joseph of Arimathea in begging the body of Jesus from Pilate (John 19:38), the fulfillment of an OT type. Another Joseph had begged the permission of Pharaoh to bury the body of the old Israel (Jacob) (Genesis 50:4-6).[29]

Although the fact of the old Israel's being a type of Christ may be much more extensively documented, this is sufficient to show that whatever is a type of Christ must also, at the same time, be a type of the old Israel as well; and we shall explore this truth with regard to Jonah, first as a type of the Lord Jesus Christ, and secondly, as a type of the fleshly Israel.

Of some forty authors and sources quoted in the notes above, nearly all of them mentioned Jonah as a type of Christ, and several mentioned that he was a type of Israel; but none of them outlined the extent and magnificence of this typical import of Jonah, hence our efforts to do so here.

---

[29]Alan Richardson, *The Gospel According to St. John* (London: SCM Press, 1959), p. 204.

Jonah and Jesus

I. Both Jonah and Jesus were on board a ship in a storm at sea. Both were surrounded by fearful men, Jonah by the mariners, and Jesus by the apostles. Both vessels were in eminent danger of perishing. Both Jonah and Jesus were awakened, Jonah by the shipmaster, and Jesus by the apostles. Both Jonah and Jesus acted to calm the turbulent sea, Jonah by commanding himself to be thrown overboard, and Jesus by fiat, rebuking the wind and the sea (Mark 4:35-41).

II. Both Jonah and Jesus gave themselves up to death for the purpose of saving others. The analogy fails to hold, absolutely, in the characters of the two men, since Jesus was altogether and totally innocent, and Jonah's life was marked by disobediences and imperfections. Nevertheless, in the case of Jonah, despite his previous rebellion, his running away from the Lord, and his repudiation of plain duty, in the last analysis, when others were threatened with eminent and impending death because of his sin, he unselfishly stepped forward, accepted the blame, freely gave himself up to death in order to save them whom he had endangered. Where in all the records of human deeds is there a *better* example of a mere man giving himself up to die on behalf of others? He is therefore in this event a noble type of the Son of God himself, despite his humanity having been marred by the common frailties of all men.

III. Both Jonah and Jesus were executed by Gentiles, Jonah by the pagan mariners, and Jesus by the platoon of Roman soldiers, acting upon the orders of the Roman governor. Like so many of these comparisons, this one also is emphasized and intensified by amazing occurrences which reveal *design* in the remarkable similarities. Although both were executed by Gentiles, the Jewish insistence upon death in each case is fully evident, not only in Jonah's command that he should be overthrown, but in the Saviour's repeated prophecy of his Passion, and in the clamoring of the Jewish mob in Jerusalem for his death. The similarity does not end there, for Gentile elements in both events declared the *innocence* of the one condemned. The mariners prayed the Lord not to lay "innocent blood" upon them (Jonah 1:14), just as Pilate washed his hands and said,

"I am innocent of the blood of this righteous man" (Matthew 27:24). If the mariners had possessed the same sense of spiritual values as Jonah, they might not have considered him innocent; but according to their light he was *innocent*, not being guilty of any violence.

IV. Both Jonah and Jesus were delivered from death, Jonah by being deposited upon the dry land after three days and three nights in the great fish, and Jesus by his resurrection from the tomb, after being interred in a sealed and guarded grave for three days and three nights! This is the great central *sign* in each case, being the one which Jesus singled out in Matthew 12:38-41 and Luke 11:29,30. Even in the barest essentials of the two events, the correspondence between them is startling and convincing; however, the exact reflection in the delivery of Jonah of that far more wonderful and greater event which it typified in the life, death, and resurrection of Jesus is so accurate, detailed, circumstantial, and amazing that a closer look at the type should be taken.

In the introduction, it was noted that there are six supportive and attendant miracles in each of these events, that of Jonah's deliverance, and that of Christ's resurrection. This is fully in keeping with the divine pattern of setting "the solitary in families" (Psalm 68:6). Also, the placement of six around one is the source of the commonest pattern in all of the natural creation; and the resulting hexagonal formation is found in most of the naturally formed crystals in nature, as well as in the honeycomb, every snowflake that ever fell upon earth, and in many other instances. It has been referred to as "the footprint of God." We should not be surprised to find it here. For further comment on materials related to this analogy, see in CM, pp. 483-497.

Not only do the six miracles in each case cited here correspond in general pattern, but there is also the most remarkable correspondence in a number of specific instances. In each instance, two of the supportive miracles are from *above*, two from the *dead level*, and two from *beneath* the earth's surface. Note that in the case of the gourd vine and the earthquake, two of the dead level miracles, that each of them reached both above and below the surface of the earth. The earthquake's high epicenter was nevertheless

below the ground, but the mighty rocks which were cast up
by the terrible force of it were heaped up above the surface
of the earth, as any traveller in Jerusalem may still see.
Likewise, the gourd vine had its tap root going down below
the surface, but the height of it reached up above Jonah's
head. This quality of being both above and below the surface requires both to be classified as surface wonders.

V. Both Jonah and Jesus, through their delivery from
death, were "signs" to the Gentiles. Jesus declared that
"Jonah became a sign to the Ninevites" (Luke 11:30), adding that, "So shall also the Son of man be to this generation." The implication of this is that Jonah's delivery from
death was the "word that came unto the king," leading to
the conversion of Nineveh. The *reason* that Jonah's message was received in Nineveh and produced such remarkable results was that this "sign" of Jonah convinced them
absolutely that God had indeed sent him. In a similar manner, the resurrection of Christ is the great wonder that
declared Jesus to be "the Son of God with power" (Romans
1:4), leading to the conversion of millions all over the world.

VI. Both Jonah and Jesus converted fantastic numbers
of Gentiles. Jonah singlehandedly converted over half a
million souls in Nineveh; and Christ, by the preaching of his
apostles, has converted literally millions and millions of
Gentiles; and, although Jews are in no manner excluded
from the gospel message, it is primarily among the Gentiles
that Christianity has been accepted.

VII. Both Jonah and Jesus had two graves. Since this
fact is so little known, we shall rehearse, briefly, the
grounds for believing it. Isaiah prophesied that, "They
made his grave with the wicked (plural) and with the rich
(singular) in his death," (Isaiah 53:9); Jesus' burial in the
new tomb of Joseph of Arimathea fulfilled the second part
of Isaiah's prophesy, but not the first; *that* was fulfilled by
the platoon of soldiers who executed Christ and whose
duties would have included the digging of three graves for
the three whom they crucified. *That grave* was, therefore,
one which "they" made for Jesus with the wicked (plural),
i.e., the two malefactors who were crucified with him. Admittedly, this is light on NT events from OT scripture, but

this is by no means the only such instance in which this occurs.

Now, with regard to the graves of Jonah:

> The mound of Kuyunjik not only covers the vast palace of Sennacherib, but ... the nearby smaller mound of Nebi Yunus (Prophet Jonah), which got its name from the tradition that the Hebrew prophet was buried there.[30]

Nineveh, in its entirety, was destroyed in 612 B.C., therefore, this mound, and the tradition of Jonah's burial there must be dated at a time prior to that; and, although there is no way to "prove" a tradition as old as this one, it admittedly fits all the facts that we have. See in CJ, pp. 421-423 and in CMK, p. 336.

> In the vicinity of Nazareth, the grave of Jonah is still shown, this place being near to Gath-Hepher, a town in Zebulun which is given in the scripture as Jonah's home (2 Kings 14:15).[31]

A great deal of material may be found in some writings about one or the other of these graves, and we certainly have no way of knowing which one of them is the "original," or where the body of the great prophet actually sleeps. Our point is simply that *he had two graves*, a truth which there is hardly any basis for denying.

As to the reason why Jonah had two graves, we pray that we may be indulged in a little speculation. Jonah, after converting the largest pagan city in the world would ever afterwards have been *persona non grata* in Israel, Jonah's wish to die probably being connected with this certain rejection in Israel. Our basis for this opinion is simply that this was surely the reaction of Israel in the case of the apostle Paul, another Jew, who converted many Gentiles. There is absolutely no reason whatever for supposing that their attitude toward Jonah would have been any different than it was toward Paul; and, if we may believe some of the

---

[30]Merrill F. Unger, *Archeology and the OT,* (Grand Rapids: Zondervan Publishing House, 1954), p. 264.

[31]J.R. Dummelow, *op. cit.*, p. 575.

traditions that have come down to us regarding Paul, how
even his wife deserted him, how the hierarchy had a public
funeral for him, disowned him for ever, and hounded him to
the ends of the earth with the avowed purpose of murdering
him — if any of this is true (and certainly, some of it is true,
being related in the NT), it is not hard to believe that Jonah
would likewise have suffered the undying hatred and animosity of his own people.

It was certainly not out of keeping with their national
custom to hold a public funeral for "deserters," bury them
in effigy, and engrave their names on a grave. It is our
speculative opinion that they surely did this for Jonah, and
that that is how his name was ever found on a grave in his
home community.

If these speculations should be allowed, and we do not
allege in any sense, that the word of God has anything like
this in it, there would then be another strange coincidence:
Jonah, honored and received by the people of Nineveh, was
given a tomb near that of their kings; and thus he, like
Jesus, actually rested in that grave which they made him
"with the rich (singular)."

The slender basis for this speculation includes the very
prophecy of Isaiah quoted above. It is possible that Isaiah,
knowing of the two graves of Jonah, in the power of the
Holy Spirit, made the deduction that it would be exactly
the same way with Jesus.

Jonah and Israel

Inherent in the fact of our Lord Jesus Christ actually
being, not merely the Second Adam, but also the Second
Israel, is the truth that any type of Christ is *de facto* also a
type of fleshly Israel. "Jonah was a type, as of Christ, so
also of Israel."[32] "He prefigured the carnal people of Israel."[33]

I. Jonah despised the Gentiles, being perfectly happy
and satisfied, enjoying the favors and privileges that undoubtedly came to him as a popular prophet of God, hold-
ing the status of a national hero for having prophesied

---

[32]Jamieson, Faucett, and Brown, *op. cit.*, p. 811.
[33]Albert Barnes, *op. cit.*, p. 423.

accurately the recovery of Israel's lost cities by Jeroboam II (2 Kings 14:15). This typifies perfectly the self-satisfied attitude of Israel, whether in Samaria or Jerusalem. Their hatred of the Gentiles was a national characteristic. When the apostle Paul made his speech upon the steps of the fortress of Antonio in Jerusalem, the great mob listened *until* Paul used the word *Gentile*, that single word exploding a riot that shook the whole city:

> And they gave him audience unto this word; and they lifted up their voice, and said, Away with such a fellow from the earth: for it is not fit that he should live (Acts 22:22).

Above, certain quotations were cited indicating the usual acceptance of Jonah as a type of secular, or fleshly Israel; but, actually, he was a type of Israel, both the old and the new, both the old secular Israel, and the Israel of God which is the church! An attempt will be made to indicate this as this study moves forward. In this very first correspondence between type and antitype, is not Jonah a perfect type of the self-satisfied, complacent and indifferent church, unmindful of its duty to preach to the heathen, in fact actually despising the entire unChristian world? How many so-called Christian ministers are there who, like Jonah, enjoy the privileges of some great earthly capital, having no love at all for the sinful, dying world just outside the periphery of their elite and charming circle!

II. Jonah's refusal to preach to Gentiles is a type of the secular Israel's absolute and adamant rebellion against God in their opposition to Christ, the apostles, and the infant church. Jonah's refusal was grounded in (a) his hatred of Gentiles, (b) his willingness to go to any length to avoid his duty, and (c) his preference of death to the hated prospect of the Gentiles accepting God. Fleshly Israel as the antitype of that refusal measured up to it fully and even went beyond it. (a) They rejected the Christ, despite their full knowledge that he was "the heir" of God and their true and legitimate sovereign (Matthew 21:38). (b) They plotted and achieved the death of Christ himself through a cunning manipulation of suborned testimony, intimidated tribunals, and mob violence. (c) They continued their opposition to the

will of God, even after the resurrection of Christ, as seen in
their murderous hatred of Paul, their murder of Stephen,
their unscrupulous opposition to the preaching on the mission field (as recorded in Acts), and in their enlistment of
the Roman government as an ally in their vain efforts to
destroy Christianity!

III. Jonah was compelled by the Lord, even against Jonah's will, to deliver God's message to the Gentiles. This is
magnificently fulfilled by the fleshly Israel, who this very
day, through their glorious scriptures, are preaching Christ
all over the world (against the will of fleshly Israel). It is the
Jewish scriptures which "testify" of Christ, as Jesus said
(John 5:39). In the very nature of things, Jonah found no
way to thwart the will of God who laid upon him the necessity of preaching to Nineveh; and, likewise, fleshly Israel
found absolutely *no way* to remove the authentic witness of
the truth and supernatural nature of Christianity from
their holy scriptures. We agree with DeHaan that:

> The greatest national miracle in all human history is
> the supernatural preservation and protection of a dis-
> persed nation, persecuted and threatened in their so-
> journ among the nations, but never to be destroyed.
> Any other nation would have disappeared from his-
> tory long ago.

IV. Jonah's opposition to God's will did not end with his
deliverance from death, nor with the actual fact of half a
million Gentiles "believing in God." No! Jonah was still
against it, even preferring death to the very sight of such a
thing. This is a perfect type of Israel's continued opposition
to God's will, even after the resurrection of Christ, after the
conversion of millions of Gentiles. It was the genius of the
apostle Paul that discovered in the very manner of Melchiz-
edek's presentation in scripture, as having neither beginning of days nor end of life, a glorious type of the Lord
Jesus Christ; and one cannot help seeing in this very same
phenomenon, i.e., the peculiar deployment of this record
upon the sacred page, a type of the perpetual hardness of
Israel, and thus we interpret it. The book of Jonah closes
with sullen and unwilling Jonah still preferring death to
God's outpouring of mercy upon anyone except Jonah and

his Jewish relatives! This is the perfect type of fleshly Israel's rejection of Christ and of Christianity throughout history.

V. Jonah's being cast overboard is the perfect type of fleshly Israel's overthrow as "the chosen people of God." The dramatic rejection of the fleshly Israel as "God's peculiar people" is inherent in the fact that all of the glorious titles which once pertained to the old Israel are, by apostolical authority, applied to the church of Jesus Christ, which is the new Israel. Thus, it is not fleshly Israel, but the church, the new Israel, who is now:

> An elect race
> A royal priesthood
> A chosen nation
> The people of God's possession
> Who in times past were no people, but are
> Now THE PEOPLE OF GOD!(1 Peter 2:9,10).

This overthrow of fleshly Israel, corresponding to Jonah's being cast overboard at sea, was quite dramatic and extensive. Their political entity was destroyed for a period of at least nineteen centuries when their capital city, Jerusalem, was sacked and destroyed by Vespasian and Titus in August of 70 A.D. Their religious economy was dramatically terminated in the total destruction of their temple, the permanent removal of the office of high priest, the final cessation of the daily sacrifices, the putting to death of the hierarchy, and the slaughter of over a million of the inhabitants of what had been at one time, "The Holy City," but which was then consigned by the Lord Jesus Christ to the sword and the heel of the invader, "until the times of the Gentiles be fulfilled" (Luke 21:24). The casting of Jonah overboard at sea in a storm is an apt type indeed of what happened to Israel as a direct result of their disobedience.

VI. God's forbearance and mercy, as extended to Jonah, even in spite of his sullen stubbornness and rebellion, is a perfect type of the same love and mercy which God is willing to bestow upon fleshly Israel, at whatever time they shall be willing to accept God's mercy upon the terms and conditions attending his proffering it to all men. We may only be amazed at the tenderness and concern for Jonah,

manifested on the part of God. That Jonah still remained
out of harmony with the will of the Father is apparent, even
after he had discharged his commission; but the Lord continued to direct and care for him.

VII. Jonah is the perfect type of the uncertainty which
clouds the future of fleshly Israel. The prophetic record in
Jonah comes to a dramatic, sudden, and startling conclusion with the issue still undecided, as to whether or not,
Jonah will accept God's will. The history concludes with
Jonah still protesting that he would rather die than see the
will of God accomplished for the Gentiles; and we simply
have no way of knowing either when Jonah changed his
mind, or even if he ever did! This is a perfect type of the
uncertainty that must for ever prevail with regard to the
future of fleshly Israel. The holy scriptures do not prophesy
the future conversion of Israel, despite, the popular misunderstanding concerning it; and, at the same time, they do
not prophesy that it will *never* occur. The wonder which we
feel with reference to the ultimate resolution of Jonah's
attitude applies with equal force to the antitype, fleshly
Israel.

There is a NT counterpart to this concluding picture in
Jonah of a sullen and unwilling prophet being tenderly
solicited and encouraged by the Father. It is in the parable
of the prodigal son, where, it will be remembered, the elder
brother, who certainly stands for Israel in the analogy, is
angered and resentful because the loving father has received the prodigal and laid out a feast for him. The elder
brother remained in the field, and outside, angered and
embittered, even protesting the justice of the father, and
laying all kinds of harsh allegations against his brother.
The parable closes with the banquet going on inside the
house, and the father going outside to entreat his elder son:

> Son, thou are ever with me; and all that is mine is
> thine. But it was meet to make merry and be glad; for
> thy brother was dead, and is alive again; and was lost,
> and is found (Luke 15:31,32).

Just as in Jonah, we are left in suspense as to the ultimate resolution of the problem. Perhaps the sacred records
of both the OT and the NT were intended to portray the

gentle, loving Father as standing for ever in an attitude of solicitation, pleading and entreating the fleshly Israel to change their hearts and restore the broken fellowship with God.

Having concluded this investigation of Jonah the Great Type, we believe it is in order to say that no infidel can laugh this off. The hand of God is so conspicuously displayed in every word of this amazing history that only those who are spiritually blind can fail to see it. The allegation that some self-seeking forger, several hundred years after the events related, could have concocted a gem like the book of Jonah is to suppose a miracle greater than that of Jonah's preservation in the fish. The discernment of the blessed Saviour in uniquely designating this book as prophetical of himself is gloriously revealed by any careful study of this portion of the word of God.

BIBLIOGRAPHY

The following sources and authors were quoted in this commentary on Jonah:

Banks, William L., *Jonah the Reluctant Prophet* (Chicago: Moody Press, 1966).

Barnes, Albert, *Notes on the OT, Minor Prophets, Vol. I* (Grand Rapids: Baker Book House, 1953).

Bickersteth, E., *Pulpit Commentary on Mark* (Grand Rapids: Wm. B. Eerdmans Publishing Company, 1950).

Bruce, Alexander Balmain, *Expositor's Greek NT, Vol. I* (Grand Rapids: Wm. B. Eerdmans Publishing Company, 1967).

Blaikie, W. G., *Pulpit Commentary, Vol. 14, Jonah* (Grand Rapids: Wm. B. Eerdmans Publishing Company, 1950).

Blair, J. Allen, *Living Obediently* (Neptune, N.J.: Loizeaux Bros., 1963).

Butler, Paul T., *Minor Prophets* (Joplin, Mo.: College Press, 1968).

Clarke, Adam, *Commentary on the Whole Bible, Vol. V* (New York: T. Mason & G. Lane, 1837).

Deane, W. J., *Pulpit Commentary, Vol. 14, Jonah* (Grand Rapids: Wm. B. Eerdmans Publishing Company, 1950).

DeHaan, M. R., M. D., *Jonah, Fact or Fiction* (Grand Rapids: Zondervan Publishing House, 1957).

Draper, James T., Jr., *Living Obediently* (Wheaton, Ill.: Tyndale House, Publishers, 1971).

Dummelow, J. R., *Commentary on the Holy Bible* (New York: The Macmillan Company, 1937).

Ellul, Jacques, *The Judgment of Jonah* (Grand Rapids: Wm. B. Eerdmans Publishing Company, 1971).

Encyclopaedia Britannica, Vol. 16 (Chicago: William Benton, Publisher, 1961).

Graham, William C., *Abingdon Bible Commentary* (New York: Abingdon Press, 1929).

Griffiths, Michael C., *The New Layman's Bible Commentary* (Grand Rapids: Zondervan Publishing House, 1979).

Haley, John W., *Discrepancies of the Bible* (Nashville: B. C. Goodpasture, 1951).

Henry, J. E., *Pulpit Commentary, Vol. 14, Jonah* (Grand Rapids: Wm. B. Eerdmans Publishing Company, 1950).

Henry, Matthew, *Commentary on the Bible* (Old Tappan, N.J.: Fleming H. Revell Company).

Hillis, Don W., *Jonah Speaks Again* (Grand Rapids: Baker Book House, 1967).

Jamieson, Faucett, and Brown, *Commentary on the Whole Bible* (Grand Rapids: Zondervan Publishing House, 1961).

Josephus, Flavius, *Antiquities and Wars of the Jews, translated by William Whiston* (New York: Holt, Rinehart, and Winston).

Keil, C. F., *Commentary on the OT, Vol. X* (Grand Rapids: Wm. B. Eerdmans Publishing Company, 1978).

Livingston, G. Herbert, *Wycliffe Bible Commentary* (Chicago: Moody Press, 1962).

Martin, Hugh, *The Prophet Jonah* (Grand Rapids: Baker Book House, 1979).

Methodius, *Fragment, Ante-Nicene Fathers, Vol. VI* (Grand Rapids: Wm. B. Eerdmans Publishing Company).

Monser, Harold E., *The Cross-Reference Bible* (New York: The Cross-Reference Bible Company, 1910).

Myers, Jacob M., *The Layman's Bible Commentary, Jonah* (Atlanta: The John Knox Press, 1979).

Nicholson, William R., *The Calvary Miracles* (Chicago: Moody Press, 1928).

Pinches, T. G., *ISBE* (Chicago: Howard-Severance Company, 1915).

Richardson, Alan, *The Gospel According to St. John* (London: SCM Press, 1959).

Robinson, W. B., *New Bible Commentary, Revised* (Grand Rapids: Wm. B. Eerdmans Publishing Company, 1970).

Smart, James D., *Interpreter's Bible, Vol. VI* (New York: Abingdon Press, 1957).

Smith, George Adam, *Twelve Prophets, Vo. II* (New York: Jennings & Graham).

Summers, Ray, *Commentary on Luke* (Waco: Word Books, Publisher, 1973).

Tertullian, *Appendix, Ante-Nicene Fathers, Vol. IV* (Grand Rapids: Wm. B. Eerdmans Publishing Company).

Unger, Merrill F., *Archaeology and the OT* (Grand Rapids: Zondervan Publishing House, 1954).

Unger, Merrill F., *Unger's Bible Dictionary* (Chicago: Moody Press, 1957).

Vine, W. E., *An Expository Dictionary of NT Words* (Old Tappan, N.J.: Fleming H. Revell Company, 1940).

Wycliffe Bible Encyclopedia (Chicago: Moody Press, 1975).

Young, Edward J., *Introduction to the OT.*

*Asterisk by entry indicates special treatment of subject on page indicated.